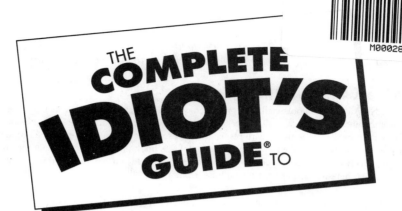

THE COMPLETE IDIOT'S GUIDE® TO

Aircraft Carriers

by C.A. Mobley and Michael Benson

ALPHA

A member of Penguin Group (USA) Inc.

M000287476

To Curt Kentner, for helping me contemplate all things Naval—M. B.
To the men and women, officers and crew, who still serve in the world's finest Navy—C. M.

Copyright © 2003 by C.A. Mobley and Michael Benson

All rights reserved. No part of this book shall be reproduced, stored in a retrieval system, or transmitted by any means, electronic, mechanical, photocopying, recording, or otherwise, without written permission from the publisher. No patent liability is assumed with respect to the use of the information contained herein. Although every precaution has been taken in the preparation of this book, the publisher and authors assume no responsibility for errors or omissions. Neither is any liability assumed for damages resulting from the use of information contained herein. For information, address Alpha Books 800 East 96th Street, Indianapolis, IN 46240.

THE COMPLETE IDIOT'S GUIDE TO and Design are registered trademarks of Penguin Group (USA) Inc.

International Standard Book Number: 1-59257-094-1
Library of Congress Catalog Card Number: 2003111941

05   04   03   8   7   6   5   4   3   2   1

Interpretation of the printing code: The rightmost number of the first series of numbers is the year of the book's printing; the rightmost number of the second series of numbers is the number of the book's printing. For example, a printing code of 03-1 shows that the first printing occurred in 2003.

Printed in the United States of America

Note: This publication contains the opinions and ideas of its authors. It is intended to provide helpful and informative material on the subject matter covered. It is sold with the understanding that the authors and publisher are not engaged in rendering professional services in the book. If the reader requires personal assistance or advice, a competent professional should be consulted.

The authors and publisher specifically disclaim any responsibility for any liability, loss, or risk, personal or otherwise, which is incurred as a consequence, directly or indirectly, of the use and application of any of the contents of this book.

Most Alpha books are available at special quantity discounts for bulk purchases for sales promotions, premiums, fund-raising, or educational use. Special books, or book excerpts, can also be created to fit specific needs.

For details, write: Special Markets, Alpha Books, 375 Hudson Street, New York, NY 10014.

Publisher: *Marie Butler-Knight*
Product Manager: *Phil Kitchel*
Senior Managing Editor: *Jennifer Chisholm*
Acquisitions Editor: *Gary Goldstein*
Development Editor: *Jennifer Moore*
Production Editor: *Megan Douglass*
Copy Editor: *Michael Dietsch*
Illustrator: *Chris Eliopoulos*
Cover/Book Designer: *Trina Wurst*
Indexer: *Julie Bess*
Layout/Proofreading: *Ayanna Lacey and Donna Martin*

Contents at a Glance

Contents

Foreword

There is no more-compelling icon of American military power than the aircraft carrier. From the war-winning "flattops" of World War II; through a half-century of major conflicts from Korea, to Vietnam, to Desert Storm; through a host of smaller conflicts that Max Boot famously describes in *The Savage Wars of Peace*; to the just-completed Operation Iraqi Freedom where six United States Navy aircraft carriers delivered the majority of the ordnance dropped on Iraqi forces; these military marvels have been the centerpiece of U.S. military power. It is no wonder that since the days of Franklin D. Roosevelt, U.S. presidents have repeatedly responded to international crises with the query, "Where are the carriers?" From World War II onward, aircraft carriers and their embarked air wings have enabled forward presence and ensured global access.

While most people are aware of how important aircraft carriers are to the nation today, and many have some recollection that aircraft carriers were central to the United States's victory in World War II, few recognize that the idea of having aircraft operate from mobile bases at sea is nearly a century old! Carrier aviation was born when civilian pilot Eugene Ely landed on the makeshift wooden deck of the USS *Pennsylvania* in January 1911 and became institutionalized when the United States Navy commissioned its first aircraft carrier, the USS *Langley* (converted from the collier USS *Jupiter*), in 1922. From these humble beginnings (*Langley* was too slow to keep pace with the centerpiece of the U.S. Navy fleet in that day, the battleship, could operate only a few airplanes, and had so many other deficiencies that her senior officers called her "this poor comic old ship"), the aircraft carrier rapidly developed into the principal striking arm of U.S. maritime power in World War II. In that conflict, the U.S. Navy won four great carrier battles over the Imperial Navy in one year (1942) alone—the Battle of the Coral Sea, Midway, the Battle of the Eastern Solomons, and the Battle of Santa Cruz; sent over 500 enemy ships to the bottom of the ocean; and destroyed over 9,000 enemy aircraft in the air. World War II ended with the U.S. Navy preeminent on the world's oceans, and the aircraft carrier was firmly established as the centerpiece of U.S. military power.

But why, almost sixty years after the end of that conflict, does the U.S. Navy aircraft carrier—symbolized by the USS *Abraham Lincoln*, the authors' centerpiece of this book—*still remain* the icon of U.S. combat power and still represent the first military asset that U.S. presidents call on in time of crisis? C.A. Mobley and Michael Benson take you through the reasons for this preeminence in this lively and entertaining book.

You will learn that there are three primary reasons for the ongoing preeminence of aircraft carriers in the United States's military arsenal: the inherent mobility and survivability of this floating airbase, the ability of the aircraft carrier to rapidly adapt new technology, and the ability of the aircraft carrier to change its mission profile.

Aircraft carriers thrive because they can remain alive—even in the face of a determined foe. Since the end of World War II, through major wars and innumerable smaller crises, no U.S. aircraft carrier has had to absorb an enemy shot fired in anger. Why? Today's aircraft carriers can move over 35 miles per hour, are surrounded by a defense cordon of surface combatant warships, can launch dozens of fighters in their own defense, and can shoot down enemy aircraft and missiles with a variety of point defense systems. Invulnerable? No. An incredibly tough target? Absolutely!

Some of the most cutting-edge technology in the U.S. military has been adapted to make aircraft carriers both more lethal and more defendable. From nuclear reactors, to more powerful catapults, to advanced radars, to advanced landing systems, to a host of other technologies, the aircraft carrier has *adapted*. While the *Langley*'s two sister ships, *Lexington* and *Saratoga*—which served so prominently in World War II—don't look that much different from today's Nimitz-class super carriers, a fleet of World War II aircraft carriers didn't carry the offensive striking power of the newest U.S. Navy aircraft carrier, the USS *Ronald Reagan*, commissioned this year.

The ability of the aircraft carrier to adapt and change its mission profile is another reason why the aircraft carrier remains the centerpiece of U.S. military power today. From the World War II fighter and bomber planes, to the Vietnam era workhorses such as the F-4 Phantom (featured prominently in the book and movie *The Great Santini*) and A-6 Intruder (immortalized in the book and movie *Flight of the Intruder*), to the F-14 Tomcat (of Tom Cruise's *Top Gun*) to the newest all-purpose fighter/attack aircraft that performed so superbly in Operation Iraqi Freedom, the F/A-18E/F "Super Hornet," to tomorrow's Joint Strike Fighter and the coming Unmanned Combat Air Vehicle (UCAV), aircraft carriers are all about adaptability. When they are not loaded with over 70 of these high-performance aircraft, these large, mobile airbases have served as platforms carrying Army helicopters in Haiti and special operations helicopters in Operation Enduring Freedom.

If this much is known about aircraft carriers, why is this book necessary? For one simple reason. The carrier's preeminence as an instrument for war—and for preventing war—makes it arguably the most used asset in the U.S. military inventory. Accordingly, these aircraft carriers are almost always gone, deployed to literally the four corners of the world—far from view of the public. When they are in their home ports—in this new era of worldwide terrorism—military officials must throw up a vast security screen to protect these multi-billion-dollar assets from would-be terrorists, further limiting the public's access to them. This is a policy that is unlikely to be changed soon.

That is why C.A. Mobley and Michael Benson have provided such an invaluable service to all of us. They take us *inside* a super carrier, the USS *Abraham Lincoln*, and explain the intimate details of that ship—its steel and sensors, its technologies and its gadgetry, its marvelous aircraft, and, perhaps most importantly, its people, from the 17-year-old aviation boatswain's mates who exercise an amazing choreography on the ship's four-and-one-half acre flight deck, to the men *and* women who fly the high-performance aircraft, to the admiral in charge of the entire strike group. This book is the next best thing to being there.

George Galdorisi

George Galdorisi began his navy career flying search and rescue helicopters off the USS *Lexington*—the navy's oldest aircraft carrier—and completed it serving for five years as chief of staff for a carrier battle group embarked in one of the navy's newest aircraft carriers—the USS *Abraham Lincoln*. He is the author of two novels of naval adventure—*The Coronado Conspiracy* and *For Duty and Honor* and two books on the Law of the Sea; has contributed to other books such as the hugely successful *The Navy*; writes regular columns in a number of naval professional journals; and has written over 100 articles and op-ed pieces on naval matters in military journals and national newspapers.

Introduction

I was and remain fascinated by aircraft carriers. While some (too much, by my way of thinking) of my time at sea was spent on smaller combatants, I took every opportunity to get onboard one of the carriers and to stay onboard for as long as possible.

The sheer complexity of the vessel is exhilarating. Then there's the hum of energy resonating in the hulls, the size, the constant cycle of flight operations. I hated to go to sleep on an aircraft carrier. I was afraid I might miss something—and there's always *something* happening on a carrier.

Aircraft carriers are at the very center of naval power. They're the resource that enables the United States Navy to do everything that every other service can do. We fly, we carry troops, we have a full medical center, and we don't need refueling. How much better can it get than that? Dare I say it? With enough carriers around, you don't need anything else.

My favorite aircraft carrier is the USS *Abraham Lincoln*, and that's the one we've chosen to use as an example in this book. Oddly enough, most of my time on the *Abraham Lincoln* was as a sand crab. That is, I was a technical analyst for a defense contractor providing reconstruction of virtually every phase of combat operations.

It was an ideal position for spending a lot of time roaming around and asking questions. I knew enough about the Navy and ships to ask better questions than a pure civilian and to understand the answers. On the other hand, since I wasn't a traditional carrier sailor, there were huge chunks of it that were fresh and new to me. I had the advantage of inexperience, of being able to see carrier operations without prior prejudices, to know what would be of interest to someone who'd never been on one. And if there's anyone who's reflexively curious, it's me.

Also, since I was a civilian, the officers and crew weren't always entirely sure just how polite they had to be to me and tended to answer my questions patiently. The mistakes or errors that survived to find their way into this book are solely the result of my not paying enough attention to their explanations.

So I'm your tour guide for carriers of today. But for the history of aircraft carriers I've teamed up with a military historian first-class, Michael Benson, who previously served in that role for *The Complete Idiot's Guide to Submarines* and who was the editor-in-chief of the not-as-stuffy-as-it-sounds newsstand magazine, the *Military Technical Journal*. Together, we've got you covered.

What You'll Find in This Book

This book is divided into five sections. In the first you'll learn what the parts of an aircraft carrier are. You'll come aboard and go on a guided tour. Then you'll get a quick overview of not just how carriers have changed over the years, but the changes in how they have been viewed and used as well.

In the second section you'll learn about carrier aircraft of yesterday and today, plus a special chapter about the greatest and most influential carrier aircraft of all time: The Carrier Aircraft Hall of Fame.

The third section details a day in the life of an aircraft carrier as seen and experienced by three very different crewmen, two sailors and an aviator. By the time you've followed the three of them through 24 hours you'll have a pretty good idea of what life aboard a flattop is like.

The fourth and fifth sections are The History of Aircraft Carriers 101, all the way from the first takeoff and landings from a ship to the role of the carrier in Operation Iraqi Freedom. You'll learn that it was during World War II that the aircraft carrier took over from the battleship the role of strongest ship in the fleet. It is a position it will hold for the foreseeable future.

Note: All opinions are my own and do not reflect official navy or government policy.

A Word of Definition

A word of definition before I go further. Many modern naval frigates, found all over the world, have a helicopter landing pad and sometimes they carry their own helicopter.

But I will not be counting these ships as aircraft carriers. To qualify as an aircraft carrier, a ship's primary function must be to carry aircraft, to be a floating air base, and take air power closer to the battlefield.

Along the Way ...

Along the way, you'll see the following boxes, which contain information designed to aid your learning experience. Regular sidebars will include:

Flattop Facts

Just the facts—perhaps a few surprising ones.

Ship's Log

Here you'll find observations and quotes that lend additional insight into the subject matter.

Naval Lingo

These boxes will help define aircraft carrier terminology that you might not otherwise be familiar with.

Fact Box

Fact Boxes will contain ship and aircraft specifications. That's the length, width, weight, and other statistics pertaining to the military wonders you'll encounter.

Acknowledgments

The authors wish to thank the following individuals and groups for their help in the creation of this book: Megan Douglass, Jake Elwell, Gary Goldstein, Norman Jacobs, Timothy J. Kutta, Jennifer Moore, Jim Pearson, Profile Entertainment, Captain Bud Weeks, USN (ret.), The Naval War College, and the men and women of Mobile Inshore Undersea Warfare Unit 106.

Trademarks

All terms mentioned in this book that are known to be or are suspected of being trademarks or service marks have been appropriately capitalized. Alpha Books and Penguin Group (USA) Inc. cannot attest to the accuracy of this information. Use of a term in this book should not be regarded as affecting the validity of any trademark or service mark.

Part 1

A Guided Tour

Before you can learn anything else about an aircraft carrier, you'll need to know your way around, so our first step is a guided tour of a huge floating airport called the USS *Abraham Lincoln*.

The carrier can seem like an impossible maze. The truth is: It is. But if you know a few basics, you'll at least be able to nod knowledgeably when someone tells you to meet them in "zero three tack one seven eight tack four Lima."

After your tour, you'll learn about how the role of the aircraft carrier has changed over the years, how today's carriers are powered by a nuclear reactor, and how a new, smaller type of carrier is being used to deliver marines onto the battlefield.

Chapter 1

Welcome to an Aircraft Carrier

In This Chapter

- ◆ What everyone who visits an aircraft carrier notices
- ◆ The modern aircraft carrier's mission and chain of command
- ◆ A quick tour of the USS *Abraham Lincoln*
- ◆ The impressive air control and radar features of a carrier
- ◆ How and where carriers are built

There are a few things you notice instantly about any aircraft carrier:

First, it's big. Impossibly big. That's why they refer to a full-sized aircraft carrier as a "supercarrier." It seems invincible. It might as well be an iceberg. It's a skyscraper turned on its side—unbelievably massive.

Second, it's alive. Even in port, a carrier hums, sort of. You can hear it, muted, and it feels like an animal tethered, one that won't put up with that for too long.

Third, you'll notice that almost everyone onboard is young. The average age in the U.S. Navy is somewhere around 22. These men and women get *lots* of responsibility very young.

Fourth, and finally, you'll notice that nobody has a name while on duty. Everyone is referred to by their job and not by their given name.

What's in a Name?

Most folks are called by their function and it may take on an abbreviated format, or initials only—for example, the Chief Engineer is called the "ChEng" (pronounced just like it's spelled). The officer of the day is addressed as "OOD"—or "Sir" or "Ma'am."

Ship's Log

Even the captain of the ship is never referred to by his or her name. As the captain arrives or departs, the announcement is "*Abraham Lincoln*—Departing," which can give you sort of a weird feeling if you're down on the mess decks watching a movie. Heck, if they didn't have nametags on their uniforms or stencils on their dungarees, you could go for years without knowing anyone's last name.

The boatswain's mate of the watch is called "Boats." Junior officer of the deck, "JOOD" (it's pronounced J-O-O-D, not *jood*), and so on. The person watching the surface radar is "surface plot," or just "surface." The Air boss is called "boss," "the mini-boss," or "mini" (even before the Austin Powers movies).

Similarly, all ships have abbreviations indicating their duty, or the kind of ship that they are. An aircraft carrier is known as a "CV" and her hull number will be CV-(number), as in CV-72 (CV doesn't stand for anything). If she's nuclear-powered, her hull number will be CVN-(number). You'll see carriers referred to as CVs frequently throughout this book. Similarly, a cruiser is a "CG" (that doesn't stand for anything, either).

Flattop Facts

My ship, the USS *Abraham Lincoln* (designated ship CVN-72) is really a big city in which 6,275 men and women live. Two hundred of them are officers, the remainder (and vast majority) are enlisted personnel. Construction on the ship began in 1984, and, after many tests (trials, they are called) was commissioned as a member of the Navy five years later. The ship is 1,092 feet long, more than three times the length of a football field. At its widest point (called the extreme beam) the ship is 252 feet wide. It is 134 feet wide at the waterline. The ship stands 206½ feet high and pushes 42 feet below the sea when it is full. When full the ship displaces more than 100,000 tons of water. (Displacement is how the weight of a ship is measured. Displacement is the volume of water that is pushed aside by the floating ship.)

The hull is made of steel, but vital spaces are protected by 63½ millimeters of Kevlar, a bullet-proof material.

There is room for more than 90 planes, it can travel more than a million miles without refueling, and it has a maximum speed of greater than 30 miles per hour. The nuclear power plant produced the equivalent of an amazing 280,000-plus horsepower.

Types of Missions

Ever since World War II, the aircraft carrier has been the king (or queen, if you prefer) of the ocean. As both ship and aviation technology have progressed, the power of the aircraft carrier has grown exponentially.

The USS Abraham Lincoln.

(Courtesy U.S. Navy)

As we saw during the War on Terrorism in Afghanistan in 2002 and in the liberation of Iraq in 2003, the aircraft carrier can be used to deliver bombs, troops, supplies, or humanitarian aid to an area, as needed.

Let's take a look now at how aircraft carriers are used as part of a military strategy.

Your Mission, Should You Choose to Accept It ...

The modern aircraft carrier's mission can be divided into three themes:

◆ To provide a credible, sustainable, independent forward presence and conventional deterrence in peacetime.

Forward presence is a big deal in terms of fighting a war. It means that you've got the equivalent of a small, heavily-armed city in the bad guy's backyard. *Conventional deterrence* means the bad guy knows this small, heavily-armed city is quite capable of bombing the you-know-what out of you with non-nuclear weapons if you get out of line. Immediately. That's supposed to make said bad guys think twice before they do anything stupid.

The reason we talk about conventional (always a code word for "not nuclear") deterrence is that we don't have conventional weapons we can launch from the United States at somebody else. All we have for that is really long range nukes. The only way to bomb someone with conventional weapons is to get an aircraft or ship into the area, i.e., forward presence.

◆ To operate as the cornerstone of joint/allied maritime expeditionary forces in times of crisis.

That is, to team up with both our own Army, Air Force, and Marines and those of friendly nations to put troops on the ground at or near the scene of a battle.

◆ To operate and support aircraft attacks on enemies, protect friendly forces, and engage in sustained independent operations in war.

At the Center of Forward Presence

Aircraft carriers are the centerpiece of the forces necessary for forward presence. They operate the aircraft that are capable of attacking airborne, afloat, and ashore targets that threaten free use of the sea. They are deployed worldwide in support of U.S. interests and commitments. They can respond anywhere in the world in a wide variety of modes.

 Flattop Facts _____

Presence missions are of great importance in the military, and nothing does it better than an aircraft carrier. Sure, the bad guys notice when air force and army assets are moved toward a trouble area, but nothing says, "You're about to get your butt kicked," like an aircraft carrier in the area. Sorry, five satellites refocusing their lenses on an area just doesn't do it. Heck, they can't even fly in formation.

The carrier is effective in all roles from peacetime presence to full-scale war. Together with their onboard air wings, the carriers have vital roles across the full spectrum of conflict.

But this hasn't always been the case ...

Born in the Era of Battleships

When aircraft carriers were first used in warfare, battleships were the kings (or queens, if you prefer) of the sea. The battleships did most of the heavy lifting at sea, including providing blockades, engaging in sea warfare, and bombarding the enemy.

Early Carriers Were Subordinate

Whereas battleships performed the primary work of war, aircraft carriers were used only for surveillance purposes. Planes would take off from the carriers' flight decks and scout the area in search of the enemy. This would help the accompanying battleships know where to go and where to point their guns.

The big guns of the navy's battleships and battle cruisers had a range of about 20 miles. It would be years before the potential of carrier-based aircraft as offensive weapons was fully realized.

Everything Changed During World War II

It wasn't until the Second World War that the bombs and torpedoes dropped from carrier aircraft became more dangerous to the enemy than the big guns of battleships. Not only could they dish out more damage, but they were better at evading retaliation. That's because battleships had to get closer to the enemy in the first place in order to carry out an attack.

Because World War II ended with the use of the atom bomb and the beginning of the nuclear age, there were those who thought the new superweapon would render both the battleship and the carrier obsolete, but this didn't turn out to be the case.

Carriers Now Dominant

The story of how the aircraft carrier took over from the battleship the role of *numero uno* in the navy is the same as the story of air power taking over from sea power the role of principle advantage. That is, the guy who can fly with a gun has an advantage over the guy who can just float with a gun.

In days of yore, the navy that controlled the sea usually won the war. Today that rule has changed. Now, the country that controls the sky wins the war.

> **Ship's Log**
>
> According to carrier historian Antony Preston, "The aircraft carrier is a hybrid creation which enables Man to conquer both air and sea simultaneously."

Uses of Battle Groups

Aircraft carriers do not move from place to place as part of a military operation on their own. They move as part of a battle group, a group of other ships designed to support the needs of the aircraft carrier and enhance its strength.

The carrier battle group (CVBG) can be employed in a variety of roles, including the following:

- To protect economic and military shipping.

- To protect a marine amphibious force while en route to, and upon arrival in, an amphibious objective area (we will learn more about Marine amphibious forces in Chapter 3).

- To establish a naval presence in support of national interests.

There is no precise definition of a battle group. It can be any combination of ships deemed necessary to help an aircraft carrier carry out a particular mission. In recent years, however, there has been a more or less standard version of a battle group. It consists of …

- One aircraft carrier.

- Two guided missile cruisers equipped with Tomahawk missiles.

- One guided missile destroyer used for antiaircraft warfare (to combat an enemy's air attack).

- One destroyer, to combat enemy submarines.

- One frigate, also to be used in an antisubmarine role.

- Two attack submarines, to seek out and destroy enemy ships and subs.

- One supply ship to keep the group supplied with oil, ammunition, and other provisions.

The Concept Behind Power Projection

The aircraft carrier battle group best exemplifies the military tactic known as "power projection." This means maximizing the outward mobility of a military force from its base.

The carrier is a military base that is, in itself, mobile—capable of going anywhere accessible to oceangoing vessels. But, beyond that, the carrier's air wing can project the military force even further, outward from the carrier to the range of the aircraft.

Don't Need Permission

One of the best things about aircraft carriers in times of tension and conflict is that we don't need anyone's permission to use them, as long as they stay in international waters. During the war in Afghanistan there was tension over whether Pakistan would allow us to use its air bases. This happened again in the 2003 war against Iraq, when Turkey waffled about allowing the United States to overfly Turkish air space.

But with flattops, the United States has to worry about none of this. The carrier battle group, operating in international waters, doesn't need the permission of host countries for landing or overflight rights. This characteristic isn't lost on our political decision makers, who use Navy aircraft carriers as a powerful instrument of diplomacy.

> **Ship's Log**
>
> Former president Bill Clinton said during a visit to the aircraft carrier USS *Theodore Roosevelt*, "When word of crisis breaks out in Washington, it's no accident the first question that comes to everyone's lips is: Where is the nearest carrier?"

The Layout

An aircraft carrier is a floating air base. It should be noted, however, that not all planes can take off and land on an aircraft carrier. Carrier-based planes are specially made for that purpose. Very large and heavy planes cannot be adapted for carrier use because they need prohibitively long runways to take off and land (we talk about carrier takeoffs and landings in Chapter 4).

The front of an aircraft carrier is the bow. The hind end is the stern. The left side is called the port side. The right side is called starboard. To move toward the front of the ship is to move forward. To move toward the rear is to move aft.

The part of the CV that sticks up is the island. This is where the ship's radar and air traffic control instruments are. If the ship is at war, its battle plans will be executed out of the island as well.

The flat part of the ship is the flight deck. It is on this flat surface that planes take off and land. One of the runways is angled so that it goes slightly off the side of the ship.

The angled runway was quite an innovation for CVs because it meant that, for the first time, planes could take off and land at the same time.

Just below the flight deck is the hangar deck. That's where the aircraft are stored, and, if necessary, repaired. There are other decks below the hangar deck, which we'll get to in a second. That's where the residents of this floating city live, eat, and sleep.

Also down there is a full-fledged nuclear-power reactor. Because of the power and efficiency of that reactor, the ship can operate for 15 years between refuelings.

Getting Around

Every compartment onboard every ship has a series of numbers followed by a letter that tells you where the compartment is and what it's used for. They're written like this: 03-178-4L. It'll be written over the top of the hatch to the compartment and you'll see other cryptic designations stenciled along the passageway. Allow me to interpret.

The first two digits tell you which deck you're on. Decks above the waterline are preceded by a zero. The 03 deck is the third deck above the waterline. The 3 deck is the third deck below the waterline. The deck *at* the waterline is 01. It's called the damage control deck, sometimes, or the main deck.

The second set of digits—178, in this case—tells you how far aft (i.e., toward the stern, the back, the nonpointy end) you are. The strakes of the ship, the vertical support members, are numbered from one at the bow (the pointy end) all the way back to the stern.

The third set of digits tells you the port/starboard (right or left, as determined while facing the pointy end of the ship) location of the compartment. Actually, it's not all that uncommon to lose a sense of which way is forward on a carrier. Try looking at the numbers on the strakes—remember, they get smaller as you go forward.

Remember this acronym: PESO. Port Even, Starboard Odd. The compartments with even numbers are on the port side of the ship, the odd ones on the starboard side. The compartments are numbered outward from the centerline of the ship, so 1 is just next to the centerline, 4 is nearer to the skin of the ship. The last bit, the letter, tells you what the compartment is primarily used for. "L" indicates it's a living space, so if someone mentions meeting at 03-178-4L to look at some etchings, you can be pretty sure they're not talking about machinery repair specs.

Chain of Command

It might surprise you to learn that a carrier is not commanded by an admiral, but by a senior captain, one who has already been the commanding officer of a squadron.

It's sometimes a point of controversy, having aviators command a ship, but they're in fact quite experienced and have a lot of training. They attend nuclear-power school and have also had command of a deep draft ship, such as an oiler or underway replenishment ship of some sort, before getting the CV command. (Remember, CV does not stand for anything. It's the Navy's designation for a ship that is an aircraft carrier.)

> **Ship's Log**
>
> When carrier battle groups are traveling in international waters, they are sovereign U.S. territory. Under international law, any military ship is sovereign territory of that nation.

These folks are front-runners—most of the time, they are selected for flag rank (naval shorthand for any of the admiral ranks) after their CV command tour.

A battle group or other collection of ships under the command of one officer is called a task unit. (Each ship is a task element. More than one ship is a task unit, with each ship being element of that unit.) Here's a quick run-through of the chain of command for a battle group:

- ◆ The admiral commands the battle group.

- ◆ The commanding officer (CO) of the aircraft carrier reports to the admiral, as do the COs of all the other ships. The admiral and his staff are located on the carrier.

- ◆ The commanding officers of the squadrons, usually commanders, report to the Carrier Air Wing Commander (CAG), who reports to the admiral. Sometimes—oh, when was it … during the 1990s some time—we went to the Super CAG concept, a very senior aviator captain as commander of the airwing, and transferred additional responsibilities to him.

> **Flattop Facts**
>
> The area for the admiral and his staff on the USS *Abraham Lincoln* is set off from the passageway with blue plastic curtains. It has blue tile, too. They're on what is called the 03 (zero three) level, just below the flight deck. It's noisy during flight operations (flight ops).

> **Flattop Facts**
>
> Names change all the time in the navy. My specialty was antisubmarine warfare (ASW). It is now called USW, for undersea warfare.

Visitor Arriving

Now that you know a little bit about the elements, both structural and human, that make up a functioning aircraft carrier, it's time for you to visit a CV and have a look around yourself.

If you are visiting an aircraft carrier in port rather than one at sea, you'll climb up a rickety sort of temporary staircase with one or two landings and then cross a metal bridge just barely large enough to accommodate two people. It'll shake under your feet. The cement pier is a *long* way down.

Right before you board the ship, you'll pass over a strip of water between the ship and the pier. The ship is held off of the pier by a bunch of heavy rubber fenders. There's all sorts of crap in the water below you. There may be an inflatable sort of tubing going all around the ship, meant to contain any oil or grease that gets discharged into the water.

> **Ship's Log**
>
> On September 11, 2001, on the day of the terrorist attacks, the *Abraham Lincoln* was in the Puget Sound Naval Shipyard. Because of the security crisis that day, the ship was put into a temporary lockdown. That meant no one could board or depart the ship. The lockdown was called off the following day and life returned to normal aboard the ship. The ship was scheduled to remain in Puget Sound for another month, but rumors were flying that it would be deployed immediately as part of the new War on Terrorism. Whereas other aircraft carriers were sent to take part in the War on Terrorism within days of the attacks in New York and Washington, the *Abraham Lincoln* had to wait for a year before it got to take part in the action.

The first place you step onto is the quarterdeck. This is often a section of the flight deck, one of the elevators, that's lowered down to hangar level. (That's how they get the airplanes from the flight deck down to the hangar deck.) It'll be fancy. Pictures of all the important people mounted on a display board, a junior officer in a spiffy uniform hoping nothing's going to get screwed up on his or her watch, a few petty officers around to maintain logs and greet visitors, and some junior *nonrates* to run errands, messages, and such.

> **Naval Lingo**
>
> **Nonrates** are sailors, usually relatively new to the ship, who are of the lowest ranks and therefore make appropriate go-fers.

You'll see some very nice "fancy work." That's the term used to describe the intricate knots and lines that boatswain's mates do—sort of like naval macramé, although you'd probably be beaten to a pulp if you referred to it as that.

" " Ship's Log

The normal job of a boatswain's mate is to operate, maintain, and fix all the deck gear. This would include the small boats and life boats, the anchors and the lines, the anchor winches, and all the exterior surfaces of the ship.

One of the first things you learn if you are a sailor on a carrier is that most boatswain's mates, including the aviation boatswain's mates, are capable of kicking serious butt any time, anywhere. Not that they have to—the fear factor works in their favor. That aside, boatswain's mates are some of the very best leaders in the United States Navy today. You want something done, find a BM. If you can't find one of those, a gunner's mate will do.

The quarterdeck is the nerve center of any ship in port, and a carrier is no different. It is to a ship in port what the bridge is underway—being the location from which the commanding officer or officer of the day controls the ship. The officer of the deck reports to the command duty officer, or CDO, and is responsible for …

◆ Carrying out the ship's routine.

◆ Initial response in an emergency.

◆ Receiving reports from the other parts of the ship.

◆ Notifying the CDO of anything that goes wrong.

One other big thing: The officer of the deck is also responsible for military courtesies and honors, and it's a rare OOD who will not break into a cold sweat when he sees a car with flags on the front and headlights on drive on to the pier (it's a bigwig) if there's nothing in the *pass down log* (an informal journal about expected visitors, unusual events, and just general good-to-know information) about expecting a VIP.

A Quick Look Around My Flattop: The USS *Abraham Lincoln*

The *Abraham Lincoln* was the fifth-built of the Nimitz class of aircraft carriers. (When a defense contractor designs a new warship, usually more than one of those ships is eventually built, and all of those ships are thought of as being in the same class of ships. The first ship built determines the name of the class.) There are eight Nimitz-class ships. They are, in the order they were built, the USS *Nimitz, Dwight D. Eisenhower, Carl Vinson, Theodore Roosevelt, Abraham Lincoln, George Washington, John C. Stennis,* and *Harry S. Truman.*

USS ENTERPRISE CVN-
ENTERPRISE CLASS NUCLEAR AIRCRAFT CARRIER

BUILDER: Newport News
LAID DOWN: February 4, 1958
LAUNCHED: September 24, 1960

COMMISSIONED: November 25, 1961
HOME PORT: Norfolk, Virginia
Enterprise Is Part Of The Atlantic Fleet

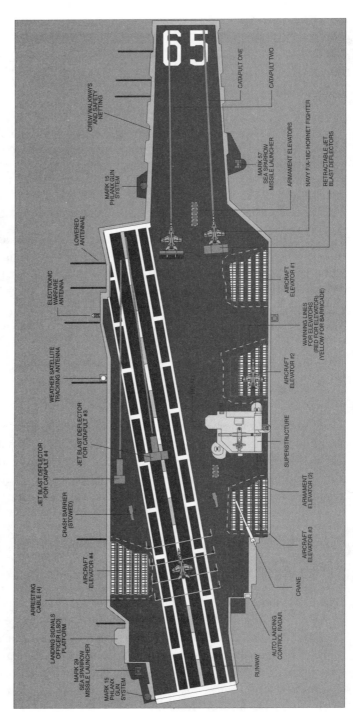

DRAWN BY JIM A PEARSON

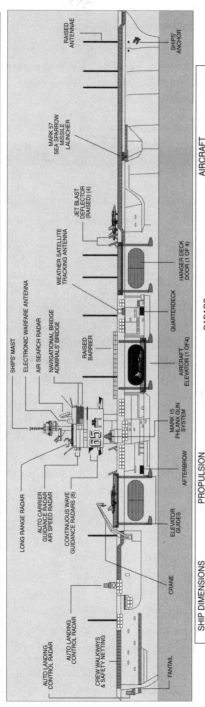

USS ENTERPRISE CVN-
ENTERPRISE CLASS NUCLEAR AIRCRAFT CARRIER

Labels on diagram:
AUTO LANDING CONTROL RADAR
AUTO LANDING CONTROL RADAR
CREW WALKWAYS & SAFETY NETTING
FANTAIL
LONG RANGE RADAR
AUTO CARRIER GUIDANCE RADAR AIR SPEED RADAR
CONTINUOUS WAVE GUIDANCE RADARS (8)
SHIPS' MAST
ELECTRONIC WARFARE ANTENNA
AIR SEARCH RADAR
NAVIGATIONAL BRIDGE ADMIRALS' BRIDGE
RAISED BARRIER
WEATHER SATELLITE TRACKING ANTENNA
JET BLAST DEFLECTOR (RAISED) (4)
MARK 57 SEA SPARROW MISSILE LAUNCHER
RAISED ANTENNAE
SHIPS' ANCHOR
CRANE
ELEVATOR GUIDES
AFTERBROW
MARK 15 PHLANX GUN SYSTEM
AIRCRAFT ELEVATOR (1 OF 4)
QUARTERDECK
HANGER DECK DOOR (1 OF 4)

DRAWN BY JIM A PEARSON

SHIP DIMENSIONS
Length(O/A) :
- 1,123' (design)
- 1,101' (1998)
Length(W/L): 1040'
Beam: 132.9'
Draft: 37'
Flight Deck Length: 1,101'
Flight Deck Width:
- 255.0', 248' (1998)
Flight Deck Area: 4.4 acres
Hangar Dimensions:
- 216,000 sq.feet

DISPLACEMENT
Full Load:
- 89,084 tons (design)
- 93,284 tons
Standard: 75,730 tons
Aviation Fuel: 8,500 tons

USS Enterprise CVN-65 To Be Decommissioned in 2013
Ship To Be Replaced By CVN 78

PROPULSION
Nuclear reactors:
- 8 Westinghouse
A2W Pressurized-Water
Turbines: 4 GE steam turbines
Endurance:
- 200,000+ miles (original)
- 1,000,000 miles (After last refit)
Horsepower: 280,000 shp
Shafts and Propellers: 4 Each
Propeller Diameter: 21' across
Max Speed: 30+ knots

ARMAMENT
- Three Raytheon GMLS Mk 29
8 tube launchers w/Sea Sparrow Missiles
(Added 1979)
- Three GE/GD 20mm/76 Phalanx
6-barreled (Mk-15) (added early.1980s)
2 starboard 1 port

RADARS
AIR SEARCH:
-SPS-32/23 phased-array
"Billboard" radars
(removed in 1979 reconstruction)
-Replaced by Raytheon SPS 49(V)5
- ITT SPS 48E 3D
- Hughes Mk 23 TAS

SURFACE SEARCH:
- Norden SPS 67

FIRECONTROL:
- 6 Mk 95

NAVIGATION:
- Marconi LN 66
- Raytheon SPS 64(V)9
- Furuno 900

AIRCRAFT
HELICOPTERS:
- 8-SH-3G/H Sea King
or SH-60F Seahawk

FIXED WING AIRCRAFT:
- 1 Squadron
F-14 A/B/D Tomcats
- 3 Squadrons
F/A-18C Hornets
F/A-18 E/F SuperHornets
- 4 EA-6B Prowlers
- 4 E-2-C Hawkeyes
- 6 S-3-A/B Vikings
- 2 E-3B Shadows

SHIPS COMPLEMENT
3,319 Navy
2,625 Air Wing
72 Marines

Flight Deck

It's pretty obvious why aircraft carriers are called flattops. They make for a better pool table than a skiing slope. The flat area on top of an aircraft carrier, where the planes take off and land, is called the flight deck. The *Abraham Lincoln*'s flight deck is 4.5 acres in size.

Although it may look like the flight deck is stiff as a board for the entire length of the carrier, it is actually constructed in pieces, with flexible expanding joints. That way, the flight deck can better withstand the stresses of bad weather and rough seas.

The whole flight deck can move atop the rest of the ship for the same reason. To accomplish this rolling effect of the flight deck atop the hull, the flight deck is attached to the hangar deck with vertical structures that are capable of moving independently of one another.

Naval Lingo

A **knot**, a unit of speed, is a nautical mile per hour. A nautical mile per hour is equivalent to 1.15 statute miles per hour, or the miles per hour that we associate with a car traveling down a road. You just say knots. You never say knots per hour, which would be redundant.

The Island

Just as the air traffic controllers at an airport perch themselves in a tower, so do those who work on an aircraft carrier. A carrier's air traffic controllers work in the tower that sticks up out of a carrier's flight deck, off to one side of the ship. This is called the island.

The island rises 150 feet above the flight deck. It is about 120 feet long, but only 20 or so feet wide, in order to leave as much room as possible on the flight deck. There are hatches on either side of it, one facing the flight deck, the other opening onto the side facing away from the flight deck.

Navigating Bridge

The person in command of the aircraft carrier is stationed at the navigating bridge, which is part of the aircraft carrier's island. This section is also known as the *conn*. The commander sits in an elevated chair on the port (left) side of the navigating bridge. From this perch, which is known as the barber's chair, the commander can see both the movements of the ship and all activities on the flight deck.

The CDO is the direct representative of the captain and has release authority, meaning that he or she can fire weapons without asking the captain, often referred to as the "skipper." Each squadron and command aboard the carrier also has an OOD or an SDO (squadron duty officer) and those all report to the ship's CDO as well.

Flattop Facts

The chain of command on an aircraft carrier is different depending on whether the ship is in port or at sea.

If you look up as you approach the ship, you'll see flags and pennants flying. They'll tell which ship of those in port has the most senior officer assigned to it; whether the CO is onboard the ship or not; whether the XO (executive officer), admiral, and chief of staff are onboard; and whether there's anything special going on—for example, church services, transferring oil or ammunition, and that sort of thing.

When you get to the quarterdeck, if you're assigned to the ship or an embarked command (a command that is stationed on the ship but not actually part of the ship, e.g., an aircraft squadron, the admiral's personal staff), you turn to the stern (the back end, the one that's not pointy) and salute the flag. Then you salute the OOD and say, "I report my return aboard."

If you're not assigned to the ship or an embarked command, you request permission to come aboard. The OOD will return your salute and *then* you step onto the quarterdeck. Savvy civilians and retired military contractors turn for a respectful moment toward the flag before addressing the OOD.

From the quarterdeck, you'll step into the hangar bay, the huge interior aircraft hangar inside the ship. That background hum of air compressors, power, and pumps is all around you now, and you can even feel it through the soles of your shoes. From there, you'll probably go through a hatch somewhere and head off to wherever you're supposed to be.

If the CV doesn't have your clearance data, you'll be escorted. Your badge, temporary or issued by ship, is color-coded to tell folks what security clearance you have.

Primary Flight Control

The primary flight control is on the flight deck side of the island, inside the island itself, and is always positioned so that it provides an unobstructed view of the flight deck. In sailor lingo, it is usually shortened to PriFly.

The air space in a five-mile radius and up to an altitude of approximately a mile around and above the ship is controlled from this location. In charge of the PriFly is the air officer and his or her assistant. This pair is known to the others on the ship as the air-boss and the mini-boss.

Carrier Air Traffic Control Center

Planes that are flying higher than one mile up and are more than five miles away from the ship are controlled by the carrier air traffic control center (CATCC). The walls of the CATCC are covered with radar screens, radios, and TV monitors—just like in the movies.

The CATCC is commanded by the air operations officer. If a squadron of jets are returning from a mission, it is up to the CATCC to determine in which order they will land. This is done by determining which jets are closest to running out of fuel.

Divvying Up the Air Space

To better understand what goes on in the CATCC, it helps to know how the air operations officer keeps track of all of the air space around the ship.

Air space around the carrier is divided into areas of responsibility, just as it is around civilian airports. While the exact figures and radii depend on the operating circumstances and the carrier air wing commander, generally the closer in to the aircraft carrier, the more likely the person controlling it is to be able to actually look outside and see the aircraft themselves. The reason for this is pretty clear. One of the major problems with aircraft is keeping aircraft from flying into each other, or deconfliction. In a hostile environment, you want to make sure that …

- Your aircraft are not mistaken for bad guys, and

- Vice versa.

Therefore, the folks with the big picture down on the ship or overhead in the E-2C Hawkeye (an airborne command and control and electronic surveillance aircraft) or other joint control aircraft (any aircraft that performs the same functions but that is assigned to a different command) will be running air traffic control far out from the carrier. They're the ones who'll know where the missile engagement zones are, those areas that the nearby cruiser is responsible for. They know where the no-fly areas are and the safe return corridors. They'll know what the settings on the automatic missile defense systems are and keep the friendlies out of that profile so they won't be mistaken for missiles and shot down. *Blue on blue* is a bad thing.

Naval Lingo

Blue on blue means friendly fire.

As aircraft break off from assigned missions, they may be handed off to different controllers—the operations specialist keeping track of the tanker, for instance. There's also one operations specialist responsible for queuing aircraft up in the "stack" (also known as the marshal) to await their turn to land. Finally, as aircraft break out of marshal and head for the deck, they'll be handed off to the tower and the LSO (Landing Signals Officer).

How does the aircraft carrier know where those aircraft are, anyway? Two primary ways:

◆ First, the aircraft carrier and all the other ships with radar (pretty much everyone) are tracking them as little blips in the sky.

◆ Second, each aircraft has a TACAN on it, a transponder that beeps out information read by special receivers on the ships. The information is correlated by the data link system between the ships.

Occasionally, the computer will screw it up and show different blips for each contact from each ship. But for the most part, the computer figures out that radar blip A from the cruiser correlates to radar blip Z from the carrier. The computer then decides which radar contact is stronger and displays that one on the screen instead of both of the radar blips.

Friend or Foe ID

There's also another bit of nifty gear involved—the IFF, or international friend or foe identification system. The IFF transponder on the aircraft beeps out a signal to the ship. It's a complex signal, one with information packed in layers inside it.

There are four separate layers of information, referred to as modes:

◆ Mode one tells you the country of origin.

◆ Mode two, what the craft is—ship, commercial aircraft, skijet, whatever.

◆ Mode three narrows down the mode two classification. For military aircraft, mode three tells you what squadron it's from, what sort of aircraft, all that. Mode three can also be changed manually inside the cockpit. There are specific settings you change to if you've got an emergency or are going down. All this can be read in the open, meaning that it does not require specialized encryption/decryption.

◆ Mode four is the biggie. It's an encrypted signal that tells you whether the aircraft is a good guy or not. In Naval lingo, if an aircraft is transmitting a mode four signal, we say a contact breaks for mode four or squawks mode four. You're not supposed to shoot at those, and most of our fire control electronics agree with that general principle. If you designate a radar blip squawking mode four as contact and tell a missile to go get it, the electronics are going to start screaming bloody murder. Like anything else, IFF gear can break.

Combat Direction Center

Usually abbreviated CDC, the combat direction center is where the war-making functions of the carrier are carried out. In the old days, this was known as the combat information center, but under any name it provides the same function. It's located right next door to the carrier air traffic control center (CATCC).

This is where enemy locations are determined and communicated to airborne pilots. The CDC receives its information not only from onboard radars and other sensor systems, but from satellites in outer space as well. You can't hide from the U.S. Navy.

The Planes

The planes on an aircraft carrier are called the ship's airwing. The standard airwing on a Nimitz-class aircraft carrier consists of the following aircraft:

- One squadron (12 planes) of the fighter jets called F-14s Tomcats
- Three squadrons (36 planes) of the fighter jets called F/A-18 Hornets
- Four EA6B Prowlers, which jam the enemy's electronics systems
- Four surveillance planes called E2C Hawkeyes
- Six S-3 A/B Vikings, an antisubmarine plane with electronic countermeasure capabilities
- Two ES3A Shadows, which can determine the precise location of potentially hostile missile sites
- Eight SH60 F Seahawk helicopters, which can be used for antisubmarine warfare, search and rescue, or for carrying cargo

For more info on modern-day carrier aircraft see Chapter 5.

Catapults

Airplanes that take off from airports usually have a lot of runway. They use that runway to build up speed for taking off, and to slow down after landing. On an aircraft carrier, pilots don't have the luxury of thousands of yards of runway. The plane has to go from fully stopped to takeoff speed in a very short distance.

To achieve this, carrier-based aircraft are "launched" with the help of a catapult, a device that literally throws the plane forward so that it gets up to speed right away, faster than it could using its own engines. There have been catapults for just about as long as there have been aircraft carriers. As you will learn, the invention of the steam catapult was one of the greatest innovations in carrier history. Most modern carriers, including the *Abraham Lincoln*, have four steam-operated catapults.

Retractable Jet Blast Deflectors

The *Abraham Lincoln*, like all modern U.S. Navy aircraft carriers, has four jet blast deflectors, one for each steam catapult. They are located behind the catapult and, as the name suggests, keep the blast from the jet from causing damage to anyone or anything on the flight deck—especially the jet behind the one that is taking off.

The jet blast deflector rises into place behind the jet after the aircraft has been attached to the catapult. Because of the high temperatures the deflector must withstand, it is made out of concrete—a metal deflector would melt.

Fresnel Lens

The modern aircraft carrier comes with its own lighthouse, thanks to a piece of nineteenth-century technology called the Fresnel lens. The lens acts as a magnifying glass allowing a light aboard the carrier to throw its light 20 or more miles to the horizon.

The lens is named after Augustin Fresnel, a French physicist who, in 1822, invented a lens that resembled a huge glass beehive, with a light at the center. It is flat on one side and ridged on the other. The lens has concentric rings of glass prisms above and below to bend the light into a narrow beam.

One use of the Fresnel lens is in the meatball, which is used to guide landing pilots. The meatball consists of a cross made of lights, a line of green lights going horizontally and a line of vertical yellow lights. The green lights are always lit. They represent the correct angle of approach to a pilot who is about to land.

Only one yellow light is lit at a time. If the yellow light in line with the green lights is lit, that means that the pilot's approach is perfect. If the yellow light is above the green line, the approach is too high. If it is below the green line, the approach is too low. The meatball is located on the port side of the runway.

LSO Platform

The LSO platform (LSO is short for "Landing Signal Officer") is a small area just below the level of the flight deck, hanging out over the water, but high enough so the LSO can watch the aircraft inbound without the deck blocking the view.

A large cargo net is attached to the hull of the ship below the LSO platform. If things go wrong, the LSO and his or her people can jump off the LSO platform and land in the safety net. That's the theory, anyway.

Newport News: Birthplace of Carriers

Twenty-nine of the U.S. Navy's aircraft carriers were built in the same place, the birthplace of carriers, Newport News Shipbuilding. Newport News has built every U.S. carrier since the 1950s.

During its peak years of construction, during World War II, this shipyard produced a new aircraft carrier every three months. A total of 46 Navy ships were built there during World War II. In its heyday, the yard employed 31,000 people.

Flattop Facts

Newport News Shipbuilding was founded in 1886 by railroad magnate Collin P. Huntington. The original name of the company was the Chesapeake Dry Dock and Construction Co. It has been building ships for the U.S. Navy since 1897. The first aircraft carrier built at Newport News was the light carrier *Ranger*, completed in 1933.

The escort carriers (smaller aircraft carriers designated CVEs) and the Midway-class (an earlier class of CV) were designed at Newport News and two of the three Midway carriers were built here. It was at this yard that the first post-WWII supercarrier *Forrestal* was built.

The first nuclear-powered aircraft carriers were built here as well. The first nuke flattop, the *Enterprise*, was commissioned in 1961. After building two more conventionally-powered carriers, the USS *John F. Kennedy* and the USS *America*, Newport News went on to build nine more nuclear-powered carriers, including the USS *Nimitz*.

Today, Newport News has around 18,000 employees. The shipyard covers 550 acres and includes the largest dry dock in the Western hemisphere—Dock 12, which measures 2,300 by 250 feet. (A dry dock is a dock in which the ship is completely out of the water, very useful for repairs.) This dock also features the largest gantry crane in the Western hemisphere, weighing more than 900 tons. (A gantry crane is a huge crane that travels along a track on a platform that is supported by side frames or towers.)

What Is a Ship's Birth Date?

The keel of a ship is usually the first thing built. The keel has been called the backbone of a ship. It lies along the center of the bottom of a ship, completely inside the hull, or the outer shell of a ship.

A ship has three different birthdates, as follows:

- ◆ The date that it is **laid down,** when construction begins.

- ◆ The date that it is **launched,** when construction is completed (which usually ends when the engines are installed). A brief ceremony is held and someone breaks a bottle of champagne.

- ◆ There then comes a period of time, usually about a year, when the ship undergoes a series of tests or trials to determine if it is a sound vessel and a competent war ship. Only after it has passed all of the tests is it **commissioned,** which means it has entered service and has been given an assignment.

The Least You Need to Know

- ◆ A carrier is not commanded by an admiral, but by a senior, post-squadron command captain.

- ◆ The tower that sticks up out of a carrier's flight deck, off to one side of the ship, is called the island.

- ◆ Carrier-based aircraft are "launched" with the help of a catapult, a device that literally throws the plane forward so that it gets up to speed right away.

- ◆ Twenty-nine of the U.S. Navy's aircraft carriers over the years were built at Newport News Shipbuilding.

- ◆ The keel of a ship is its backbone, and it is usually the first thing built.

Chapter 2

Powering a Carrier

In This Chapter

- ◆ How oil was used to power aircraft carriers
- ◆ Aircraft carriers move into the nuclear age
- ◆ The building of the USS *Enterprise*

Moving an aircraft carrier through the water is only slightly easier than shoving an office building through sand. Water isn't all that interested in moving out of the way, and developing enough power to get anywhere is a pretty slick engineering trick.

Here's How It Works ...

The blades on a ship's propeller are a little like the wings on an airplane. You turn them, they cut through the water at an angle. That angle means there's an area of lower pressure on one side of the blade, just like an airplane's wing creates a low-pressure area on the top of the wing. The movement of the water around each propeller blade exerts force against the propeller. That shoves the ship forward.

But How Do You Get the Propeller to Move?

All modern aircraft carriers, even the nuclear ones, have huge steam turbines to turn the propeller shaft. These turbines run at very high speeds, far too fast to turn the propeller directly. The turbine is connected to the propeller by a set of reduction gears, pretty much like you'd find on a really *really* big 10-speed bike. That steps the speed of the shaft down to a reasonable level.

The difference between a conventional (non-nuclear) carrier and a nuclear carrier is how you make the steam. On a nuclear carrier, water is heated up by a nuclear reaction. On a conventional carrier, the water is heated up in a boiler.

Obviously, it's a lot more complicated than this. For one thing, the steam is "super-heated," which means it's kept under pressure so it's far hotter than the steam you have coming out of your tea kettle at home. And it's *dry* steam—odd, but true. There's a system for removing miniscule droplets of water from the steam so that the water doesn't corrode the turbine. Engineers also spend a lot of time worrying about contaminants in the water, and the nuclear engineers are very concerned that the coolant water doesn't leak into the water they make steam out of because you don't want water that's been in close contact with a nuclear reactor getting dumped into your turbine.

Flattop Facts

Leaks are a very bad thing in nuclear reactors. Actually, they're a very bad thing in any engineering plant. The main steam, which is the steam used to turn the turbines, is under very high pressure, around 1,200 pounds per square inch. A pinhole-sized main steam leak won't just burn you—it will slice through skin, flesh, and bone like a scalpel. Which explains why you should never feel around on a main steam line to see if there's a leak.

Early aircraft carriers didn't start off with 1,200 pounds of steam and nuclear reactors. Let's look at how the technology evolved.

Power Carriers the Old-Fashioned Way

In the days before nuclear reactors, aircraft carriers were powered by oil-fired, high-pressure steam boilers—as many as a dozen of them. To keep the boilers stoked, the carriers needed to carry many tons of oil with them, stored in fuel tanks called *bunkers*.

The oil was burned in furnaces, called *fireboxes*, under a forced draft to create extremely high temperatures. Saltwater was converted into fresh water, and the fresh water was pumped through tubes that traveled through the super-heated area in the fireboxes, producing steam.

That steam then turned the ship's geared turbine engines. Such a system could produce as much as 150,000 horsepower, which is necessary to move a ship as heavy as an aircraft carrier at the required speed.

> **Ship's Log**
>
> The USS *John F. Kennedy*, which was commissioned in 1968, was the last carrier to be powered conventionally. Since then, all carriers have been powered by nuclear energy. That is, they have had a full-fledged nuclear reactor onboard.

What Is Nuclear Energy?

In modern nuclear-powered aircraft carriers, the nuclear reactor takes the place of the oil-burning firebox, but otherwise the system works the same. The heat creates steam and the steam turns the turbines.

What is nuclear energy? It is energy created through the molecular breakdown of unstable materials.

Radioactive, or molecularly unstable, materials were first discovered in 1895 when Wilhelm Conrad Röntgen discovered X-rays. The following year, Antoine Henri Becquerel found that uranium salts caused fogging and images on photographic plates. But humankind did not learn to use radioactive materials to create huge amounts of power until more than 50 years later.

The Navy first tested out the idea of nuclear power not on an aircraft carrier but on a submarine. When that worked, they started building the larger nuclear plants needed to move an aircraft carrier (a few were also used on cruisers, but all those ships have since been decommissioned). The first nuclear-powered aircraft carrier was the USS *Enterprise*. For a while, the Navy built both nuclear and conventionally powered CVs. Ever since the USS *JFK*, all CVs have been nuclear-powered.

Nuclear power is created when radioactive material undergoes a process known as exothermic chemical decomposition. That is, its molecules are made to break down and release heat. This heat is used to turn water into steam—just as coal-burning furnaces were once used to fuel steam engines. That part of the mechanics remains the same. The steam pushes a turbine connected to a generator that converts the energy into electricity. The only difference is in how the heat is created.

The *Enterprise*: First Nuclear Aircraft Carrier

The U.S. Navy and Congress argued the matter of whether the United States should build a nuclear-powered aircraft carrier from 1949 to 1956, when the barely adequate funds for the project were finally approved for six nuclear flattops. Because of budget concerns, they tried cutting costs in the areas of planning and development.

Flattop Facts

The USS *Enterprise*, the world's first nuclear-powered aircraft carrier, was commissioned by the U.S. Navy on November 25, 1961.

Flattop Facts

Here's to those of you who might want to design your own carrier some day. Ideally, you want as short a propeller shaft as possible on both conventional and nuclear CVs. A shorter shaft means less torque and more efficient operation. Less chance of damaging shafts. Fewer watertight compartments to run the shaft through, therefore fewer shock mountings and fewer seals to leak between compartments.

A Kitty Hawk–Class Carrier

The engineers did not design the ship that was to become the first nuclear aircraft carrier from scratch as a brand-new designation of aircraft carrier— although this might have seemed warranted, considering the ship's unprecedented size, power, and potential problems. Instead, they designated the first nuclear-powered aircraft carrier a Kitty Hawk–class carrier, modified to accommodate a nuclear power plant. The Kitty Hawk–class influence on the *Enterprise*'s design shows up in the location of the island and the elevators. The *Kitty Hawk*, because of its angled runway, needed to have one elevator moved forward. This meant that the island was moved aft a bit. The *Enterprise's* island and elevators are in the same place.

Despite the obvious changes that they would need to make to accommodate a drastically different power plant, planners retained style elements from the Kitty Hawk class of ships. They thought it would be cheaper than designing the *Enterprise* from scratch. However, the final price tag for the *Enterprise* would indicate that this probably was not the case.

Construction of the *Enterprise* began on February 4, 1958, at Newport News, Virginia.

Three Hundred Thousand Miles Between Pit Stops

The *Enterprise*'s power plant, which is a full-fledged nuclear reactor, is capable of sailing 300,000 miles between refuelings and is driven by 8 Westinghouse A2W pressurized-water-cooled reactors that provide heat to 32 heat exchangers. These generate steam for the 4 turbine units, which are each geared to a propeller shaft. The ship's engine is capable of producing an almost incomprehensible 300,000-shaft horsepower. The *Enterprise* has a maximum speed of 35 knots.

The reactor was a great deal larger than the oil-burning power plants that had been in the previous Kitty Hawk–class carrier, but this was made up for, and then some, by the fact that the nuclear-powered vessel didn't have to carry the oil to fuel the fire-boxes.

Fact Box
USS *Enterprise* (CVN-65) Specifications Launched: September 24, 1960 Commissioned: November 25, 1961 Overall length: 1,123 feet Maximum width: 257 feet Beam at waterline: 133 feet Maximum height: 250 feet Displacement (full load): 90,000 tons Number of reactors: 8 Maximum speed: 35-plus knots Propellers: 4 Rudders: 4 Catapults: 4 Anchors: 2 Anchor chain length: 1,080 feet Crew (total): 5,500 Aircraft: 85

The surplus space, enhanced by the fact that the *Enterprise* was larger than the previous Kitty Hawk carriers, was used to increase the aviation fuel supply by 50 percent. It isn't enough to merely have a source of power that enables you to go hundreds of thousands of miles between ports, you must have supplies for the crew to last that long as well.

Flattop Facts

The rest of the space not used for oil was used to keep the people onboard supplied during those long stretches at sea.

The principle advantage of a nuclear-powered aircraft carrier is its range. Since it rarely needs to refuel, it can report to any potential theater of war for as long as needed.

World's Largest Moveable Structure

The USS *Enterprise* was larger than any aircraft carrier that had come before, and it remains the world's largest moveable structure. The carrier displaces 75,700 tons (of water) at standard weight and 89,000 tons when fully loaded.

The overall length of the ship is 1,123 feet. The flight deck measures 1,100 feet by 257 feet. That amounts to 4.5 acres. When fully manned, the ship sleeps 3,157 ship's officers and crew and 2,628 air-wing personnel.

The hangar for the aircraft is truly awesome. It is 860 feet long, 107 feet wide, and 25 feet high. It can hold and maintain close to 100 aircraft.

The world's largest moveable structure: the USS Enterprise.

(Courtesy Warzone Magazine/Military Technical Journal)

A Classic of Design

The *Enterprise*'s original island was a classic of design. It had a dome at the top, and the sides were so flat that they were referred to as billboards. Because the ship needed no smokestack, the sides of the *Enterprise*'s island became the home of eight huge fixed planar radar arrays.

Four of them were SPS-32 search radar antennae and the other four were tracking-beam radar antennae. The large fixed antennae have proven to have greater range than their rotating Kitty Hawk predecessors. In addition, electronic countermeasure antennae were installed in circles around the top of the island's dome.

Hefty Price Tag

The *Enterprise* and the USS *Constellation*, a conventional aircraft carrier, were built simultaneously. The *Enterprise*, however, cost 70 percent more. To partially offset this cost difference, construction of the *Enterprise* was completed without any defensive armament except aircraft. The plan at the time was to retrofit the carrier with two Mark (Mk.) 10 Terrier missile launchers. (Mark 10 indicates the tenth design version of the Terrier launcher.)

To make sure everything worked properly. *Enterprise* left Newport News on October 29, 1961, for what are called "builder trials." Builder trials consist of putting the ship through her paces before she's turned over to the Navy. Such trials include a full power run, which involves going as fast as possible and exercising all power plant systems (including running a certain percentage over rated power to see if the safety factors are working); a "crash back"—going from as fast as you can ahead and then immediately kicking it into reverse; hard turns; maneuvers; and about anything else you can think of. The carrier still belongs to the builder until after the trials—it's still under warranty, so to speak.

When the carrier returned to port on November 3, a huge broom was attached to her masthead, symbolically stating that the *Enterprise* had made a "clean sweep" of her tests. Everything had gone perfectly. A second trial was planned but canceled, because it was no longer necessary (another cost-saving move).

The final price tag for the Enterprise was $451.3 million. That number frightened Congress so badly that previously approved funding for five additional ships was rescinded. It would be 10 years before construction of another nuclear carrier would be approved.

Flattop Facts

The *Enterprise* is no longer known as CVAN-65, but rather as CVN-65. The code was changed in the mid-1970s when all supercarriers lost their attack designation. (CV is the Navy's designation for aircraft carrier. CVA means attack aircraft carrier. CVN means nuclear-powered aircraft carrier. CVAN means a nuclear-powered attack aircraft carrier.)

The *Enterprise* Gets Some Weapons and a Facelift

By the end of the 1970s, the Navy had decided that the *Enterprise* would be a more secure vessel if it had the ability to shoot back. Times were changing, and other modifications, to communications and radar systems, were also called for.

Armament

The *Enterprise* was finally retrofitted for armament in late 1972, but not with the Terrier missile launchers, as had been originally planned. Instead, Mk. 25 Sea Sparrow BPDMS (pronounced *Be-po-de-mus*) launchers were put aboard.

Between 1979 and 1982, the *Enterprise* received Mk. 57 NATO Sea Sparrow launchers to replace the Sea Sparrow BPDMS launchers. Contemporaneously, three Phalanx Mk. 15 20mm multibarrel *CIWS* (Close-In Weapons Systems, pronounced *See-whiz*), as well as three Mk. 68 20mm systems, were fitted to the *Enterprise*.

> **Naval Lingo**
>
> **CIWS** is short for Close-In Weapon Systems. *SEE-whiz* is how it's pronounced. There's also a rude translation of the acronym that I have conveniently repressed. CIWS fires a lot of bullets at a really high rate of speed. It sounds like a buzz saw when it goes off

New Antennae

Also during the 1979 to 1982 refurbishing, the billboard antennae, which turned out to be ineffective and costly to maintain, were removed and the entire island was redesigned in a different configuration. The dome and mast were removed as the Electronic Countermeasure, or ECM system, they held had grown obsolete.

The original mast was replaced with a new central mast. Antenna for surface search radars (SPS 48, 58, and 10—not to be confused with SPF ratings, which are for sunscreens) and air search radars (SPS 48C, 49, and 65), plus low-level SPS 58 and search SPS 10 were mounted to the new mast.

Also in the early 1980s, an OS-82 communications satellite antenna was installed. Two Mk. 115 missile fire control systems were removed and in their place went three Mk. 91 systems. To confuse incoming homing missiles, three Mk. 36 Chaffroc RBOC were installed.

> **Flattop Facts**
>
> After the refitting, the Enterprise's maximum population shrunk to 3,100 ship's crew and officers and 2,400 airwing members.

The first nuclear-powered aircraft carrier was the eighth U.S. Navy ship to bear the name *Enterprise*. The ship turned out to be a smashing success. It proved that a nuclear-power plant could provide the power for a state-of-the-art aircraft carrier.

Even before it was officially commissioned by the Navy, the ship was doing its part to defend the United States. The *Enterprise*'s first task was to be part of the Cuban Missile Crisis quarantine in 1962.

It proved its endurance in 1964 when it went all the way around the world in 65 days. It also proved that, because nuclear power is so efficient and eliminates the need for massive fuel storage, freeing up space for additional food and water, a nuclear-powered flattop can be deployed in an action zone for much longer than its fossil-fuel predecessors. It can go three years without being refueled.

Because of the *Enterprise*'s success, more nuclear-powered ships were eventually built. Today they are commonplace.

The Least You Need to Know

- In the days before nuclear reactors, aircraft carriers were powered by oil-fired, high-pressure steam boilers.

- In modern nuclear-powered aircraft carriers, the nuclear reactor takes the place of the oil-burning firebox, but otherwise the system works the same.

- The *Enterprise* was designated a Kitty Hawk-class carrier, modified to adapt to her nuclear power plant.

- The USS *Enterprise* remains the world's largest moveable structure.

Teaming Up with the Marines

In This Chapter

◆ Moving marines from ship to shore

◆ The first amphibious assault ships

◆ A new breed of gators

◆ The rise and fall of the Osprey

This chapter is about the navy's amphibious assault ships, which are like mini-aircraft carriers. An amphibious assault ship's job is to help launch a sea-to-land invasion by the U.S. Marines. Along with marines and sailors, the ship holds the aircraft that are used to take the marines inland to the battlefield.

For years, the navy and the marines have teamed up, with marines using naval ships to launch amphibious (sea-to-land) assaults. For instance, amphibious attacks helped the United States to victory in the Pacific Ocean in history's largest war, World War II. It was also the method by which the Allies, including the U.S. Army, began the liberation of Europe, with the

D-Day invasions on the beaches of Normandy, France, in 1944. Let's take a look at how amphibious attack became the marines' forte.

Birth of Amphibious Attack

The marines' amphibious attacks in World War II surprised the enemy because never before in military history had troops been successful when moving from ship-to-shore directly into battle. Luckily for the United States, the marines foresaw the possibility of an island war with Japan, and developed the equipment and strategy necessary for an attack from the sea.

The concept dates back as far as 1921 when Marine Corps major Earl Ellis first proposed a "ship-to-shore tactical movement." The proposal stressed that troops should invade shorelines only under the cover of intense naval firepower. Troops should hit the beach on the run and should set up their initial firing positions inland, off of the beach.

Ship's Log

Covert SEAL teams operate very effectively off carriers, and they're quite tightly integrated with their counterparts in the other services. Even though it's a bit harder to sneak up on the enemy when you've got all that steel off the coast, SEALs remain particularly nasty forms of swamp bugs. You can't see 'em, but you know when you've been bit.

For the theory to work, a great deal of specialized technology had to be developed. Pilots would need to fly in dive bombers in order to execute precise strategic strikes on the beach during the first stages of the invasion. Plus, a landing craft would need to be developed that could quickly and efficiently transport troops from ship to shore. The craft, Ellis pointed out, would have to be able to beach itself, empty itself of troops, and then return to sea without a push and regardless of the tides.

During the next 10 years, the marines determined the need for three types of amphibious boats, capable of transporting troops from ship-to-shore. The first would be armored and fast, able to drive up out of the water and onto—even across—the beach. This left open the possibility that troops could embark further inland, off of the sand. The prototype for this craft was developed in 1924 by American tank pioneer—and father of the T-34—Walter Christie.

The second craft would be larger, able to transport great numbers of troops ashore during an attack's second wave. This vehicle turned out to be a variation on a Mississippi Delta boat built by the Higgins Company of New Orleans.

The third would be a ship designed to transport tanks ashore. The first plans for this craft weren't drawn up until November 1941 by John Niedermair of the United

States Navy Bureau of Ships. All three craft would double as supply shuttles once the invasion was underway.

Deadly Gators: Amphibious Assault Ships

These amphibious forces, formally somewhat of a backwater in the Navy (no pun intended), have moved to the forefront in the past 10 years or so. Despite the successes with smart weapons, unmanned aerial surveillance aircraft, and other new technology, to win you have to take land and hold it, and that's where *shallow water operations* come in handy.

Which brings us to modern warfare, in which the navy helps the marines get to the shore to engage in battle with amphibious assault ships. They are called "gators," and they resemble small aircraft carriers. They have a flight deck and an island. They launch and recover aircraft. But they are much smaller—about one third of the size of the navy's supercarriers.

> **Naval Lingo**
>
> The process of taking land and holding it is known as **shallow water operations** or **brown water operations**, named after the color of the water near the coast, as opposed to a blue water navy, when the battle group is operating completely out of range of land and independently.

Tarawa Class

The original amphibious assault ships, capable of launching aircraft used to move marines to the front, were Tarawa-class ships. Built at Ingalls Shipbuilding in Pascagoula, Mississippi, beginning in the mid-1970s, they were 820 feet long. Five of them were built. They were:

- USS *Tarawa*
- USS *Saipan*
- USS *Belleau Wood*
- USS *Nassau*
- USS *Peleliu*

The Tarawa-class ships displaced 40,000 tons when full, about a third of the displacement of the United States's nuclear-powered aircraft carriers. They held a crew of 1,731 (including marines), and were the base for 26 to 43 helicopters. The marines were passengers on these Tarawa-class craft until the ship was near the shore; they then traveled to land (the battlefield) in helicopters that were stored onboard the craft.

Tarawa-class ships had an armament of four missile systems. A typical air group might include 16 CH-46D Sea Knight helicopters, 6 CH-53D Sea Stallion helicopters, and 4 UH-1N Iroquois helicopters. All of the choppers were transport vehicles, designed to move marines from ship to land.

> **Ship's Log**
>
> Amphibious assault ships use AV-8B Harrier aircraft and anti-submarine warfare helicopters to perform sea control and limited power projection missions.

A plan to update the Tarawa-class ships was scrapped in favor of building a whole new class of amphibious attack ships, the Wasp class. The Tarawa-class ships, now obsolete, are still around, but plans are to scrap them between 2010 and 2012.

Wasp Class

The Tarawa class's replacement, and the most recent class of amphibious assault ship, is the Wasp class, which were first built in the late 1980s. There are seven of these ships, as follows:

- USS *Wasp* (LHD 1)
- USS *Essex* (LHD 2)
- USS *Kearsarge* (LHD 3)
- USS *Boxer* (LHD 4)
- USS *Bataan* (LHD 5)
- USS *Bonhomme Richard* (LHD 6)
- USS *Iwo Jima* (LHD 7)

The aircraft aboard a typical Wasp-class amphibious assault ship are …

- Twelve CH-46 Sea Knight helicopters.
- Four CH-53E Sea Stallion helicopters.
- Six AV-8B Harrier attack aircraft.
- Three UH-1N Huey helicopters.
- Four AH-1W Super Cobra helicopters.

The armament consists of …

- ◆ Two RAM launchers.

- ◆ Two NATO Sea Sparrow launchers.

- ◆ Three 20mm Phalanx CIWS mounts (two on LHD 5–7).

- ◆ Four .50 cal. machine guns.

- ◆ Four 25 mm Mk 38 machine guns.

Fact Box

Wasp-Class Amphibious Assault Ship Specifications
Builder: Ingalls Shipbuilding, Pascagoula, Miss.
Power plant: Two boilers, two geared steam turbines, two shafts, 70,000 shaft horse-power
Length: 844 feet
Beam: 106 feet
Displacement: Approx. 40,500 tons, full load
Top speed: 23.5+ miles per hour
Crew:
     Ship's company: 104 officers, 1,004 enlisted
     Marine detachment: 1,894
Date deployed: July 29, 1989

Osprey: New Breed

So far we have talked about the ships that the marines use for amphibious attacks. Now let's take a look at some of the latest aircraft used for those invasions.

The MV-22 Osprey is a new breed of military aircraft. The tilt-rotor aircraft is designed to land and take off like a helicopter and to fly like a fixed-wing aircraft. It is a transport vehicle designed to deliver marines from an aircraft carrier to an inland battle.

However, the Osprey is heavy, so heavy that it caused dangerous listing in the aircraft carriers that it test-landed on. Therefore, the newest amphibious assault ships, like the *Iwo Jima* (see discussed in the next section) take on sea water and maintain ballast when an Osprey lands, thus offsetting the weight of the aircraft.

USS *Iwo Jima*

The USS *Iwo Jima* (LHD-7) is the seventh and newest of the Wasp-class amphibious assault ships. It is 844 feet long and weighs 40,500 tons. Its beam is 106 feet and the ship travels at a speed of 23 knots. The *Iwo Jima* was commissioned on June 30, 2001.

It has a crew of 1,009 sailors and 73 officers. It can launch up to 42 troop-carrying helicopters and carries 40 amphibious vehicles. Its armament includes two Sea Sparrow launchers, two Phalanx antimissile systems, eight .50-caliber machine guns, and two rolling airframe missile systems.

Flattop Facts

The new USS *Iwo Jima* shares the same name as LPH 2, the lead ship of the first class of amphibious attack ships, the Iwo Jima class. The elder ship, laid down in 1959, was built as the first "keel-up" amphibious assault ship. (The class of ships was not named after LPH 1 because that ship had been converted into an amphibious attack ship.) Among that ship's accomplishments, one came on April 17, 1970, when it served as the primary recovery ship for the return of the crew of Apollo 13. HS-4 helicopters from LPH 2 recovered the three Apollo 13 astronauts from the South Pacific. That ship was also the first amphibious assault ship to deploy to the Persian Gulf during the first Gulf War. LPH 2 was decommissioned in 1993.

The ship was built at Litton Ingalls Shipbuilding in Pascagoula, Mississippi. Its flight deck is 2.2 acres in size, and it has a 15,000-square-foot hangar deck.

Ship's Log

The motto of the USS *Iwo Jima*—"Uncommon Valor"—is based on Fleet Admiral Chester W. Nimitz's words when he spoke of sailors and marines who fought at Iwo Jima: "Among the Americans who served on Iwo Jima Island uncommon valor was a common virtue."

The *Iwo Jima* cost $1.4 billion to build. It is the seventh LHD-class amphibious ship, bringing the navy's total of amphibious assault ships to 12. The navy-marine teaming now has 12 amphibious ready groups (ARGs). These consist of an amphibious assault ship along with supporting ships that, as a group, can land and sustain marines on any shore.

The ship works great. Unfortunately, two Ospreys crashed in 2001 killing 25 marines in test flights. As a consequence, the *Iwo Jima* fought in Operation Iraqi Freedom in 2003 without the aircraft that it was specifically designed to accommodate.

Instead of carrying the Ospreys, the *Iwo Jima* went to war with CH-53 Super Stallion and CH-46E Sea Knight helicopters. Aboard the ship was the Twenty-sixth Marine Expeditionary Unit, which was comprised of 2,200 marines. During Operation Iraqi

Freedom, marines were transported from the USS *Iwo Jima* to locations deep inside Iraq. When the war was over and it was time for most of the marines to return to the ship, they were picked up at a location near Mosul, Iraq.

The Least You Need to Know

- The marines deserve credit for the amphibious attack strategy that led to the United States's series of successes in the Pacific during World War II.

- In modern warfare, the navy helps the marines get to the battle with amphibious assault ships, which resemble small aircraft carriers.

- The original amphibious assault ships were Tarawa-class ships, which were first built in the mid-1970s.

- The most recent class of amphibious assault ship is the Wasp class, which were first built in the late 1980s.

- A Wasp-class ship, the USS *Iwo Jima*, went to war in support of Operation Iraqi Freedom.

Part 2

The Parts That Fly

Now that we have familiarized ourselves with the carrier, let's take a look at the carrier's *raison d'etre*: the aircraft. If it weren't for the aircraft, the carrier would have nothing to carry, after all. It would just be a ridiculously large barge.

First we will examine how planes take off and land from a carrier's flight deck. It isn't as easy as taking off and landing from an airport, where extralong runways give pilots lots of room for error. As you'll find out, planes are pretty much thrown into the air when they take off and they are caught and yanked to a halt when they land.

Then we'll learn about the individual planes. We'll look at how carrier aircraft must differ from their land counterparts. We'll learn of the state-of-the-art jets of today, the history of carrier planes, and the greatest carrier aircraft in history.

Chapter 4

The Planes, Boss, the Planes

In This Chapter

- ◆ Taking off and landing on a carrier
- ◆ Hoping for the best but preparing for the worst
- ◆ Meeting the rigorous demands of a carrier
- ◆ Helicopters and other vertical takeoff and landing craft

As anyone who has ever witnessed planes landing on aircraft carriers can tell you, taking off and landing on a land airstrip is a peaceful and nonviolent thing compared to the rivet-wrenching world of the carrier plane.

One of the big differences between land-based and carrier aircraft is that the carrier aircraft needs to be tougher. A plane that lands and takes off with the luxury of a long runway at an airfield will not undergo anywhere near the stress of a carrier plane.

To see why planes need to built tougher to withstand life on an aircraft carrier, let's take a closer look at how aircraft are launched and recovered on carriers.

Launches and Recoveries

On a carrier, planes don't roll into an easy takeoff or roll to a stop after a smooth landing. Instead, they are thrown into the air on takeoff and are caught and jerked to a sudden halt when they land. Even the terminology is different, reflecting the more violent nature of carrier takeoffs and landings: takeoffs are called *launches* or cat shots (short for catapult shots) and landings are called *recoveries* or traps.

> **Ship's Log**
>
> It has long been said that landings on a carrier are less like landings at an airport and more like controlled crashes.

To launch the aircraft, carriers have a nifty device called a catapult, which, as its name suggests, throws the plane into the air. Actually, most Nimitz-class carriers have four catapults on their flight decks.

Those Nifty Catapults

The Wright brothers had been experimenting with a system that used a weight, rope, and pulleys. But the first usable carrier catapult, the mechanism by which aircraft are tossed into the air and told to fly, was designed by U.S. Navy captain Washington Irving Chambers.

Chambers's catapult was very high-tech for the time, which was 1912. It used compressed air to propel the aircraft down the deck. The principle behind the carrier catapults of today is not that much different. Larger, yes—but not that different.

Off We Go!

Today's catapults are strong enough to throw an automobile 800 yards. The catapult consists of 200-feet-long tubes that have been set into the deck. At the rear of the tubes are steam-powered pistons, and these are attached to something called a shuttle, which runs along the top of the deck. This shuttle is attached to the nose wheel tow bar on the aircraft. This is a bar near the plane's front wheel that is used to tow the aircraft.

Super-pressurized steam from the ship's power plant builds up behind the pistons. When it has built up to a sufficient degree, the pressure is released all at once, which pushes the pistons. The pistons in turn push the shuttle, and the shuttle pushes the aircraft down the flight deck. The aircraft quickly achieves the speed it needs to take off. The connection between the shuttle and the plane is released, and off we go into the wild, blue yonder.

> **Flattop Facts**
>
> The catapult propels the jet from zero to 160 miles per hour in just three seconds.

Catapults are surprisingly dependable. Not all that many moving parts, when you get right down to it: steam, a big piston, and room for it to release. However, there have been notable breakdowns, which you'll learn about in Chapter 20.

Soft Cats

Probably the biggest danger of malfunction on a cat shot is a "soft cat." When there is insufficient steam pressure driving the catapult forward, the aircraft simply dribbles off the bow (the pointy end) of the ship. It takes a *very* fast reaction by the pilot to punch out (eject) in time to avoid hitting the water while still inside the aircraft. The big danger from going into the water is not the impact—it's the cold water hitting the blazing-hot jet engine turbines, which results in an immediate explosion. The blades of the jet engine can slice through the cockpit and anything (or anyone) in it.

Controlled Crash Landings

The concept behind landing an aircraft on a carrier is simple. The pilot doesn't land as much as he aims his plane (at speeds of up to 100 knots) at a spot on the flight deck, and then allows the carrier to catch the plane. This is sometimes referred to as a controlled crash.

Dangling off the back of the plane is a tail hook. Across the deck have been stretched a series of (usually four) super-strong steel wires. The plane hits the deck rear wheels first. The arresting hook catches the wires, which slams the nose wheel down, yanking the plane to an immediate halt.

The wires start close to the stern of the ship and are laid across every couple of hundred feet. This gives the pilot a margin of error—if he misses the first set of cables, he gets a couple more chances—but not much. And pilots do miss. That's why the landing strip is angled away from the ship's island and other parked aircraft—so that errant pilots will do as little damage as possible.

Ship's Log

Author Tom Clancy says that landing an F/A-18 Hornet strike fighter on the deck of an aircraft carrier is like "taking a swan dive out of a second-floor window and hitting a postage stamp on the ground with your tongue."

But don't panic just yet. A pilot who misses every set of wires on the runway won't just allow his plane to roll off the edge of the ship and into the sea. Instead, he will go full throttle, bounce his wheels off the deck, and fly back up into the air. Pilots actually accelerate into their landings so that they will be able to easily take off again in case something goes wrong with the landing.

Another safe landing on the flight deck of the USS Enterprise.

(Courtesy Warzone Magazine/Military Technical Journal*)*

Pilots always aim for one of the two middle wires, as this allows for the most margin of error. Undershoot and you can catch the first wire. Overshoot and you can catch the last wire. Aim for the first wire and you're apt to come up shy of the ship's stern and that, my friends, is not recommended.

Bolter and Wave Off

Because it's so difficult to do, not every landing on an aircraft carrier goes perfectly. In this section we will look at some of the problems that come up fairly frequently, and what's done to prevent them from turning into full-fledged disasters.

We've just described one of the most common problems: failing to catch any of the wires. This is called a *bolter* in aircraft carrier lingo, and it can be caused by many things, including the following:

- Pilot error
- A fault in the tail hook system that allows it to bounce back when it hits the deck
- A snapped cable
- Sheer bad luck

At the moment the aircraft touches down, the pilot shoves the throttles forward, applying full power. Friction starts slowing the aircraft immediately as the wheels make contact with the deck. (Hey, there's a reason they call the deck a nonskid surface, right?) That way, if the tail hook fails to stop the aircraft, the pilot can build up enough speed to take off again at the end of the ship.

Sometimes, just as the aircraft is getting ready to land, there's a reason it shouldn't. If this happens, then the pilot is *waved off*—in other words, he's told not to land. Pilots can be waved off for a number of reasons, including any of the following:

♦ A fouled deck (meaning that someone is inside the flight area)

♦ The cables have the wrong tension

♦ A really crappy approach

♦ The LSO is taking a break for a latte or potty break (just kidding, LSOs!)

The LSO or air boss will normally initiate the wave off. That is, he or she will get on the radio, tell the pilot to wave off, and go around again. The Fresnel lens turns red, meaning that the flight deck is not ready for landing. When waved off, the pilot increases airspeed and flies past the carrier, sometimes not all that far above the deck, and then follows the same path to leave the ship as he would during a normal launch.

Rigging the Barricade

Two other things can go wrong when a plane is attempting to land on a flight deck: The tail hook might not extend, meaning that there is nothing to catch the wires; and the landing gear might not come down when it is time for recovery.

If a plane is having mechanical difficulties that make recovery impossible, all is not lost. The carrier can then do something called "rigging the barricade," which is like hanging a really big badminton net strung across, with the incoming aircraft as the shuttlecock.

Barricade traps are just about one of the most fun operations you can do on an aircraft carrier. Everyone just loves doing them, looks forward to it, and can't wait for the next one.

Not!

Barricade traps are probably responsible for more pairs of soiled underwear in the ship's laundry than any other event, other than fire. *So* much can go wrong. The aircraft can hit the barricade at a bad angle and bounce around a bit, slew into other aircraft, and so on. The aircraft isn't really built to take forces coming at it from those angles and can suffer significant mechanical damage. The aircraft might even miss the barricade and hit the island.

Naval Lingo

General Quarters is the highest state of damage control readiness.

Repair Eight is the damage control team responsible for the flight deck.

Because there's so much that can go wrong while trying to stop an aircraft with a barricade, the ship will be at *General Quarters*, the highest state of damage control readiness. *Repair Eight*, the damage control team responsible for the flight deck, will be having just a really ducky day.

There's also an automatic guidance link between most aircraft and the carrier that allows the aircraft to land on autopilot. I've never known a pilot who felt it was safer than doing it himself.

So all of this throwing and catching and yanking to a halt takes its toll on the aircraft. That's why a regular land-based aircraft couldn't just be transferred to a carrier and expect to survive. Its landing gear and fuselage simply couldn't handle the stress of the controlled crashes. In addition, other modifications must be made to planes to accommodate the unique situation that aircraft carriers present.

Reinforcements Necessary

Carrier craft have always been built to be a lot more rugged than land-based craft. This, of course, comes with a price. Fuel efficiency takes a nosedive because all of that reinforcement in the landing system and fuselage is heavy. Consequently, carrier craft do not have the range, and generally cannot carry as many bombs as their land-based cousins. (Because of tanking, the ability of modern aircraft to refuel while in flight, the actual difference in range, in some cases, no longer exists.) On the other hand, carrier-based aircraft can go places that land-based craft can't get to, and that is their strength. They can go wherever their ship takes them.

It has only been recently that, through the use of new materials, engineers have been able to design carrier aircraft that are strong enough to handle the stresses of launching and recovery and are also light enough (thus having the mobility to avoid the enemy and the range to get to and back from a target) to compete with land-based aircraft. The F/A-18 Hornet would be in this category (see Chapter 5 for more information on the Hornet).

Folding Wings

Not long after carriers first hit the seas, the need for planes with fold-back wings became apparent. Because of their wingspans, too few planes could be stored in a ship's hangar. Design the wings to unlock at a hinge and fold back, like the wings on a fly, and you can fit many more aircraft into the same-sized hangar deck.

In the early days of naval aviation, a plane's wings were unlocked by hand and manually folded back. The first British plane with folding wings was the Short Folder, which flew in 1914. It had a wingspan of 67 feet. The wings folded laterally 90 degrees until they ran parallel to the fuselage.

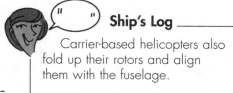

Ship's Log

Carrier-based helicopters also fold up their rotors and align them with the fuselage.

Today, the folding wings are hydraulically controlled by the pilot. After landing, the pilot presses a button and a chain of electronic wiring, electrical cable, and hydraulic tubing does the work.

Fighting Corrosion

Sure, aircraft carriers have been in battles against evil empires. They have fought to defend freedom around the globe. They have carried their air power to the four corners of the earth. Yet there are many carrier veterans who will tell you that the hardest battle an aircraft carrier ever fought was against an insidious enemy, an enemy that never relents and never surrenders: corrosion.

One of the last things you want to do is store an airplane in an overly salty atmosphere, yet when the plane is on a carrier in the middle of an ocean of saltwater, there isn't much choice. The salt in the air causes an electrolyte to form between dissimilar metals in the plane's structure. The galvanic activity that follows reminds you of what happens to a battery if it's left in your night table drawer for too long. Metal is systematically eaten away and weakened every second a plane is on a carrier at sea.

Common forms of corrosion include …

- Pitting, which causes cavities or holes in a material.

- Exfoliation, which causes a lifting or leafing type of separation along a material's natural grain.

- Crevice, so-called because it forms in crevices, such as under washers and in the thread of a bolt.

- Filiform, a process in which metal breaks down into thread-like pieces that separate themselves from the remainder of the structure.

The corrosive effect of salt has been plaguing planes since the days when the planes were made out of wood—the salty air slowly rotted and mildewed them. Not exactly corrosion, but no better. Over the years, science has advanced, and better and better coatings have been put on the metals of sea-based planes to slow corrosion. But the problem has yet to be licked. Given enough time, the sea always wins.

Vertical Launch Vehicles

The problems of launching and recovering aircraft on a carrier are lessened when that craft has the ability to take off and land vertically. It wasn't until fairly recently that the technology was developed to allow full-fledged fighter jets to get into the air and return to earth in this manner.

The British have always been at the forefront when it came to developing this technology. They began working on this revolutionary form of aircraft back in the 1950s. The jets used something called "vectored thrust" to not only take off and land vertically, but to hover in place. The first V/STOL (vertical or short takeoff and landing) craft, known as the P.1127, was flown in 1960 and it directly evolved into today's Harrier, a jet that takes off straight up like a helicopter, has the capability to hover, and can fly like a fighter jet. V/STOL aircraft demand a lot less flight deck (i.e., runway) than their conventional counterparts.

The advantages of using V/STOL aircraft on carriers are that they do not need tail hooks and the flight decks from which they take off and land do not need catapults and arresting wires. They also don't need to be reinforced to withstand the stress of catapult launches and arresting wire recoveries.

The disadvantage of V/STOL jets is that they need a tremendous amount of fuel to take off and land. To keep a jet hovering, you have to have vectored thrust. That is, the plane must be able to blast jet power in all directions to stay in one place in mid-air. All of this vectored thrust makes for one thirsty bird. The V/STOL technology is still developing. We are years away from an all-V/STOL naval air force.

Helicopters

The original vertical launch vehicles, of course, are the whirly-birds—helicopters. If I wanted to get technical on you—not much chance of that—any boat or ship that has a heliport on it could be called an aircraft carrier.

Seagoing helicopters have had two primary purposes since they first became part of the U.S. military. They …

- ◆ Carry personnel or supplies from ship to shore or from shore to ship.

- ◆ They carry personnel or supplies from one to ship to another ship.

Let's take an ever-so-quick look at the development of the helicopter and its meant-to-be marriage with aircraft carriers.

Sea Kings

The SH-3H Sea King helicopter was conceived in 1957, made its first flight in 1959, and became operational in 1961. It was built by Sikorsky Aircraft Division of United Technologies of Stratford, Connecticut. It is powered by two General Electric T58-GE-402 turbo shaft engines.

Fact Box
SH-3H Sea King Specifications
Length: 73 feet
Fuselage length: 54 feet, 9 inches
Height: 17 feet
Weight: 11,865 lbs. empty
Maximum takeoff weight: 21,000 pounds
Range: 542 nautical miles
Flight ceiling: 14,700 feet
Cruising speed: 138 miles per hour
Crew: Four
Armament: Two Mk-46 torpedoes

The Sea King gave carrier battle groups the ability to detect, classify, track, and destroy enemy submarines. Its use in this role was discontinued during the mid-1990s. Today, the Sea King provides logistical support and a search and rescue (SAR) capability.

Seahawks

The SH-3H Sea King was replaced by the SH-60F Seahawk. The switch was made during the mid-1990s. The SH-60F is the version of the Seahawk helicopter designed to operate primarily off of aircraft carriers. It offers the Navy close-in antisubmarine protection of the carrier battle group. It provides *SAR* support during carrier flight operations.

Naval Lingo

SAR means search and rescue.

The Seahawk is also used for logistics and for transporting personnel, mail, and supplies between ships in the carrier battle group. A variant of the SH-60F, the HH-60H is designed specifically as a combat search and rescue (CSAR) and naval special warfare platform.

The SH-60F can detect, localize, track, and attack enemy submarines as well as provide the task force with utility support. They have a crew of four: two pilots and two sensor operators. One crew member is always an SAR swimmer, ready for rescue operations. The SH-60F operates from the decks of every conventional-and nuclear-powered aircraft carrier in the U.S. fleet. The SH-60F's ordnance includes the MK-46 or MK-50 torpedoes and M-60D machine guns.

The Seahawk detects enemy submarines using the AQS-13F dipping sonar (essentially, an underwater microphone) which is deployed on a 1,575 foot cable while the aircraft hovers 60 feet above the ocean. Pilots maintain their 60-foot day-or-night all-weather hover with the help of an automatic flight control system.

The next chapter looks at the state-of-the-art carrier aircraft that are being used off the flight decks of today's flattops.

The Least You Need to Know

- One of the big differences between land-based and carrier aircraft is that the carrier aircraft needs to be tougher.

- Today's catapults are steam-powered pistons strong enough to throw an automobile 800 yards.

- Planes land on a flight deck and come to a sudden stop because they catch an arresting wire with their tail hook.

- Carrier planes have wings that fold back so that they take up less room and more of them can be kept aboard the carrier.

- Jets that have the ability to take off and land vertically, such as the Sea Harrier, greatly simplify the matter of launch and recovery on a carrier.

- Helicopters are the original vertical takeoff and landing aircraft.

Chapter 5

Carrier Aircraft of Today

In This Chapter

- ◆ Fighter jets
- ◆ Electronic warfare
- ◆ Radar in the sky
- ◆ Sub fighters
- ◆ Choppers
- ◆ Unmanned vehicles

Back in Chapter 1, we took a brief look at the aircraft that could be found at any given time, aboard a typical modern American aircraft carrier, such as the USS *Abraham Lincoln*. Now we are going to look at those aircraft in greater detail. First on our list is a fighter jet that has been around now more than 30 years—the F-14, the *F* standing for *fighter*.

Tomcat, the Indisputable Leader of the Gang

One squadron of 10 to 15 F-14 Tomcats can be found on today's aircraft carriers. In the late 1960s, General Dynamics had been contracted to design a new fleet defense jet for the navy. They had no previous experience building carrier aircraft, so they subcontracted the job out to Grumman, which had been making planes for the navy for decades.

The job was to convert the F-111B, a previous-generation fighter, into a carrier craft that met all modern needs. They succeeded so well at this task that the jets are still being used more than 30 years later.

Fact Box

F-14D Tomcat Specifications

Size:

> Length: 62.7 feet
>
> Wingspan: 64.1 feet
>
> Height: 16 feet

Power:

> Engines: Two F110-GE-400, capable of 27,400 pounds of thrust

Fuel capacity: 16,200 pounds

Maximum takeoff weight: 74,348 pounds

Armament:

> Any combination of Phoenix, AMRAAM, Sparrow, and Sidewinder missiles weighing up to 14,500 pounds.
>
> 20 mm M61 cannon

The war in Vietnam was going on at the time and the navy was learning valuable lessons in what was needed in a modern fighter. They knew that they needed more than a good radar/missile platform. They needed a fighter with all the long-range/high-endurance attributes of a fleet defense missile carrier, a long-range radar/missile system, plus dogfight/fighter escort capabilities.

Grumman looked at more than 6,000 configurations before deciding on the design, using the best of designs from previous Grumman aircraft. The F-111's variable-geometry wings, TF30 engines, AWG-9 radar/fire control, and Phoenix missiles were combined with the F-4's tandem crew seating, and Sparrow and Sidewinder missiles. The variable-geometry wings, which can change their alignment with the fuselage (the body of the aircraft) from virtually sticking out at 90 degrees to swept-back along the fuselage to almost touch it, were retained in later fighters. Pilots launch with the wings making the greatest angle with the fuselage, giving them more lift. Sweeping the wings back during flight decreases air drag on the airframe, resulting in greater speed.

The navy's experience in Vietnam had taught it the need for an internal gun so, in the F-14 Tomcat, Grumman included the combat-proven M61 Vulcan 20mm six-barrel Gatling gun. Grumman also built in provisions for up to 14,500 pounds in air-to-ground or air-to-air weapons on the weapons stores stations. Over the years, Grumman made several changes in the design. The F-14D, which is the version that is still being flown, made its debut in 1990.

Flattop Facts

The first Tomcat took to the skies on December 21, 1970. That aircraft crashed due to hydraulic failure, and the tests resumed in May 1971.

The Tomcat continues to receive incremental improvements, and new software upgrades are regularly being installed. Although there are no immediate plans for an F-14E—that is, no major upgrades are planned—the Tomcat is still scheduled to perform the navy's "outer air battle" mission well into the twenty-first century.

These Hornets Have a Big Sting

There are three squadrons of F/A-18 Hornets on the flight deck of the USS *Abraham Lincoln*. The most recent version of this jet is the F/A-18E/F, also known as the Hornet Strike Fighter.

The new jets come in both one-seat and two-seat versions. They were a significant improvement over the earlier Hornets. They deliver greater fighting capabilities over a greater range, can carry more fuel, and are 25 percent larger. They also have increased engine power, which allows for a quick response time.

The new design has altered the Hornet's airframe structure, lengthening the fuselage and tripling the size of the payload.

The new Hornets are propelled by two General Electric F414 afterburning turbofan engines, which provide 22,000 pounds of thrust. This robust engine tolerates intense abuse and comes back for more. The Hornet had proven itself to be a reliable combat aircraft even before these upgrades. With them, they have a much improved speed, range, and efficiency.

Fact Box

F/A-18 Hornet Specifications

Size:

> Length: 60.3 feet
>
> Wingspan: 44.9 feet
>
> Height: 16 feet

Performance:

> Maximum speed: Mach 1.8+
>
> Combat ceiling: 50,000 feet
>
> Combat radius: 660+ nautical miles

Propulsion: 2 General Electric F414 afterburning turbofan engines (for a total of 22,000 pounds of thrust, with a nine-to-one thrust to weight ratio)

Armament:

> Internal: Lightweight M61A1 20mm cannon with 400 rounds of ammunition.
>
> External: 17,750 pounds maximum. Weapons include AIM-9 Sidewinder; AIM-7 Sparrow; AIM-120 AMRAAM; Harpoon; HARM; Shrike; SLAM-ER; Walleye and Maverick TV, laser and infrared-guided missiles; joint standoff weapon (JSOW); joint direct attack munition (JDAM); and various current and future general-purpose bombs, mines, and rockets. (When adapted as an electronic warfare aircraft, the Sidewinders would be replaced by receiving pods, and a Satcom receiver would be added directly behind the cockpit.)
>
> Weapons stations: 11 wing and fuselage stations.

Prowlers on the Deck!

Also on the flight deck you'll see four EA-6B Prowlers. Made by Grumman, the EA-6B Prowler is a twin-engine aircraft. Its airframe is modified from that of the A-6 Intruder airframe.

Flattop Facts

The EA-6B first saw action in the Vietnam War in July 1972.

It is a fully integrated electronic warfare system combining long-range, all-weather capabilities with advanced electronic countermeasures. More avionics equipment is located in a forward equipment bay and in pod-shaped faring on the vertical fin. The cockpits are side-by-side for maximum efficiency, visibility, and comfort.

Fact Box

EA6B Prowler Specifications

Size:

       Length: 59 feet 10 inches

       Wingspan: 53 feet

       Height: 16 feet 3 inches

       Weight: Max gross takeoff: 61,000 pounds

Primary function: Electronic countermeasures

Contractor: Grumman Aerospace Corporation

Propulsion: Two Pratt & Whitney J52-P408 engines (11,200 pounds thrust each)

Performance:

       Speed: Max speed with five jammer pods: 610 miles per hour

       Climb rate: 10,030 feet per minute

       Range: More than 1,000 nautical miles

       Ceiling: 38,000 feet

Crew: Four: Pilot and three electronic countermeasures officers

Armament: Up to 4 AGM-88A HARM missiles

Date deployed: First flight, May 25, 1968

Operational: July 1971

The Prowlers received a major *ICAP* in 1976. This upgrade involved new displays, AN/ALQ-126 multiple-band defensive and radar deception gear, better jamming equipment, and a new *hard kill* capability with AGM-88A Harm missiles.

Seeing Farther: Hawkeyes

Next on out list of aircraft carried aboard the USS *Abraham Lincoln* is the E-2C Hawkeye. Usually four of these are on the flight deck.

The E-2C Hawkeye is not a weapon. It carries no arms. Instead, it is part of the carrier's sensory system—the eyes and ears of the ship. Introduced in 1964, the Hawkeye's dominant feature is its radar dome mounted on top of the plane. It works closely with both the F-14 Tomcat and the Carrier combat information center.

Naval Lingo

ICAP is short for improved capability. That means it can fly higher, faster, longer; see and hear better; and packs more of a punch.

Hard kill means the target is converted into a smoking hole in the ground. A **soft kill** simply destroys the target's capabilities, e.g., knocks off an antenna that could be replaced.

Fact Box

E-2C Hawkeye Specifications

Size:

        Length: 57 feet 6 inches

        Wingspan: 80 feet 7 inches

        Height: 18 feet 3 inches

        Weight: Max. gross, takeoff: 53,000 lbs.; 40,200 lbs basic

Primary function: Airborne early warning, command and control

Contractor: Grumman Aerospace Corp.

Unit cost: $51 million

Propulsion: Two Allison T-56-A427 turboprop engines; (5,000 shaft horsepower each)

Performance:

        Speed: 300+ knots (345 miles, 552 km. per hour)

        Ceiling: 30,000 feet (9,100 meters)

Crew: Five

Armament: None

Date deployed: First flight, October 1960

Operational: January 1964

The Hawkeye provides all-weather airborne early warning and command-and-control functions for the carrier battle group. It extends the detection range of a battle group by 298 miles for aircraft and 160 miles for missiles. It can also detect ships.

Flattop Facts

E-2C Hawkeyes directed the F-14 Tomcat fighters flying combat air patrol during the two-carrier battle group joint strike against terrorist-related Libyan targets in 1986.

E-2Cs were very important during the Persian Gulf War of 1991. They provided the command and control for successful operations, directing both land attack and combat air patrol missions over Iraq and providing control for the shoot-down of two Iraqi MIG-21 aircraft by carrier-based F/A-18s in the early days of the war.

With These Vikings, You Leave the Horn Helmet at Home

Also onboard are six S-3A/B Vikings. The S-3A Viking entered fleet service in 1974, replacing the S-2 Tracker. An all-weather, long-range, multi-mission aircraft, it operates primarily with carrier battle groups in antisubmarine warfare zones. It carries automated weapon systems and is capable of extended missions with in-flight refueling.

Fact Box

S-3 Viking Specifications

Size:

> Length: 53 feet, 4 inches
>
> Wingspan: 68 feet 8 inches
>
> Height: 22 feet 9 inches
>
> Weight: Max design gross takeoff: 52,539 pounds

Performance:

> Maximum speed: 439 knots
>
> Ceiling: 40,000 feet
>
> Range: 2,300+ nautical miles (2,645 statute miles)
>
> Endurance hour: 7 hours 30 minutes

Primary function: Antisubmarine warfare and sea surveillance

Contractor: Lockheed-California Company

Unit cost: $27 million

Propulsion: Two General Electric TF-34-GE-400B turbofan engines (9,275 pounds thrust each)

Armament:

> Weapon bay: 4 MK 46 torpedoes or four MK 36 destructors
>
> > or four MK 82 bombs or two MK 57
> >
> > or four MK 54 depth bombs or four MK 53 mines
>
> Underwing pylon: Flare launchers, mines, cluster bombs, and rockets

Crew: Four

Date deployed: First flight, January 21, 1972

Operational: February 1974

The S-3 Viking, developed to counter the hard-to-hear Soviet nuclear submarines, consists of four crew members (pilot, copilot, tactical coordinator, and acoustic sensor operator). Debuting in 1972, it uses the AN/APS-116 search radar, OR-89 FLIR. The APS-116 radar is built to search the surface of the water, with superior capabilities for detecting targets amid the clutter of the waves, a problem that air search radars don't have. The FLIR, or Forward Looking Infrared Radar, detects infrared differences in the area, sort of like night-vision goggles. The Viking carries 60 *sonobuoys* and is capable of carrying torpedoes, bombs, and depth charges.

Naval Lingo

Sonobuoys are sonic detectors.

Chaff consists of strips of metal foil or wire that is ejected from an aircraft into the air in order to confuse an enemy's radar.

The current version, the B version, has been around since 1981. The new version has improved acoustic processing, expanded ESM coverage, increased radar processing capability, new sonobuoys receiver system, and the capability of housing the AGM-84 Harpoon ASM. The main difference between the A and B versions is that a *chaff* dispenser has been added to the aft fuselage of the updated Viking. Most A models have been converted to B standards.

The Viking is one of those aircraft that really *loves* to fly. In fact, if you get in serious trouble with it, often the best thing to do is nothing. I knew a pilot who got into serious trouble at one point during his flight—a spin he couldn't pull out of. He bailed out—that is, he ejected. Once deprived of its expert airmanship, the aircraft pulled out of the spin, regained level flight, and continued flying until it ran out of gas. Fortunately, it was headed out to open ocean when its crew bailed out and floated on parachutes back to Earth.

Flattop Facts

Ejection seats are a fascinating subject themselves. The canopy (roof over the cockpit) is held on with explosive bolts. Once the ejection handle is jerked down, the bolts blow. The canopy tumbles away in the slipstream—that is, the suction caused by the rapidly moving aircraft.

Less than a second later, rockets under the crews' seats fire, shooting them up and out at an angle from the aircraft. The rockets are configured so that the exhaust and flame from one rocket doesn't fry the other folks ejecting.

In the S-3 Viking, which has two rear seats, the top of the backseats punch through a thin place in the overhead to get them out.

Ejection seats can be configured so that only the pilot can initiate ejection or so that either the front or the back seat can initiate it. The control is in the pilot's area of the cockpit.

If the pilot initiates it, both seats go. The backseater can initiate his own ejection or both. More than one senior backseater has threatened to punch out when irritated by a hot-dogging junior pilot and let the pilot explain to CAG after landing why he's back without his backseater.

Choppers, Too

Our inventory of aircraft on the flight deck of the USS *Abraham Lincoln* concludes with helicopters. You'll find eight SH-60F Seahawk helicopters, which you learned something about in the previous chapter. The Seahawk is a twin-engine helicopter used for antisubmarine warfare, search and rescue, anti-ship warfare, cargo lift, and special operations.

It's an airborne platform based aboard cruisers, destroyers, and frigates and deploys sonobuoys and torpedoes in an antisubmarine role. They also extend the range of the ship's radar capabilities. Although use of this helicopter dates back to 1979, the version that is currently used, the SH-60F, made its debut in 1988.

Eyes Like a Global Hawk

In the year 2000, the USS *George Washington* took part in a test flight of a *UAV* that will play a major part in future wars.

A UAV called the Global Hawk took off from Eglin Air Force Base in Florida, flew nonstop along the East Coast, crossed the Atlantic to Portugal, and finally flew back to Eglin, a 29-hour test flight that set an endurance record.

The entire mission to Portugal was programmed on a laptop and downloaded to the UAV's main controls. The vehicle's sensor suite took hundreds of detailed radar and infrared images en route and transmitted them via satellite to Fort Bragg, North Carolina, and to the aircraft carrier *George Washington* underway in the Atlantic. Global Hawk took photographic images capable of distinguishing vehicle tire tracks from 65,000 feet.

Naval Lingo

UAV stands for un-manned aerial vehicle, a remote-controlled aircraft that can spy on or attack an enemy without putting any of the good guys in harm's way.

Global Hawk can fly 1,200 nautical miles and orbit the area of interest at 60,000 feet for 24 hours in a single 32-hour mission. The system can gather imagery of a 200 × 200 mile area in 24 hours, or alternately, it can observe up to 1,900 smaller areas.

System operators have demonstrated the capability to send imagery from Global Hawk to an F/A-18 in as little as nine minutes.

So there's a quick rundown of the aircraft you'll find on today's U.S. carriers. In our next chapter we'll look at some of the great planes that have flown off the flight decks of carriers past.

The Least You Need to Know

◆ F-14 Tomcats first flew in 1970, and their use is planned to continue well into the twenty-first century.

◆ The F/A-18 Hornet had proven itself to be a reliable combat aircraft even before it was upgraded—and now it is new and improved.

◆ Prowlers and Hawkeyes offer a carrier battle group eyes and ears on the sky— in order to see or hear the enemy before it does them.

◆ The Hawkeye provides all-weather airborne early warning and command and control functions for the carrier battle group.

◆ The S-3 Viking was developed to counter hard-to-hear Soviet nuclear submarines.

Chapter 6

The Hall of Fame of Carrier Planes

In This Chapter

- ◆ The B-25 Mitchell as a World War II workhorse
- ◆ The navy's first dive-bomber
- ◆ Zeroing in on the Japanese Zero
- ◆ Hornets and Super Hornets' sting

Hundreds of different types of planes operated off of aircraft carriers over the years—too many to discuss individually here. But here are some of my favorites, the Carrier Aircraft Hall of Fame.

B-25 Mitchell

The B-25 Mitchell was the bomber that executed the famous "Doolittle Raid" during World War II. (We'll be discussing that more in Chapter 15.) The B-25 first flew in 1940. This twin-engine bomber has been called the most versatile aircraft of the war. At various times it was used for both

" " Ship's Log

The design and development stage of building the first B-25 was extensive. According to North American Aviation, 8,500 drawings and 195,000 engineering man-hours were needed to build the prototype.

high- and low-level bombing, strafing (the rapid firing of bullets from a plane at the ground), photoreconnaissance, submarine patrol, and as a fighter.

Almost 10,000 B-25s were built during World War II. It was a twin-tail, mid-wing land monoplane (that is a plane with one set of wings that lands and takes off from a land-based air strip) powered by two 1,700-horsepower Wright Cyclone engines. It held two and a half tons of bombs and some versions were further armed with 75mm cannon, machine guns, and added firepower of 13 .50-caliber guns in the conventional bombardier's compartment. One version carried eight .50-caliber guns in the nose in an arrangement that provided 14 forward-firing guns.

Fact Box
B-25 Mitchell Specifications
Wingspan: 67 feet, 6.7 inches
Wing area: 610 square feet
Length: 53 feet
Crew: Five: pilot, copilot, bombardier, radio operator, gunner
Power plant: Two 1,700-hp Wright Cyclone supercharged 14-cylinder radial engines, driving 12-foot-7-inch full-feathering, constant-speed Hamilton Standard three-bladed props
Maximum speed: 300-plus miles per hour
Range: 3,000-plus miles
Weight empty: 20,305 pounds
Weight gross: 27,051 pounds
Landing gear: Hydraulically operated tricycle

Douglas Dauntless

The navy's first dive-bomber was conceived in 1934 when the U.S. Navy Bureau of Aeronautics invited several aircraft manufacturers to submit proposals. The job finally went to the Northrop Aircraft Company, which designed the XBT-1. When the head of Northrop, John K. Northrop, sold his company to Douglas Aircraft in 1938, the dive-bomber became known as the SBD-1 Douglas Dauntless.

Fact Box

Douglas Dauntless Specifications

Wingspan: 41 feet, 6 inches

Wing area: 325 square feet

Length: 32 feet, 2 inches

Height: 13 feet, 7 inches

Power plant: One Wright R-1820-32 nine-cylinder air-cooled radial engine producing 1,000 horsepower

Maximum speed: 253 miles per hour

Range: 1,165 miles per hour at 142 miles per hour

Perforated diving flaps on the wings allowed the Dauntless to dive. The result was a bomber that handled like a fighter. The windshield was bulletproof. The landing gear retracted hydraulically.

Two versions of the Dauntless were built, the SBD-1 and SBD-2. They were very similar. The SBD-2 had a machine gun in its rear cockpit whereas the -1 did not. The -2 also had armor plate for the crew, self-sealing rubber-lined fuel tanks, and two 65-gallon fuel tanks in the outer wing panel. Thus, the -2 had greater range than the -1. The -2 also had added to its design an outer wing panel for 100-pound bombs.

The Dauntless became the workhorse of the Pacific campaign and participated in every major engagement against the Japanese.

The navy planned to replace the Dauntless with a newer dive-bomber called the Helldiver. The Curtiss SB2C Helldiver was a two-seat, carrier-based dive-bomber. The prototype flew for the first time on December 18, 1940, and the navy ordered them into large-scale production before the year was out. They were assigned to the new Essex-class carriers.

The first Helldivers didn't see action until late in 1943 when they flew from the deck of the *Bunker Hill* for a raid over the major Japanese base of Rabaul. It didn't take long for problems with the Helldiver, in particular with the handling, to reveal themselves. The plane had poor low-speed stability, and its stability during high-speed dives wasn't great either.

The Dauntless was the more accurate of the two bombers. However, the navy stuck with the Helldiver, despite its shortcomings, and it ended up dishing out a whole lot of damage against the Japanese.

The Curtiss SB2C Helldiver was a two-seat, carrier-based dive-bomber.

Hellcats of the Navy

One of the premiere U.S. carrier-based planes during World War II was the Grumman Hellcat. It flew for the first time on June 30, 1941, five months before the United States entered the war. Grumman delivered the first Hellcats to the military in October 1942, and in January 1943 they were assigned to the aircraft carriers, *Essex*, *Yorktown*, and *Independence*.

Fact Box
Grumman Hellcat F6F-3 Specifications Wingspan: 42 feet, 10 inches Length: 33 feet, 7 inches Height: 11 feet, 3 inches Weight empty: 9,042 pounds Weight gross: 12,186 pounds Maximum speed: 376 miles per hour at 22,800 feet (324 miles per hour at sea level) Range: 1,090 miles at 179 miles per hour Armament: six 0.50 caliber Colt-Browning machine guns

Although the Hellcat got off to a late start in the war, by 1945 it was one of the United States's most valuable carrier-based planes. A total of 2,545 of them eventually went to war.

An F6F Hellcat on the flight deck of the USS Yorktown.

The plane was upgraded in 1944 to the Hellcat FF6-5, which had a stronger engine and additional armor installed behind the pilot. The new version could carry a ton of bombs and, in dogfights, proved itself again and again to be superior to the Japanese Zero (discussed later in this chapter).

The Avengers

The Grumman TBM Avenger was originally designed to be a torpedo bomber. However, during its extensive use in World War II in the Pacific theater, it was used predominantly as a glide bomber. In that capacity it attacked Japanese ships and provided air support for U.S. troops on the ground. It also searched for enemy submarines in both the Pacific and Atlantic, where both the United States and Great Britain used it.

During the years leading up to America's entrance into World War II, its primary torpedo bomber was the Douglas TDB Devastator. But, after only a few short years of operation, the Devastator quickly proved to be obsolete.

> **Flattop Facts**
>
> George Herbert Walker Bush flew the Avenger off the aircraft carrier USS *San Jacinto*. He was shot down during September 1944 while flying his fifty-eighth mission but survived to later become the Director of Central Intelligence and the forty-first president of the United States.

*The Grumman TBM
Avenger was originally
designed to be a torpedo
bomber. However, during its
extensive use during World
War II in the Pacific theater,
it was used predominantly as
a glide bomber.*

Grumman won the contract to design its replacement. The navy ordered its first Avengers in December 1940. During the summer of 1941 the prototype made its first test flight. A little more than a month after the Japanese attacked Pearl Harbor in December 1941, the Avenger was operational.

The Avenger could carry bombs in an internal bomb bay and could carry depth charges and rockets under its wings.

Ship's Log

Her crews did not refer to the plane as the "Avenger," and more frequently referred to it by its affectionate nickname, "Turkey."

Grumman produced more than 150 Avengers per month during 1943. Later, Grumman was kept busy building Hellcats, so the production of Avengers was switched to Eastern Aircraft, the airplane-producing wing of General Motors. By the end of the war, almost 10,000 Avengers had been built, about three quarters of them by Eastern.

Fact Box
Grumman TBM Avenger Specifications

Crew: 3

Wingspan: 54 feet, 2 inches

Length: 40 feet, 9 inches

Height: 13 feet, 9 inches

Power plant: Wright R-2600 Cyclone producing 1,900 hp

Armament: Three .50 caliber machine guns; up to one ton of ordnance

Maximum speed: 276 mph

Range: 1,130 miles

Service ceiling: 23,400 feet

Wildcats

The Grumman F4F Wildcat was first designed in 1935. It was the first all-metal, carrier-launched monoplane (single-wing) fighter ever to be used by the U.S. Navy. This was the U.S. Navy's and the Marine Corps's primary fighter plane when America entered World War II. The plane had a reputation for seldom having mechanical difficulties, and when it did, it could be repaired with a Band-Aid and some bubblegum.

The Wildcat was the first all-metal, carrier-launched monoplane fighter ever to be used by the U.S. Navy.

This plane was originally designed as a biplane, but soon lost one of its wings. The U.S. Navy didn't go for the original design, choosing instead the Brewster Buffalo as its new fighter plane. But Great Britain and France both liked Grumman's design, and so the first Wildcats (although they were known as Martlets at the time) were shipped over to Europe.

When France fell to Germany, the planes were moved to England. The plane scored its first victory on Christmas Day, 1940.

Fact Box
General Motors FM-2 Wildcat Specifications Wingspan: 38 feet Length: 28 feet, 9 inches Height: 11 feet, 5 inches Weight gross: 8,221 pounds Power plant: Wright R-1820-56 developing 1,350 horsepower Maximum speed: 322 miles per hour Range: 1,350 miles Service ceiling: 35,600 feet

The carrier-based Wildcat, a version with folding wings, debuted in time for the attack at Pearl Harbor, and the Wildcat first saw action for the U.S. Navy at the battle of Wake Island. The plane was upgraded several times during the war, with the FM-2 being the most abundantly produced (4,777 of them were made). As would later be the case with the Avenger, the manufacturing of the plane was shifted from Grumman to General Motors.

Naval Lingo

HVARs are high-velocity aircraft rockets.

The FM-2 had a lighter, yet more powerful, Wright R-1820 radial engine. Additionally, the plane carried four rather than six .50 caliber machine guns and was often fitted with *HVARs* for use against ground targets, ships, or surfaced submarines. The FM-2 also had a larger tail than the standard F4F to counter the increased torque produced by the Wright engine.

In the Pacific they were perfectly suited for use off of escort carriers. They won numerous dogfights against Japanese Zeroes and sunk several Japanese submarines and one cruiser. The Wildcat was America's primary naval fighter through the end of 1942. However, during 1943 most Wildcat squadrons were re-equipped with either the larger Grumman F6F Hellcat or the Chance-Vought F4U Corsair.

Chance-Vought F4U Corsair

Although the great majority of Corsairs were land-based and supported the marines, they were also the United States's most successful carrier-based fighter planes. The one-seater had a *kill ratio* of better than 11 to 1.

The first germ of an idea leading to the development of the Corsair came about almost three years before the United States entered World War II, in February 1938. It was then that the U.S. Navy Bureau of Aeronautics requested proposals from aircraft manufacturers for a high-speed, single-engine fighter with a stalling speed not higher than 70 miles per hour. (The stall speed of an aircraft

Naval Lingo

A **kill ratio** for a plane is the number of enemy aircraft shot down compared to the number of its own type shot down by the enemy.

depends on its angle of attack—whether it's ascending, descending, or in level flight— and its airspeed. A plane flying too slow at any angle will stall its engine. It's important that the pilot know what that speed is as a stalled engine can cause a sudden loss of altitude!)

The Corsair was the United States's most successful carrier-based fighter plane with a kill ratio of better than 11 to 1.

The request specified that the plane should have a range of 1,000 miles, four guns, and provisions under the wings to carry antiaircraft bombs. The winning design came from Chance-Vought, who designed bent wings that resembled those of a sea gull. The plane was the first U.S. fighter to fly faster than 400 miles per hour.

Flattop Facts

The Chance-Vought F4U Corsair became legendary during the Pacific War, striking fear into the hearts of Japanese pilots who came to call the aircraft "Whistling Death."

The Corsair wasn't immediately assigned to the navy's carrier fleet, however. Because of its long nose, which restricted pilot visibility, especially during takeoff and landing, it was considered unsuitable as a carrier craft. That's why the Corsair's earliest victories were in support of the marines, who used them to replace the Wildcats.

Fact Box
Chance-Vought F4U Corsair Specifications
Wingspan: 41 feet
Length: 33 feet, 8 inches
Height: 14 feet, 9 inches
Weight empty: 9,205 pounds
Weight gross: 14,669 pounds
Power plant: Pratt & Whitney R-2800-18W producing 2,100 horsepower
Armament: Six .50 caliber machine guns
Range: 1,005 miles
Maximum speed: 446 mph
Service ceiling: 41,500 feet

As it turned out, Corsairs worked fine off of aircraft carriers. They came in particularly handy during the final weeks of the war as they could out-duel kamikaze Zeroes before the Japanese suicide pilots could reach U.S. ships.

Mitsubishi A6M "Zero"

The Mitsubishi A6M Zero-Sen was the most famous of Japan's combat aircraft. This one-seater carrier-borne fighter was manufactured by Mitsubishi Jukogyo KK. It received its power from a 925-hp Nakajima NK1C Sakae 12 engine.

The Zero had a wingspan of 39 feet, 4 ½ inches. It was 29 feet, 9 inches long and stood 9 feet, 7 inches at its highest point. The plane weighed 3,704 pounds when empty and 5,313 pounds when fully loaded.

With a top speed of 316 mph and a service ceiling of 33,790 feet, the Zero was armed with two 20mm Type 99 cannons and two 7.7mm Type 97 machine guns. It also had the capability of carrying two 66-lb. bombs.

The Zero was designed by Jiro Horikoshi in 1937, who envisioned a short war. He adhered to the exacting specifications laid down by the Imperial Japanese Navy. The navy commissioned the design to replace the Mitsubishi A5M Claude carrier-fighter.

Oh-oh, Here Comes the A6M2 Reisen

The prototype for the Zero first flew in April 1939. When the plane first went into production in 1940 it was known as the A6M2 Reisen (Type 00). The 00 signified the year on the Japanese calendar, 5700, and soon the plane began to be called the Zero-Sen.

The plane first saw combat in July 1940 over China in the Sino-Japanese War, where it quickly outclassed all other fighter aircraft, including the Curtiss P-40s being used in that theater on December 17, 1941, by the American volunteer force, Claire Chennault's Flying Tigers.

At the time of the Pearl Harbor attack in December 1941, more than 400 Zeroes had been delivered to the Imperial Japanese Navy. In air combat, the United States, to its dismay, quickly discovered that the Zero could outfight the Grumman F4F Wildcat, as well as the American land-based fighters.

Less Than Zero

That isn't to say that the Zero was perfect. It did have its flaws. It was poorly armored and, because of its lack of self-sealing fuel tanks, it proved to be dangerously flammable. Plus, it was constructed of a light alloy that didn't stand up well against enemy bullets. U.S. Navy pilots in their F4Fs soon learned that diving through Zero formations while continuously firing at them brought satisfactory results.

The Zero was the supreme fighter plane in the Pacific only until the Battle of Midway in June 1942. In the following year two new U.S. planes, the F4U Corsair (first action over the Solomon Islands in February 1943) and the F6F Hellcat (first production delivery, January 1943), gave the Allies air superiority.

To compensate, Mitsubishi developed new versions of the Zero. The A6M5, introduced in August 1943, could dive faster than its predecessor because of a stronger wing—and the A6M5b came with an armored windscreen and fuel tank fire extinguishers.

By June of 1944 the Zero was once again lagging behind the new U.S. planes. At the Battle of the Philippine Sea, in what became known as the "Marianas Turkey Shoot," U.S. Navy F6Fs shot down 315 Zeroes and lost only 23 aircraft in exchange.

Converted for Kamikaze

In 1944 Mitsubishi again upgraded the Zero, introducing the A6M5c, which featured pilot armor, larger fuel tanks, and heavier caliber guns. This model proved too heavy to be effective until the end of 1944 when the 1,130-hp Sakae 31 engine was mated with it.

By that time the Zero was no longer a carrier-based plane, for the simple reason that all of Japan's aircraft carriers had been sunk. Continuing as a land-based plane, with experienced pilots becoming fewer and fewer in number, the remaining Zeroes were converted into kamikaze planes and, in the spring of 1945, took a horrible toll on the Allied armada off Okinawa.

Fact Box
Mitsubishi A6M5 Specifications Wingspan: 36 feet, 1 inch Length: 29 feet, 9 inches Height: 11 feet, 5.75 inches Power plant: One 1130-horsepower Nakajima NK1C Sakae 21 radial piston engine Weight empty: 4,175 pounds Weight gross: 6,504 pounds Maximum speed: 346 mph Service ceiling: 35,100 feet Range: 1,118 miles with internal fuel Armament: Two 20-mm cannon and two 7.7-mm machine guns Number built: 10,500

There you have the "historical" wing of our Hall of Fame. Now we move to the present, planes that have already earned their way into our hallowed halls, but that are still being used.

The F/A-18 Hornet

In 1974, the U.S. Navy initiated a study to find a new, lightweight, multi-mission carrier-based fighter.

At the time, the requirement to carry out the various missions had often resulted in several different types of aircraft equipping the squadrons. Each carrier air group was usually composed of fighter aircraft, attack aircraft, reconnaissance aircraft, and patrol aircraft. Each different type of aircraft required spare parts, special tools, and specially trained pilots and mechanics.

If the navy could find one aircraft that could carry out many different roles, it could save millions of dollars on spare parts and personnel. In addition, the carrier air group would become more efficient.

The study was just underway when funds were withdrawn from the program. The U.S. Air Force had just gone through a study of its own to develop its next fighter. In the course of the development, several major aircraft manufacturers had submitted designs that had the potential to meet the navy's requirement without undergoing a lengthy and costly development study.

The navy looked at all the prototype aircraft and decided that the General Dynamics YF-16 and the Northrop YF-17 were the closest to its needs. However, both would need substantial revision to make them acceptable for work aboard an aircraft carrier. The firm that could best modify its design for work on the high seas would win the new contract.

F/A-18 launches from the deck of the USS Constellation.

(Courtesy the U.S. Navy)

McDonnell Douglas, whose F-4 Phantom aircraft was to be replaced by the winner, approached Northrop with an offer to team up to develop not only a navy version of Northrop's design but one with many improved design features.

The new design was christened the Navy Air Combat Fighter. Melding McDonnell Douglas's naval aircraft experience with Northrop's design led to a superior aircraft. In January 1976, the design was accepted as the winner of the competition, and the navy ordered prototypes built for testing.

There were two distinct versions ordered. The first was a two-seat version to be known as the F-18. The other was a single-seat attack version to be known as the A-18. The navy also ordered a trainer version that was designated as the TF-18.

First Flight

The first of 11 prototype aircraft flew its maiden flight on November 18, 1978. The prototypes were very impressive. The new aircraft, which was nicknamed the Hornet, was a mid-wing monoplane with a twin tail. The aircraft had twin General Electric F404-GE-400 engines with afterburners. Each engine generated 16,000 pounds of thrust.

Packed into the airframe were the most advanced communications, flight controls, radar, and navigational equipment McDonnell Douglas and the navy could find.

Of course, the aircraft was adapted for carrier use. It was equipped with carrier launch and arresting gear. The wingtips could be folded up to increase storage space aboard ship, and the landing gear was specially strengthened to allow for the shock of carrier landings. The prototypes were quite successful and after a full range of tests, the aircraft was accepted into the navy.

The success of the Hornet's new design convinced the Marine Corps that the Hornet would also be used to replace its aging McDonnell Douglas F-4 Phantom fighter and fighter-bomber jets. Since the Marine Corps routinely embarks its squadrons aboard aircraft carriers, the standardization made sense.

Flattop Facts

The first production version of the Hornet was delivered in May 1980 to VFA-125 stationed at Lemoore, California. This squadron was a joint U.S. Navy and Marine Corps squadron that would transition pilots to the new aircraft. By the time the first production version arrived, the nomenclature of the aircraft had changed to F/A-18. The difference between the two versions was a small amount of operational equipment on the aircraft and the ordnance load it carried.

The F/A-18 Hornet had a wingspan of 40 feet, 4 inches, with sidewinder missiles mounted on the outer wingtips. The fuselage was 56 feet long and the aircraft was 15 feet, 3 inches high. It had an empty weight of 23,050 pounds and could get in the air with a fully loaded weight of 50,064 pounds. Without any ordnance creating drag, it had a top speed of 1,190 miles per hour. It had a combat ceiling of 50,000 feet and in the fighter configuration had a range of 460 miles.

The business end of the F/A-18 was quite impressive. It carried an M61 20mm six-barreled cannon with 570 rounds of ammunition. The gun was mounted in the nose. In addition to M61, the aircraft had nine external *hard points*. The Hornet could carry 17,000 pounds of missiles, bombs, sensor pods, or extra fuel tanks. Among the weapons it could carry were the AIM-7 and AIM-9 air superiority missiles.

The new Hornet was quite successful in operational use. By 1984 three Marine Corps squadrons—VMFA 314, VMFA 323, and VMFA 531—had transitioned to the Hornet along with several navy squadrons. In that same year, a reconnaissance version was introduced.

Naval Lingo

Hard points are locations on an aircraft's wings where weapons can be mounted.

Improved Version

Within a few years, the navy and McDonnell Douglas were at work to build an improved version. The two-seat trainer had been redesignated as the F/A 18B, so the next version would be the F/A-18C.

On September 3, 1986, the new F/A-18C was unveiled. It featured improved avionics for night flights, new General Electric F404-GE-402 Turbofan engines, and improved hard points, which allowed the aircraft to carry the AIM-120 Phoenix Missile and the AGM-65 Maverick ground attack missile. The first F/A-18C was delivered to the Naval Warfare Center and was an immediate success.

The next improvement was to the two-seat night-attack version. The aircraft had a Forward Looking Infrared Radar unit and improved attack computers for work at night. The new version was designated the F/A-18D and flew for the first time on November 1, 1988.

Within a few years the navy and marines had fielded 37 tactical squadrons of the Hornet from air stations worldwide and from 10 aircraft carriers. The U.S. Navy's Blue Angels Demonstration Team also chose the Hornet as its mount. However, as impressive as the aircraft was, it had yet to prove itself in combat, but its combat debut wasn't far off: During the Gulf War of 1991 the Hornet proved its immense value and versatility.

Over Iraq

During Operation Desert Storm, the first war with Iraq in 1991, F/A-18s en route to bomb enemy targets were attacked by enemy fighters. Without jettisoning their bomb loads, they engaged and shot down the fighters and then went on to bomb their assigned targets. (Complete air dominance was the rule in Operation Iraqi Freedom as well.)

In the high-threat environment, the Hornets were certain to take damage from enemy antiaircraft guns and antiaircraft missiles. Several F/A-18s were damaged by enemy action. Despite the extent of the damage, all were able to make it back to their aircraft carriers or friendly airfields.

The vast majority were quickly repaired, and most flew combat missions the next day. Such was the ruggedness of the aircraft that during the course of the war they broke all records for mission availability and reliability.

After the design of the F/A-18D, the engineers at McDonnell Douglas decided that the added weight of new ordnance would require a longer and stronger airframe. The new requirements prompted the navy and McDonnell to create the F/A 18E and F. These versions were officially designated the "Super Hornet."

The new airframe had 11 hard points and 17 cubic feet of "growth space" for electronic systems. The new versions could carry the improved APG-73 radar. The new aircraft seemed to be everything that the navy wanted or needed, and the navy authorized initial development of the aircraft. After carefully reviewing the design, the navy authorized the production of 10 prototype aircraft.

The Super Hornet made its first flight at Patuxent River, Maryland, in September 1995. Of the total of 10 test aircraft being used for the test program, 7 were flying test aircraft and 3 were ground test aircraft.

The F/A-18E/F is quite impressive. The design team not only enlarged the fuselage but also incorporated new technology into the aircraft. The Super Hornet incorporates low observable technology with its improved radar and state-of-the-art defensive electronic countermeasures.

With these changes, the F/A 18 E/F has reduced its own vulnerability while increasing its lethality against air and ground targets. In practical terms the aircraft can carry 3,600 pounds or 33 percent more fuel. This allows the Super Hornet to fly up to 40 percent farther on a typical interdiction mission and to stay "on station" (patrolling an assigned area of the air) for 80 percent longer on a combat air patrol, or CAP. The gain is greater for the CAP than on the bombing missions or interdiction because the weapons required to fight other aircraft weigh less than weapons you drop on the ground.

All tests were successful and with that the navy ordered the F/A 18 E/F into production.

Ship's Log

In the second war with Iraq, the F/A-18 E/F led the navy's attack on the Iraqi defenses.

The first operational cruise of the Super Hornet was with VFA-115 onboard my old ship, the USS *Abraham Lincoln* (CVN 72) on July 24, 2002, and it saw initial combat action on November 6, 2002. That action came when E models participated in a strike on hostile targets in the "no-fly" zone in Iraq.

The navy's Super Hornet gives this nation both a "first day of the war" and an "every day of the war" dominance, and a precision strike fighter that meets and beats the best jets possessed by any of our potential enemies through the first part of the twenty-first century.

The Super Hornet can carry every tactical air-to-air and air-to-ground weapon in the navy's inventory. With the Advanced Medium Range Anti Air (AMRAAM) missile, enhanced radar, and advanced onboard sensor fusion capability—which correlates all of the aircraft's sensors, such as the radar and the electronic emissions detections— there is not a threat fighter in the world today—or projected to exist in the next 20 years—that Super Hornet cannot decisively defeat and totally dominate in combat.

S-3B Viking

The S-3B Viking is based on the S-3A, which was formerly configured for antisubmarine warfare (ASW). Today's Viking, however, is a top surveillance and precision-targeting platform with modern precision-guided missile capabilities.

Fact Box
S-3B Specifications
Primary Function: Force Protection, Organic overhead/mission tanking
Contractor: Lockheed-California Company
Unit Cost: $27 million
Propulsion: Two General Electric TF-34-GE-400B turbofan engines (9,275 pounds of thrust each)
Length: 53 feet, 4 inches
Wingspan: 68 feet, 8 inches
Height: 22 feet, 9 inches
Weight: Max design gross takeoff: 52,539 pounds
Speed: 450 knots (518 mph)
Ceiling: 40,000 feet
Range: 2,300+ nautical miles (2,645 statute miles)
Armament: Up to 3,958 pounds of AGM-84 Harpoon, AGM-65 Maverick and AGM-84 SLAM missiles, torpedoes, rockets, and bombs
Crew: Two/Four
Service Entry: 1975

The S-3B Viking is an all-weather, carrier-based jet aircraft. It provides protection against hostile ships while also functioning as the carrier battle groups' primary overhead/mission tanker. Extremely versatile, the aircraft is equipped for many missions, including day/night surveillance, electronic countermeasures, command/control/communications warfare, and search and rescue (SAR).

Among its features are several high-speed computer system processes that display information generated by its targeting-sensor systems. These systems include the inverse/synthetic aperture radar (ISAR/SAR), the infrared (IR) sensor, and an electronic support (ESM) system.

The S-3B Viking employs an impressive array of airborne weaponry to engage and destroy targets. These include the AGM 84 Harpoon antiship missile, AGM 65 Maverick IR missile, and a wide selection of conventional bombs and torpedoes.

In the future, planned Viking aircraft will have a control capability for the AGM 84 standoff land-attack missile extended-range (SLAM-ER).

E-2C Hawkeye

For almost 40 years, the E-2C Hawkeye has been the navy's all-weather, carrier-based tactical warning and control system aircraft. The concept of an airborne early warning and command and control aircraft was born in the mid-1950s, due to the continuous improvements in early airborne radar. The first plane to perform this mission was the Hawkeye's daddy, the Grumman E-1 Tracer, which was based on the S-2 Tracker, an antisubmarine aircraft.

The E-1 performed from 1954 until 1964, when it was replaced by the Hawkeye. The E-2 was the first carrier-based aircraft designed from the outset for the all-weather airborne early warning and command and control function.

The Hawkeye has performed other missions as well, such as surface surveillance coordination, strike and interceptor control, search and rescue guidance, and communications relay.

The Hawkeye made its combat debut in Vietnam, and also directed F-14 Tomcat fighters flying combat air patrol during the two-carrier battle group joint strike against terrorist-related Libyan targets in 1986.

Flattop Facts _____

The navy calls the Hawkeye the "eyes of the fleet."

During the first Persian Gulf War the Hawkeye directed both land attack and combat air patrol missions over Iraq and provided control for the shootdown of two Iraqi MIG-21 aircraft by carrier-based

F/A-18s in the early days of the war. The latest model of the aircraft, the E-2C, has been around since 1973.

Fact Box
E-2C Hawkeye Specifications Primary Function: Airborne early warning, command and control Contractor: Grumman Aerospace Corp. Unit Cost: $51 million Propulsion: Two Allison T-56-A427 turboprop engines (5,000 shaft horsepower each) Length: 57 feet, 6 inches Wingspan: 80 feet, 7 inches Height: 18 feet, 3 inches Weight: Max. gross, takeoff: 53,000 pounds, 40,200 pounds basic Speed: 300+ knots (345 mph) Ceiling: 30,000 feet Crew: Five Armament: None Operational: January 1964

So there you have it, the Hall of Fame of ship-based aircraft, featuring both the warplanes of today and those of yesteryear. Without the proper aircraft to "project the power" during times of war, the aircraft carrier could never have developed, as it has, into the king of the sea.

The Least You Need to Know

- The B-25 Mitchell altered the course of World War II with bombing missions flown off the flight decks of aircraft carriers.

- Grumman made superior carrier-based aircraft before and during the Second World War.

- The Mitsubishi A6M Zero-Sen, the most famous of Japan's combat aircraft, began World War II as a competitive fighter, but didn't keep up.

- Today's Super Hornet is a strike fighter that dominates the competition.

Part  3

A Day in the Life of an Aircraft Carrier

Now we are going to get down to the nitty-gritty. This section of the book is about what it is like to live on an aircraft carrier. You'll find out where you sleep, where you eat, and what there is to do when you're not doing your job (which, as you'll also learn, isn't all that often).

Since life on a carrier is different for different people, we are going to follow three very different occupants of the carrier through a typical 24-hour period, two sailors and one aviator.

So, with the help of our three heroes—Airman Carl Schmuckatelli, Lieutenant Commander Joe Blow, and Chief Petty Officer Frank Sands—you'll learn a slice of what a day in the life of an aircraft carrier is like.

Chapter 7

Living on a Carrier

In This Chapter

- ◆ What all that noise is about
- ◆ The never-ending sequence of emergency-preparedness drills
- ◆ Leisure time activities
- ◆ Where sailors get their grub

In this chapter, I am going to try to give you a little idea of what it is like to live on an aircraft carrier. Compared to the life you are living now, it is probably a noisy and chaotic existence, but there are ways to relax—and I'll discuss them as well.

Finally, I'll take you on a tour of the various places to eat onboard, the food and ambiance you can expect there, and who you have to be to qualify to eat there.

What? I Can't Hear You, I'm on an Aircraft Carrier

One of the first things you'll notice about life on a carrier is that it's noisy, but by the time you get to your rack—that is, your bed—you're usually too tired to care. Even if the carrier isn't launching or recovering aircraft, there's always machinery at work.

Ship's Log

An aircraft carrier wants to keep the amount of noise it puts into the water at a minimum. This is so the ship will be harder to pick up by a potential enemy's listening devices.

Flattop Facts

After a few days, you don't even have to hear the noise to know what's taking off or landing. Particularly takeoffs. A Tomcat will rattle your computer monitor far more than a Hornet will.

If it's not the carrier's aircraft landing and taking off, it's the pumps that provide water or the blowers circulating the air. Or the shifts of people who work different hours, coming and going into compartments or down the hallway. This is particularly true for the more junior ratings (that is, the lower-ranked crew members), who live in large compartments with around 60 men in each.

Despite sound isolation and other quieting measures, noises travel easily through the steel of the ship's hull. The main silencing and shock-absorbing measures are devoted to isolating the interior from the exterior—that is, reducing the amount of noise the carrier puts into the water. While that certainly relates to the amount of noise inside the carrier, they're not necessarily the same thing.

Oddly enough, you can get used to anything. I normally lived on the 03 level, right below the flight deck. Takeoffs and landings will rattle everything you have in your stateroom.

More Drilling Than a Dentist's Office

In addition to the noise of day-to-day living, there are the drills—the incessant, continuous drills. For the most part, they're pretty necessary. You fight the way you train, and most major disasters at sea have been made far less serious because the crew was trained to deal with them.

But training means practice, and it's not something you can do by walking through the scenarios in a classroom—although there is a fair amount of classroom damage control training, too.

In an emergency, every person onboard the ship has an assignment. Those assignments are listed on a big chart in every workspace for the people who work there. The chart is called the WQSB, or watch, quarters, and station bill. It shows where the person stands normal watches, where they sleep, and what their assignment is during an emergency (their station).

No, you have to actually experience being dead asleep in your rack and being jolted awake by the clamor of the general quarters alarm, or the collision alarm, or the chemical and biological alarm.

You go from a dead sleep to fully dressed and moving in a few seconds, and it's all reflex. You're out of the compartment and running for your general quarters station before the first 10 gongs are over, running with the traffic.

In Case of Chaos, Stay to the Right

You can imagine the chaos as every single sailor is trying to get to his or her general quarters station at the same time. It's worse than Wal-Mart the day before Christmas. For that reason, there are rules about how you travel on a carrier during general quarters.

If you're going up or forward, you stay on the right side of the ship. If you're going down or aft, you stay on the left side of the ship. The two sides of the ship are connected at intervals with cross passageways, but they aren't at the same place on every level, so that's got to be factored into your planning.

Not that you have to plan at this point. You've done this drill so many times that you're moving by reflex, going with the flow of the crowd.

Know the Route with Your Eyes Closed

That's because the first thing you learn on a carrier, the first basic bit of damage control and safety, is how to get from your berthing compartment and your work center to the outside of the ship. You memorize the route—two routes, if you're smart.

You have to be able to do it blindfolded, know how many steps there are between your compartment and the first turn, where the ladders are, what the next turn is. In all probability, your division leading petty officer will require you to do it blindfolded several times before he or she is satisfied with the results.

He or she will stand you in the middle of your compartment blindfolded, turn you around several times until you're disoriented, and say, "go." It's up to you to find your landmarks within the compartment so you know where you are and make your way to the outside world. You'll do the same thing from your work center.

> **Ship's Log**
>
> You won't find many apartment complexes that require you to be able to get from one place to another without being able to see where you're going. But on a carrier, your rent is low—nonexistent, actually—and there's no security deposit required, so it evens out.

Things You Don't Have to Worry About

One thing about being at sea, as distant as you are from your family and friends, there's a lot you don't have to worry about. The navy does a fair job of keeping people focused on their jobs. For instance, you don't have to cook for yourself.

Ship's Log

A wide range of food is provided, including low-fat choices, and there is some place 24 hours a day that you can go to eat.

And laundry—no laundry to worry about unless you're one of the people who works in the laundry. There's a set schedule and you simply leave your dirty laundry in your laundry bag, all pieces clearly marked with your name and social security number, and it's picked up, cleaned, and returned to you.

Variety of Activities

The isolation of being at sea on an aircraft carrier is made a little easier by the variety of activities that are available. Today, the Internet is even available for sailors who want to surf the web.

There's virtually everything you could want to do onboard the ship. Here's a list of the facilities available:

◆ A well-equipped gym, including Stairmasters and treadmills

◆ Movies

◆ A library

◆ A store for junk food, books, and magazines

◆ TVs

◆ A wide range of religious services

Flattop Facts

It used to be that the only way you could talk to your family was via the ham radio folks, but now almost every sailor gets an e-mail account just by asking for it.

Movies are shown at several spots around the ship. For the crew, it's in the galley. Squadrons normally have their own movie schedule, with the junior officer in the squadron being responsible for the nightly movie show.

The chief's mess also shows movies, as does the wardroom on occasion. The flag mess will also show movies for flag staff. Back in the old days, before women were assigned to ships, there were a lot of stag films (dirty movies) on the schedule. They were called training films. They're banned now but still are shown under surreptitious circumstances.

On my ship, the *Abraham Lincoln*, there was always a competition between squadrons as to who could produce the best popcorn, and each one of them had a large popcorn popper in the ready room.

Movies are one of the carrot-and-stick motivators onboard a ship. Normally, if you haven't completed whatever qualifications (quals) you're supposed to be working on, you're not allowed to watch movies. For junior officers on the ship, these quals may be surface warfare officer qualifications or damage control qualifications.

Working the You-Name-It Shift

The other thing that you normally get used to quickly is working odd hours. Not only do you have your regularly assigned billet onboard the ship (your job, if you like), but you're also part of a watch section as well.

Your normal job may require a regular seven in the morning to five in the afternoon workday but your watch-standing hours may interrupt that as well as your off-duty hours. Officers, in particular, may have significant "collateral" duties, including the miscellaneous programs that keep a ship or a squadron running, such as human relations council and that sort of thing.

Day and Night: What a Concept!

Many crew members on a carrier can go for days without seeing daylight. It's easy to get your *circadian* rhythms mixed up until you're really not sure whether you're waking up for breakfast, lunch, or dinner.

It's not a problem for air crews or surface officers, or at least not as much of one, as they see the daylight regularly. But engineering ratings (called snipes) can stay below the waterline for days on end.

Naval Lingo

Circadian means pertaining to a 24-hour cycle.

You learn to sleep when you can. During flight operations, it's not unusual to see a small cluster of exhausted junior sailors, plane captains, and deck personnel stretched out in the passageway for a quick nap, their sound-powered phones

Flattop Facts

Sailors quickly learn to at least get outside occasionally to reset their internal clocks.

still clamped to their head and plugged into the circuit, a small part of their mind listening to the traffic in case they're needed as the rest of their body catches a nap.

These young men and women work incredibly long hours, and during intense flight operations they seem to be on duty for days at a time.

Places You May Never See

There are many parts of the carrier you'll probably never see. And you'll never run into most of the crew, either. There are only three primary groups of people you'll associate with, other than those you meet through special interests. The people you will primarily be in contact with include those who occupy …

- ◆ Your work center.

- ◆ Your living space.

- ◆ Your watch section.

You get to know people very quickly living in such close quarters, and you'll be exposed to cultures and ways of life that you'd never see otherwise.

How close those quarters are depend on how senior you are. If you're a junior sailor, you share a compartment with 30 to 60 other people. The compartment is filled with bunk beds, three deep in some ships, just two deep in others. You've got a bunk and usually a locker about three feet tall and a foot wide. There may also be a big shallow drawer or storage area under your mattress.

The bathroom, called the head, may be attached to the berthing compartment or it may be a short way down the passageway. It will contain showers, toilets, urinals, and sinks (usually no urinals in the women's berthing compartments, although they may be left in place in case the compartment has to someday be used for men again). The more senior you get, the fewer people you have to share a compartment with. By the time you're a chief petty officer, you may have a room of your own (you'll still be sharing a bathroom, or head, with others, though).

Junior officers may get lucky and get housed in a six-man berthing compartment, or they may be in larger compartments known as JO Jungles, or Junior Officer Jungles. Officers normally have bunk beds, a full-length locker, and a few drawers under the bed. Normally, there will be a pull-down desk built in to one of the locker compartments. There's usually a safe as well, for storing classified material.

With officers, RHIP (Rank Has Its Privileges). By the time you're a full commander, you may have a compartment to yourself. Your bed may fold into a distinctly uncomfortable couch during the day. You're still sharing a head with others, though. It's not until you're a captain, or the commanding officer of a squadron, that you can be pretty sure you'll have a room to yourself—and maybe even a private head!

A Cross-Section of America

You'll learn to understand every sort of accent from a Boston whine to a Valley Girl lilt. You'll meet people from the inner city and from the wide-open spaces, from every socioeconomic part of the country.

Inevitably, since the carrier population is a reflection of the United States in general, you get the bad as well as the good. Like the rest of the world, "the bad" is a small part of the population, but they can have a disruptive effect.

Oblivious to the Elements

The other thing you miss about being on a carrier is the weather. The carrier is so massive that it takes a very rough sea for its motion to be felt at all. You'll primarily notice the weather predictions as they affect your job. Here are some examples:

◆ For the engineer, the sea intake temperature may affect the distillation of water and cooling processes.

◆ For the mess management specialist, cold weather topside means being ready to take hot drinks to those standing watch on the weather decks and feeding them more calories.

◆ For meteorologists (and they do usually look out the porthole to see if their predictions make sense) it means advising the air commanders on how the weather may impact operations.

◆ For the combat system specialist, weather may affect how tight the formation of ships traveling together should be, a scheduled underway replenishment, or the range of radars and other sensors.

◆ For the Destroyer Squadron DESRON commander, the weather affects the ability to detect sound signals and longer ranges and to conduct surface surveillance. The DESRON is in charge of coordinating aircraft and surface ships to fight surface and subsurface threats. The destroyers and frigates, along with the ship's airwing S-3B and shore-based P-3 aircraft, usually work for him once they're launched.

Where to Eat

The first thing you learn about eating is that if you're on watch or going on watch, you have front-of-the-line privileges. This is significant in the crew's mess, where the lines at peak hours can be formidable, and use of this privilege is generally controlled by the master at arms (MAA), the equivalent of the ship's police force.

You may have a special chit (chit is a generic name for any piece of paper that asks for a privilege or grants you one) or be on a list, or the MAA may just take your word on it, counting on peer pressure to keep everybody honest. Nobody likes line cutters.

If you're on watch, and it's one of those endless ones, you may have 15 minutes to leave your station, get below and eat, and get back to work. Thus, front-of-the-line privileges.

The Finest Restaurant: CPO Mess

There's really no dispute about the best place to eat onboard a ship: it's the chief petty officer's mess. Although the CPO's mess generally obtains staples such as fruits and vegetables from the main galley, it has its own cooking area.

Flattop Facts

Junior officers know that they are blessed indeed when their chief petty officer brings them a crab leg or bit of steak from the chief's mess.

The chief petty officers contribute to their messing fund, and their mess treasurer plans the menus. Rumors of the delicacies and gourmet treats served there abound.

Captains and admirals yearn for the opportunity to mess with the chiefs, but it is by invitation only if you're not one of the enlisted khaki crowd.

A Side Note on Rank and Rating

There are three terms you need to know when discussing how senior an enlisted sailor is—paygrade, rating, and rate. Paygrade defines the sailor's actual seniority in the service, how high their rank is, e.g., Petty Officer Second Class. Rating is their job field, e.g., Sonar Technician. Rate is the combination of the two, e.g., Sonar Technician Second Class.

Enlisted paygrades fall into three basic categories—nonrated sailors, petty officers, and chief petty officers. Nonrated sailors are in paygrades E-1, E-2, and E-3 (the E stands for enlisted). Nonrated sailors *may* or *may not* have a rating. If they don't have a rating, a job specialty, then they are part of a general apprentice field (see more on this in Chapter 8). Non-rated sailors are promoted based on time in service and satis-factory performance and completion of a few training courses.

Petty officers are paygrades E-4 through 6. These two groups, E-1 through 6, pretty much dress alike. The paygrade insignia on the left shoulders are the same, and those who have a rating will have the insignia for that rating as part of the paygrade in-signia. The insignia for a petty officer is 1, 2, or 3 chevrons with an eagle above them. This insignia is known as a crow.

Chief petty officers wear khaki-colored uniforms, the same uniform that officers wear. They are berthed in a separate area of the ship and have their own mess. They are composed of paygrades E-7 through E-9, or chief, senior chief, and master chief. They wear an anchor on their collar, if they're wearing their khaki uniforms, or chevrons and a rocker on their uniform in dress uniforms.

Chiefs run the navy.

Officer paygrades start with O. Paygrades O-1 through O-4 (Ensign, Lieutenant [jun-ior grade], Lieutenant, and Lieutenant Commander) are considered junior officers. Paygrades O-5 through O-6 (Commander and Captain) are senior officers. Above that are the admiral ranks, O-7 through O-10, known as the flag ranks. They're called the flag ranks because every admiral has a flag that is "broken" or displayed on the ship to which the admiral is assigned or that he's temporarily on.

A few odd interservice notes:

In other services, an O-4 is considered a "field grade" officer, their equivalent of a senior officer.

Be polite to any officer on the phone who announces that he or she is "Captain so and so." In any other service, that denotes an officer of paygrade O-3, not O-6, so don't give them a special parking sticker if they're not navy. Conversely, be very polite until you find out whether you'd dealing with a navy captain or a junior officer.

Captain is not only a paygrade term—it's also the term used to denote an officer in command of a unit. For a small unit, the captain or commanding officer may actually be a lieutenant commander.

Confused? Of course. Just be polite until you see if there are eagles or railroad tracks on the collar.

Next Best Depends

The next best place to eat depends on what you're after. If you like atmosphere, you want to eat in the flag mess. Of course, you have to be on the admiral's staff or a high-ranking civilian to have that privilege, but you get tablecloths, waiters, and some fairly decent grub.

> **Ship's Log**
>
> I remember one cruise where the admiral, an avid hunter, brought aboard a large number of quail which were later served in the flag mess.

> **Naval Lingo**
>
> The **dirty shirt mess** is called that because you're not required to be in a normal, spiffy uniform. You can show up grimy because you've been working, in a flight suit because you've been flying or you're about to fly, or because you're an aviator and that's all you have in your closet.

After that, it's a matter of personal preference. My favorite was always the *dirty shirt mess*, located aft on the 03 level.

The dirty shirt is quite egalitarian, and you may find yourself sharing a long stretch of tables with very senior officers and very junior ones. It's a bit rowdier than the other officers' messes, too.

The dirty shirt is an officers' mess, one built along the lines of the crew's galley. Officers eat in a mess, enlisted sailors eat in the galley. The difference is that an officers' mess is run by a committee that decides what sort of food the mess will serve. All officers must join the mess. At sea, the monthly cost to feed everyone is split between all members. When the ship is in port for an extended period of time, sometimes the mess will allow officers to pay by the meal. If the mess votes to serve lobster at every meal, mess bills will be astronomical. Conversely, eight straight days of chili mac will probably lead to a revolt amongst mess members.

The galley, however, is provided a certain amount of money each day for each sailor—not a lot, around $3 or so. There's usually an advisory committee of some sort, but the menu is primarily under the control of the senior enlisted Mess Management Specialist. The sailors have less say in what is served, but they don't get billed for it, either. On a CV, however, there's usually something for every taste.

There's a serving line, trays, portions scooped up by sailors behind the hot line, and there's normally a soft-serve ice cream machine somewhere in the vicinity. There's also a small hot line set aside for 24-hour food operations.

> **Naval Lingo**
>
> Soft-serve ice cream is often referred to as **auto dog** for reasons that are beyond the scope of the classy tone we're trying to maintain in this book.

The serving line normally has one or two entrees (don't ask for the chili mac or anything with the word "veal" in it—it's not veal, it's mystery meat), vegetables (stay away from anything that says mixed or spring) and starches, a dessert area, and almost always hamburgers (known as sliders). Pizza may also be on the menu.

The dirty shirt will be open for regular meals and a small, detached steam line for 24-hour service will usually have chili, spaghetti, peanut butter and jelly and bread, or some other quick food, as well as salads.

In addition to regular mealtimes, the regular steam line will also be open for mid-rats, or midnight rations, at around—you guessed it—midnight. Count on leftovers and continue to avoid the chili mac and veal. Go with the peanut butter if you're desperate.

Crew's Galleys and Officers' Mess

There will normally be two crew's galleys on the ship as well; a portion of one might be set off for a petty officer first class mess and there may be a petty officer *first-class association* that many of them belong to.

Naval Lingo

The **first-class association** recognizes the time that a petty officer first class has in service and provides training for their eventual ascension to the lofty ranks of chief petty officer. It's a good thing, on general principles. A lot of work gets done at the petty officer first class level. They are the leading petty officers of divisions, and many coordination or interdivision problems can be ironed out at that level before they reach the attention of the more senior ranks.

Finally, there's the regular officers' mess. One should be decently attired to eat there, and there will be a head table with a *cloth* tablecloth that is reserved for senior officers. The atmosphere is a bit stuffy, so go for the dirty shirt if you're given a choice. If you're a surface warfare officer, you may want to turn up there for the required face time.

Flattop Facts

In many messes, but not all, discussing work is absolutely forbidden. You may get fined if you bring it up.

In the flag mess, you have a small photocopied menu next to your plate and you check off what you want or give your order to a snappily attired mess cook. Everywhere else, you're on your own with a steam line.

One thing you should try to figure out early on: If you're eating in the enlisted messes, you should know ahead of time when the marines eat. They eat a lot, and they burn the calories off in the gym, so count on getting to chow early if you have any hope of getting good desserts.

You'll also want to figure out when the marines work out and try to go to the gym at a different hour. Not only do they take up most of the equipment, putting heavy weights on everything, but it's also somewhat discouraging to try to keep up with them.

One final note: Never take a gunny sergeant up on an invitation to work out with him. You won't be able to get your arms down by your sides for several days. (And yes, this would be the voice of experience speaking.)

The Least You Need to Know

- ◆ Despite sound isolation and other quieting measures, sound travels easily through the steel of the ship's hull—so it's a noisy place.

- ◆ There is so much drilling and practicing that everyone knows exactly what to do in case of an emergency.

- ◆ The isolation of being at sea on an aircraft carrier is made a little easier by the variety of activities that are available.

- ◆ There are several places to eat on a carrier, but where you go depends both on what you want and who you are.

Chapter 8

Meet Our Three Heroes

In This Chapter

- Three very different sailors
- The airman
- The pilot
- The cook

Before we go through a day in the life of an aircraft carrier, let's meet the three sailors we'll be following. By looking at three different individuals we'll get a glimpse of the diverse ways in which one might find himself or herself aboard an aircraft carrier, and we'll have a more complete look at what 24 hours aboard a flattop is like. Let me introduce you to three people: Airman Carl Schmuckatelli, Lieutenant Commander Joe Blow, and Chief Petty Officer Frank Sands.

For starters, a bit about each one of them.

Flattop Facts

Don't ask me why, but this is a fairly common surname used in hypothetical examples in the navy—no offense to any actual Schmuckatellis who may be reading this.

Ship's Log

Schmuckatelli's score on the ASVAB will follow the potential recruit around for quite some time, determining what navy training schools he's eligible for in the future, what military career he can plan on, that sort of thing.

Airman Carl Schmuckatelli

Airman Schmuckatelli is from Tennessee. He grew up on a small farm outside the city, attended high school and did well, and is trying to decide whether he wants to go to the University of Tennessee, to a technical school, or straight into the workforce.

For some reason, some throwback genes have surfaced in Airman Schmuckatelli, and he feels the call of the sea. Carl goes down to his local recruiter's office, picks up some material, and talks to a very impressive, understanding, and generally all-around squared-away petty officer, who is a recruiter there.

The first order of business, before they can discuss Airman Schmuckatelli's possible future with the United States Navy, is to find out what he's eligible to do in the navy. This is accomplished by administering a basic battery of tests known as the ASVAB (Armed Services Vocational Aptitude Battery).

Processing and Testing

At a centralized processing center, Carl Schmuckatelli takes the tests with a bunch of prospective recruits from all services. It's an armed services test, not one unique to any service. The test yields both a raw score and a percentile score.

It's also supposed to catch any really odd character traits, like complete psychosis, but there are some doubts about how well that works. (I still remember the young recruit who flipped out in boot camp after eating mushrooms he found in the grass in front of his barracks. He spent a good 30 minutes running around the barracks screaming, "I'm from Uranus!" before we could catch him and get him to Medical.)

Flattop Facts

The requirements for test scores change from year to year, depending on how many recruits the service needs and what they think they can live with.

So Schmuckatelli takes the tests and does fairly well. He scored in the seventieth percentile, which means that out of 100 people who take the test, 69 percent will score below him and 30 will score above him.

That's a good score, which puts him squarely in the desirable recruit category, and makes him eligible for just about everything the navy has to offer with the exception of some very technical fields, such as nuclear power.

Now that the recruiter knows he's dealing with quality goods, his attitude changes. In an ideal world, the recruiter would give Airman Schmuckatelli a realistic idea of what life in the navy will be like, assess his personal interests and capabilities, and work with him to get a guaranteed technical school upon graduation from boot camp.

The Needs of the Navy

Depending on who you're dealing with or talking to, the recruitment results can be quite different. There may be a push to recruit certain job skills. ("The needs of the navy" is a phrase Airman Schmuckatelli will come to know well.) All the schools may be full up for the next year or so—or recruiters might be behind quota and very eager to sign up more recruits.

But really, how can the recruiter give the future Airman Schmuckatelli a real feel for what navy life will be like? It's not possible—too much of it is beyond the potential recruit's experience, and even with telling him that he will stand watches in addition to his normal duties and have a chance to work on aircraft, none of it will make much sense. Not until Schmuckatelli has been there, has stood cold midwatches, or been assigned to the galley for three months.

Ship's Log

You'll find many people who claim recruiters lied to them about what they would be doing in the navy. That probably occurs, but more often the answer lies in selective listening or simply an inability to convey what military life is all about. Recruiter fraud allegations are investigated and are prosecuted if they're warranted. If there has been out-and-out fraud, the recruit can request to be released from active duty.

Schmuckatelli's friend is one of those people who doesn't do very well on the tests. He may not be able to get a guaranteed basic school (called an A school) straight out of boot camp.

Instead, he'll go to a general apprenticeship training of some sort where he'll learn the basics of one of several broad occupational fields. Those are seaman, airman, and fireman.

There are three other occupational fields that do not have apprenticeship training, since A school is required: constructionman (the source of Seabees), hospital corpsman, and dental technician. Other ratings in the navy are open only to those above a certain pay grade from certain source ratings. For instance, a sailor must reach pay-grade E-5 before he or she can apply to become a master at arms, sort of a military policeman in the navy. In the aviation community, a wide range of structural repair technician ratings merge to become a new rating at the chief or senior chief petty officer paygrade.

If Carl Schmuckatelli is assigned to a seaman apprentice program, he'll be learning traditional naval skills. He'll probably be assigned initially to the deck division, where he'll help …

◆ Maintain the ship's hull by chipping paint and rust.

◆ Take care of the small craft onboard the ship.

◆ Work with the boatswain's mates and quartermasters.

◆ Stand lookout or bridge watches.

Naval Lingo

The seaman rating also includes most of the shipboard electronics ratings, such as electronic technician, operation specialists—the guys who watch the radar—and all folks to work on the computers. These technical specialties are referred to as **twidgets.**

Naval Lingo

All engineers are known as **snipes,** no matter what their pay grade.

While he's on the ship, he will be evaluated for his aptitude and potential for one of the ratings in the seaman occupational field and he will be eventually encouraged to "strike" for a particular rating, such as boatswain's mate, gunner's mate, sonar technician, or one of the clerical ratings, e.g., yeoman. (Don't ask me why yeomen are part of the seaman occupational field. They just are.)

He'll have to complete several correspondence courses and be recommended to take the petty officer third class test. Once he passes it, whether or not he is advanced, he will be called a "designated striker" and add the insignia of that rating to his rank badge on his sleeve.

If he chooses the fireman apprentice program, Schmuckatelli will be working on machinery. He'll be a *snipe,* an engineer in training, below the waterline most of the time, assigned to the engineering department and doing everything from learning damage control procedures to repairing machinery.

The Wild Blue Yonder

Finally, there's the apprentice program that calls out to Carl Schmuckatelli, visions of high-powered combat aircraft dancing in his head, and he sees himself boldly striding across the flight deck, controlling the entire evolution of flight operations with a single nod of his head or a gruff word.

The recruiter may tell him at this point that if he wants to actually fly aircraft he'll have to go to college and get a degree. The recruiter will also hasten to point out that the navy has a wide variety of college programs both onboard the ship and working with civilian institutions. And they pay for it.

For whatever reason, Carl Schmuckatelli decides his future lies in the wild blue yonder and signs on the dotted line (several dotted lines, actually) of a recruitment contract providing for an aviation designation.

Now, suppose Schmuckatelli fails out of his A school for any reason. If that happens, he'll normally be sent straight to a ship as a nondesignated airman, and have to start the striking process all over again.

The requirements for striking for rating when you're already in the fleet differ from those required for A school. Some ratings require that the sailor attend an A school, but the vast majority of them are taught by on-the-job training and off-duty study.

Remember, we said that Airman Schmuckatelli scored in the seventieth percentile on his standard tests. In all probability, he's going to go to an A school, and that can last anywhere from four weeks to a year or so, depending on the technical complexity of his field.

Flying Blind

Airman Schmuckatelli will choose his A school based on a couple of factors: first, the needs of the navy (that ever-present overriding consideration) and then a brief description of each job in the recruiter's catalog.

The recruiter himself may or may not have any first-hand experience with that rating, although he will generally know a lot more about it than Airman Schmuckatelli simply by virtue of his training and experience in the navy.

Nevertheless, a catalog cannot really convey what life in any of the ratings is like, and unless Schmuckatelli has a relative or friend who's been in the navy, he's going to make his career choice without really knowing much about what he's going to be doing.

For instance, he may not know that the rating has been clogged at the midgrade petty officer grade for years and because of that advancement is slow. He may not know that the rating has extensive sea duty requirements, that he will always be on a carrier rather than a small ship, and that he'll be away from home and deployed most of the time.

Let's say that Airman Schmuckatelli decides he wants to be an aviation ordnanceman, to work on weapons and bombs carried on aircraft, maintaining them, keeping track of them, loading and unloading them off aircraft. So he goes to his A school after boot camp, comes out with his designation patch on his sleeve, and reports to either a squadron or a ship, depending on whether he's with a squadron or assigned as ship's company.

So Airman Schmuckatelli immediately begins to work on bombs, right? Not so fast. There's a variety of jobs onboard the ship that have to be done and never enough people to do them. Most non-petty officers, those sailors in paygrade E-1 through E-3 will spend three to six months in one of those sorts of billets.

Schmuckatelli may be in the galley or assigned as a compartment cleaner, cleaning living spaces while everyone else is working. There is a wide variety of temporary duties for any non-rated sailor, but those are the most common.

We'll rejoin Aviation Ordnanceman Airman Schmuckatelli after he's completed those tours of duty and is back with his squadron, working in his rating.

Naval Lingo

ROTC stands for Reserve Officer Training Corps. If you're a student and want to be an officer, a good way to enter the navy is through an ROTC program. The navy offers officer-training courses at many colleges. These are called ROTC programs. (Some high schools offer what are called Junior ROTC Programs that can help you get into a ROTC college.) For middle school students interested in a naval career, the Sea Cadets offers exposure to navy life, including a short summer boot camp.

Lieutenant Commander Joe Blow

Twelve years ago, Lieutenant Commander Joe Blow (another name used in many navy hypotheticals) was in the same position that Airman Schmuckatelli is now. They have roughly the same intelligence, but Joe Blow came from a family where going to college was pretty much a given.

Even so, the costs were high and Joe was looking for a way to offset the expense. He applied for and was accepted to navy *ROTC*, and in exchange for having his tuition paid, picked up a four- to six-year obligation to the navy.

There was no guarantee of what specialty he would be assigned to or whether he would be able to enter the aviation community at all. If he had dropped out of college for any reason, he would have immediately been subject to being called to active duty in the enlisted ranks.

Planning Ahead

Joe did well in college and took a variety of math and science courses, knowing that those would look good on his record when the time came to determine what he would be doing in the navy. He spent some time each summer on active duty as a midshipman, gaining exposure to a variety of navy stations, including ships, and when the time came to choose, he had a far more realistic idea of what he was getting into than Airman Schmuckatelli.

The career gods smiled on Joe Blow. Tests revealed that he had perfect eyesight, above-average intelligence, and an excellent spatial relationships ability. After passing a few interviews with classification officers, Joe was designated as a prospective naval aviator.

Brown Shoes and Black Shoes

The aviation community is divided into several broad career paths. There are the pilots, of course, and then there are the *naval flight officers* (NFOs).

There are those who make the mistake of referring to NFOs as "nonflying officers." Nothing could be further from the truth. Often, they are people who wanted to be pilots but didn't have the perfect eyesight or reflexes required.

In addition to aviators and NFOs, there are other career fields within the aviation community, including the following:

- Specialized aviation maintenance officers, who serve as maintenance operations within the squadron, maintenance department heads for the ships with extensive maintenance facilities, and commanding officers of shore maintenance stages

- Specialized air intelligence officers, skilled in the interpretation of aerial photographs and imagery and their application to target planning

- Peculiar crossbreeds such as flight surgeons who perform flight physicals and are experts in the odd sorts of medical issues that arise in pilots and NFOs

Naval Lingo

The **NFOs** are the backseaters, the experts who run the sophisticated electronics and warfare gear inside the aircraft. In the F-14, they are called a bombardier/navigator, or BN. In an S-3 Viking, an NFO is called a TACCO or tactical officer.

Ship's Log

NFOs will often say that their intelligence was too high to be a pilot, but the pilots will disagree.

No matter what they do, they're "brown shoes." Aviators and others within the aviation community traditionally wear brown shoes with their khaki uniforms rather than black shoes as the surface sailors wear. (Obviously, surface officers and sailors are referred to as black shoes.) Later, brown high heels and brown pocketbooks were added for the female aviation officers.

> **Flattop Facts**
>
> In accordance with some unknown cycle, probably correlated with sunspots, the navy periodically changes officers' uniforms. Last I heard, black shoes were now allowed to wear brown shoes with their khakis. There was also a move to abolish the specialized formal uniforms known as the aviation greens, a very spiffy uniform in—you guessed it—green, fitting far more like a marine officer's uniform would than the standard coat and tie a black shoe would wear.

Flight Jackets

Even more important than the brown shoes is the issue of flight jackets. They come in two styles: the brown leather with fake fur collar and the ever-popular green nylon. In the old days, acquiring one for a black shoe took a bit of skullduggery, a large number of pounds of coffee changing hands, and perhaps a white lie or two told to the supply officer—a beady-eyed soul with the heart of an accountant.

These days, flight jackets can be routinely purchased anywhere and the glamorous air of an aviator can be had by anyone. But it only really counts if you have one issued to you by a squadron.

Learning to Fly

Back to Joe Blow, who came by his flight jackets the honest way. Joe graduated from college, doing well—low grades would be sufficient to get him tossed out of ROTC, and, if they were bad enough, out of college entirely.

> **Ship's Log**
>
> Officers candidate school is academically more demanding but far less grueling than enlisted boot camp. I know. I've been to both.

He's made the cut and will be a naval aviator. He's called to active duty, and, because he attended ROTC, he skips a 16-week officers candidate school (OCS) course that is the officer equivalent of boot camp.

Joe is sent to a shore station to wait for a date for flight basic, which I'll tell you about in a minute. He is what is called a "stash," an officer waiting for orders. It is somewhat the equivalent of Schmuckatelli doing time in the galley when he reported aboard ship except that Lieutenant Commander Blow won't get as dirty.

He will be an SLJO (Shitty Little Jobs Officer) until he goes to basic. Joe is lucky and spends only a month assigned to local recruiting station processing paperwork before his orders arrive sending him to basic.

Basic is the first cut for all aviators. It's where they find out whether they have inner ear problems, a tendency to puke when upside down, or any variety of emotional, psychological, or physical problems that would keep them for being an aviator.

Basic is just what it sounds like—you learn the basics of learning to fly. The newly minted would-be pilots do not wear aviation wings on their uniforms. They attend ground school and a wide range of instructional flights. They are watched closely, graded strictly, and washed out if they can't cut it.

Basic is a critical point in a young aviator's career. Depending on the needs of the navy (surprise, surprise), aviators will be allowed to choose which community they go into based on their class standing in basic.

Ship's Log

An officer who washes out of either basic or later courses is known as a "fallen angel" and is often reassigned as either an aviation maintenance officer or sent to the surface warfare community.

At the top of the list, of course, are jet fighters, followed by such things as the S-3 Viking and the turboprop Greyhound COD, a carrier onboard delivery aircraft. Usually, everyone's last choice is helicopters.

There are times when the navy desperately needs more helicopter pilots in the pipeline (which is what the course of training and career paths is called) and, according to some helicopter pilots I've talked to, an entire class will be sent to helicopters.

Wings to Wear

Joe comes out of basic in fine form, standing high in his class, and opts to take an open F/A-18 Hornet slot. Joe's next assignment will be at the Hornet RAG, or Replacement Air Group.

Some speculate that there's a basic personality difference between pilots who choose Hornets versus those who opt for Tomcats. The Tomcat is the two-seater, with electronics and sensors

Flattop Facts

Now, I don't care what you saw on the TV show *JAG*. Except for a few specialized trainers, the guy in the back seat *cannot* land an F-14. There are no controls there. Just radar screens, sensor controls, and a variety of other gear designed to keep the guy in the back from bothering the pilot.

run by an NFO. The Hornet is a single-person aircraft, pilot alone. (At least, this is true within the navy. The marines have a two-seater version in the fleet, and the training commands do, too.)

While he's waiting for his seat at the RAG, Joe is once again a stash—a much more useful stash, though, since he now sports a pair of wings on his uniforms. If they can, the navy will stash him at his next training facility, or somewhere nearby. Joe will again take on a wide variety of duties, most notably supervising the other SLJOs.

Carrier Quals

After all his pipeline training is completed, while he's still at the RAG, Ensign Blow has one final test, or qual, to pass, and it's a critical one. He must qualify onboard the carrier. The carrier quals, or CQ, is one of the most dangerous periods of carrier operations.

Each pilot must get a certain number of "traps" or landings on the carrier during the day and night, something like 10 successful day traps and 6 successful night traps. Any serious safety infraction or problem qualifying, and Joe faces either being recycled through his pipeline or being booted out of the community altogether.

By this time, the Navy has spent a fair amount of time and money teaching him to fly, so Joe will be given every opportunity consistent with safety to qualify.

If carrier quals are among the most dangerous times in operations, with so many new pilots getting their first look at the boat, it's also among the most interesting ones. An observer will see a wide variety of interpretations of good airmanship.

It's possible to pick up an entirely new vocabulary listening to the CAG and the air boss make their assessments of the new pilots in their pithy and concise ways. Not for the tenderhearted.

Remember, during carrier quals, the danger is not only to Joe Blow and whoever is flying with him. He has a multimillion-dollar aircraft that the carrier really doesn't want to end up in the drink.

There's also the prospect of doing significant damage to the carrier, to the deck, to the island, and to other aircraft that are positioned on the deck, not to mention all the people near those things.

All in all, the stakes are quite high, and everyone from the admiral on down keeps a close eye on the plat camera, the camera that protrudes from the flight deck and gives a deck-level view of everything that happens. Damage control teams, particularly damage control locker No. 8, which is responsible for the flight deck, are edgy. The potential for disaster is enormous.

Joe's First Squadron

Depending on the schedule, time of year, and available aircraft, Joe will spend up to a year and a half getting through flight basic and his RAG. From there, he will go to the wide variety of other schools the navy requires of a prospective pilot, including weapons schools, survival schools, and others.

Joe makes it through CQ, successfully completing the required number of traps both day and night, and is now officially designated a member of the F/A-18 community. His next set of orders will be to his first squadron, one that deploys at sea somewhere.

If they are already on deployment, he will catch up with them. Ideally, they'll be ashore, just starting workups for the next deployment, and Joe will have plenty of time to warm up before slipping into a full flight schedule. During his first sea duty tour, Joe will probably make two or three deployments.

After the initial tour at sea, probably a two-year commitment or so, Joe is probably assigned to shore station for awhile. He gains additional experience in maintenance and tactics and two years later heads back to sea as a second tour pilot. No longer is he a "nugget," a new pilot. Now he's a seasoned veteran.

As a lieutenant commander, Joe is probably on his third or fourth sea assignment, and has made six to eight six-month deployments already. He is a department head within the squadron, perhaps a junior one, but already looking forward to the day that he'll be up before the command screening board, a group of senior aviators that convenes yearly to select the next crop of executive officers and commanding officers of squadrons and aviation commands.

Ship's Log

Squadrons are unusual in the navy in the way command of a squadron is passed on. The aviator selected as executive officer, the number two in command, will eventually "fleet up" to serve as the commanding officer of the same squadron.

This ensures a degree of continuity and stability within the squadron. Surface warfare officers and submariners, on the other hand, screen for executive officer and commanding officer separately, and the XO does not "fleet up" but rather goes to command of an entirely different ship if he's selected by the command screening board.

Chief Petty Officer Frank Sands

Chief Petty Officer Sands started his career much the way Airman Schmuckatelli did, with an A school and subsequent assignment to a ship. Chief Sands is a mess management specialist—a cook. While Chief Sand may not be ex-SEAL, he's far more than a burger flipper. He's been in the Navy for 15 years and has been a chief petty officer for the last two.

Up until the pay grade of E-7 (chief petty officer), advancement within the navy is determined by the (say it along with me, now) *needs ... of ... the ... navy*, meaning the available slots projected over the next year, and a score that is a composite of an individual's test results, performance evaluations, and time in service, with a few brownie points thrown in for awards, medals, and other such things. If an individual's "final multiple" is above the cutoff score, the individual will be promoted.

But for chief petty officers, it's different, and it works more like the officers' system. Yes, there is an exam, and there is a final multiple, but the result of making the cut is not that you get promoted. There's another step involved.

The service records of all petty officers first class who are eligible for chief and have passed the test go before a board. Each board has a number of different reporting officers assigned to it, and their job is to review every record within a particular rating, summarize individual service records, and present the candidates to the selection board.

By dealing with only one or two ratings, the presenting officers develop a good deal of expertise in the range of experience and qualifications that exist within a rating.

Every year, a "zone" for selection is determined, a range of time in service requirements. Most of the people who are selected for promotion will be "in zone," but a board is allowed to dip below that time in service requirement to select a "below zone" candidate if it deems necessary.

Promotion board deliberations are completely secret. Each board member swears not to reveal the details of any discussion or how any member voted. The CNO does release a "precept," which is a message that tells the board to look for certain things—for example, college courses, unusually challenging assignments, duty at Recruit Training Command, but the general consensus is that it's hard to know exactly what sways a board one way or another.

Chief Sands made the board the first two times he took the exam and was promoted the second time. Now, as a chief petty officer, he has a broader range of responsibilities. He may supervise a shift of cooks, but more than likely that falls to a first class.

Chief Sands will be responsible for the overall planning of the meals; determining requirements and working with the supply officer to ensure there are sufficient stores onboard; staying within the budget; coordinating with operations personnel for special needs or requirements; and, in addition, making sure that the meal plans provide a range of nutritious and healthy foods and overall tastes.

He's also in charge of accounting for all the food, making sure it's stored properly, and on a ship such as a carrier, supervising numerous work centers—for example, the bakery, the entire section devoted to fresh fruit and salad preparation, and the scullery, where the dishes are cleaned. The main galley will also supply a number of staples to the various officer and chief's messes.

Feeding that many people three meals a day as well as making allowances for providing food around the clock and standing by with bag lunches for those trapped at watch stations is a challenging job.

The mess chief is also usually the first chief petty officer to get a good look at the newly reporting junior sailors, since they often do a tour in the galley before being assigned a billet in their work centers or squadrons.

The Least You Need to Know

- ◆ Where a sailor ends up depends, more often than not, on the needs of the navy.

- ◆ Airman Schmuckatelli is an aviation ordnanceman who works on weapons and bombs carried on aircraft, maintains them, keeps track of them, and loads and unloads them off aircraft.

- ◆ Lieutenant Commander Joe Blow is a pilot and a department head within the squadron.

- ◆ Chief Petty Officer Frank Sands is a cook, responsible for the overall planning of the meals.

Chapter 9

Rockin' Around the Clock

In This Chapter

- ◆ Billets, quals, and collateral duties
- ◆ Schmuckatelli's responsibilities
- ◆ How Sands feeds 7,000
- ◆ Blow's surface and air duties
- ◆ From reveille to taps

Now that we have met our three heroes, let's follow them on a typical day aboard an aircraft carrier. But before we get into matters of the clock, perhaps a quick lesson in military time is in order.

What Time Is It?

Almost everyone has watched enough war movies or the TV show *JAG* to know how military time operates. It's a twenty-four-hour clock and using it prevents sailors from getting six in the morning and six in the evening confused. (Not all that difficult to do when you don't see daylight for days sometimes.) The simple way to do it—anything after 12 noon has 12 hours added to it. Thus 6 P.M. becomes 1800, 8 P.M. is 2000. Easy enough, and after you've used it for a while it'll come automatically.

If you're mathematically impaired, try this—if someone says an unnatural number to you, just drop the first digit and subtract two from the second one. Thus 1800 becomes 800 becomes 600—or 6 P.M. Please. I beg you. Do not say "1800 hours" unless you're talking to someone in the army or air force. We don't do that. Just 1800. That's sufficient.

And it's not "oh four hundred." It's "zero four hundred." Try not to sound like a telephone operator and get your zeros and the letter *O* mixed up. Might sound like an odd pet peeve, but using the letter and the numeral interchangeably can lead to deadly confusion if you're reading times over a circuit. Completely logical, right?

Unless … someone tells you to show up at eight o'clock reports. Having mastered the twenty-four-hour clock, you figure you don't have to ask what time, right? Clearly it's a meeting at eight in the morning, right? Nope. Eight o'clock reports, where all the duty department heads meet with the officer of the day, are held in the evening. And usually not at 2000—more like 1930 or so, so that the OOD can brief the captain at 2000. So if you're invited to eight o'clock reports, ask what time they want you there. Go figure.

Don't Bounce the Bombs

Aviation Ordnanceman Carl Schmuckatelli is assigned to a squadron to handle aviation ordnance, which includes everything that goes boom or makes holes in the ground. That's his primary billet (and we've already seen how he spent a couple of months working in the galley, right?).

On days that he doesn't have duty, Schmuckatelli will be gently roused from his rack (bed) by the dulcet tones of the boatswains mate of the watch piped over the 1MC, the shipwide announcing system at some ungodly hour, like 0600:

Reveille, reveille! All hands turn out and trice up. On deck, duty section three.

The wording varies from ship to ship and the "trice up" bit (which I've always liked) is a reference back to the days when sailors slept in hammocks. And if you're in duty section three, the last phrase is bound to strike terror into your heart, because it means you're late for the duty section muster that occurred an hour ago. When you eventually *do* find the duty section chief and make your appearance, you'll blame it on the roving patrol from the previous watch section, who *should* have woken you up in time to make muster.

Assuming Schmuckatelli doesn't have the watch, he rolls out of his rack, careful not to step on the head of the guy below him doing the same thing, checks his locker or the storage compartment under his rack for some clean skivvies (undergarments, all stenciled with his name), and heads for the shower. There, along with 30 other guys, he can take care of the *four S's*.

Then he heads to morning chow, followed by "mustering on station"—that is, going to his workstation or other designated location for morning muster. He'll fall into line with the rest of the group for morning quarters, which consists of a headcount (muster) to make sure no one's fallen over the side in the middle of the night, a quick briefing on the POD (plan of the day), and any other special evolutions that the whole squadron or workcenter needs to know about. If his squadron holds a squadron muster, his department or workcenter will probably hold a short briefing after that to go over the day's work.

Naval Lingo

The morning routine is known as the **four S's**: poop, shave, shower, and shine shoes.

Too Much Work, Too Few People

There's always too much work and too few people to do it: scheduled maintenance, repairs, uploading and downloading munitions onto aircraft, cleaning the workspaces, and general and rating-specific training. It is not your normal eight-to-four job (or 0800–1600). He may be finished up in time for evening chow or he may not be.

The upside to it all is that there's not a whole lot else to do. Someone else is taking care of feeding you, doing the laundry, and paying the electricity bills. Sure, there is a host of activities onboard a carrier, but there are far fewer normal everyday tasks to worry about.

Other than the trice-up bit, it doesn't sound too tough, does it? Lots of folks ashore put in overtime. But wait, there's more, and I ain't talking Ginsu knives. Remember, I mentioned the watchbill?

Watchbill

Airman Schmuckatelli is also on a squadron watchbill of some sort. The watchbill is a set of people who take care of the running of the ship while everyone else is racked out—that is, asleep—and handle routine functions during the day. In a squadron, watch standers make rounds on the ship's aircraft to make sure they're secure, not in the psychological sense but physically. They have a checklist:

◆ Are the aircraft tied down and are extra tie-down chains in place if heavy weather is expected?

- Is anyone messing with them?

- Is oil, hydraulic fluid, or fuel leaking out of them?

> **Ship's Log**
>
> When I left active duty and joined the civilian world, it gave me an odd turn at the end of the day to realize that everyone just *left*. They went *home*. Nobody stayed at the office all night to make sure it didn't burn down. Nobody made hourly rounds to check all the locks. They just ... left. Whenever they wanted to—within reason, of course.

Different departments and workcenters have different watchbills. If Schmuckatelli's workcenter or squadron is undermanned or has had an influx of new people, our valiant airman may be in three section duty, meaning every third day he's on duty. Worse still, he could be in port and starboard, standing duty every other day. Or, when there's a crisis, port and report, which means he's *never* off.

> **Flattop Facts**
>
> Depending on which watch you have, you sleep for a while before or after it, or you just stay up waiting for it. More experienced sailors eat and sleep whenever they get the chance, because it may be a while because you have the chance again.

Watches are usually four-hour chunks of time, with the exception of the dog watches, which are two hours long. Whoever makes up the watchbill usually tries to rotate the hours so you're not pulling the 0000 to 0400 watch every duty day, but that doesn't always work out. (This is one person you don't want to annoy.)

Personal Qualifications Standards

In addition to the watchbill, Schmuckatelli has one other primary concern: qualifications. *Every* watchstation aboard the carrier has a list of things you have to know about and tasks you have to know, known as personal qualifications standards, or PQS. Our airman's progress in finishing up his PQS will be closely monitored by his supervisors, because he can't stand watches alone until he does finish them. (He'll be UI, or under instruction, until then, and that means more watches for everyone else.)

And not only does he have PQS for his watch station, he also has them for his billet (his day job) and a set that everyone on the ship completes—for example, damage control. And then there are PQS for PMS (planned maintenance systems), for his next advancement exam, for just about every phase of his professional navy life.

Emergencies and Drills

Finally, there are the emergencies and drills that are a constant part of life at sea. The navy operates on the theory that you fight the way you train, and nowhere is that more true than at sea in an emergency.

Most true emergencies are not thoughtful enough to occur during normal waking hours. The first clue you'll have of them is an alarm over the 1MC, followed immediately by an announcement as to the nature and location of the problem.

When you're jolted out of a deep sleep by a a hard, constant bonging noise piped throughout the ship, the general quarters alarm, your body immediately starts pumping adrenaline. You lose fine motor control and become very focused. The point of training is to turn your immediate reactions into reflex, to teach you to scramble into clothes and head for your emergency station before you're even entirely conscious, and the only way to do that is through repetition.

Damage Control

Airman Schmuckatelli will mostly likely be part of a damage control team, perhaps assigned to Repair Eight, which has responsibility for the flight deck. He might start off as a messenger or phone talker (guess what? more PQS).

Eventually he will work his way up to a position on the hose or as the person who does the initial assessment of the emergency (the primary investigator). He may be assigned to report to the weapons storage spaces to maintain security, or to DCC (damage control central).

Distinctive Alarms

In addition to the general quarters alarm, there are a host of other emergencies ranging from in-flight emergencies that may result in emergency landing procedures and rigging the barricade to chemical attack, collisions, or man overboard. Most have their own distinctive alarm sounded over the 1MC.

Alarms and what they mean:

♦ The general quarters alarm is the one known to most folks, a constant bonging sound.

♦ The chemical alarm is a series of three electronic beeps repeated again and again.

- An "in extremis" ship-handling situation—for instance, a collision may be imminent—is a set of five blasts from the ship's whistle

- Man overboard is a set of six blasts from the ship's whistle.

Where Schmuckatelli runs to is determined by the alarm—six blasts, and he's headed for a designated mustering point for a headcount. Five and he's scrambling to get above the waterline and away from wherever the collision is about to happen.

As Schmuckatelli gets some seniority in the navy via promotion or simply longevity, he can expect to have his time invaded by another critter, the bane of every officer and senior enlisted sailor's life: collateral duties. More about those a little later in the chapter.

Flattop Facts

Since five blasts on the whistle indicates an "in extremis" ship-handling situation, the moment between counting five and six blasts is a tense one.

Like Sands Through an Hourglass

Chief Sands has not woken up to reveille in years. By the time the other sailors are grumbling about tricing up, he's already been at work for hours. His billet, supervising the night shift in the galley, means that he's on station and managing things at around 0400, just as the cinnamon buns are coming out of the bakery.

The chief's day is filled with paperwork and mess management duties. In addition to the main food prep areas, the carrier's galley complex includes a separate bakery, vegetable prep area, scullery (dishes and such go through several commercial dishwashers, but there are always tons of pots and pans that get washed by sweating young sailors), and myriad freezers and dry goods storage areas. All those have a supervisor, usually a petty officer first class, and they all report to the chief.

Ship's Log

Remember that the ship is feeding folks 24 hours a day.

Safety Above All

Safety is foremost in Chief Sands's mind. The last thing he needs is a tub of potato salad going bad on him and incapacitating a chunk of the crew. Items served on the steam lines have to be kept at 140°F, chilled items have to be chilled, the coffee pots have to be kept going, and there's always the next day's meals to prep for.

Chief Sands also has a ton of personnel paperwork to do. Writing quarterly performance evaluations; rewriting them after his boss has sent them back; compiling daily musters; monitoring PQS progress; making sure PMS charts are filled out and all tasks completed; accounting for all the stores issued on his watch, what happened to them, how much was left over, when they are put back on the serving line, and what went into box lunches for sailors who can't leave their watch stations—all are in his in-basket.

Flattop Facts

Potatoes are no longer peeled by hand. There's a machine that does it, a cylinder that looks like a grater inside—toss the potatoes in and turn it on.

Feeding the Ship in General Quarters

One colossal task—feeding the ship while it's at general quarters. During GQ, the entire ship is buttoned up tight. Watertight hatches are secured, turning the ship into a honeycomb of spaces to prevent flooding or toxic gases from spreading in the event of taking a hit. Traveling through the ship requires calling DCC for permission to "break Zebra," to undog or open a hatch that's supposed to be shut. The ship is at maximum readiness to both fight incoming threats and control damage if she takes a hit.

Flattop Facts

Today's supercarriers carry 40,000 gallons of drinking water.

This, as you can imagine, is not conducive to business as usual in the galley. The radar operator can't leave his or her watchstation just because it's easier for the galley to serve everyone in a chow line, and during an antiair emergency that can mean staying on station for hours and hours. On the other hand, a hungry sailor isn't a good thing, either.

The fine art of feeding 7,000 people box lunches on a few hours' notice requires extensive preparation, and Chief Sands has to be ready to produce that many box lunches, making sure they are nutritious and designed to keep a sailor going, on short notice.

Ship's Log

Eighteen thousand hot meals a day are served aboard a flattop!

Most box lunches have ...

- Two sandwiches.
- A piece of fruit.
- A couple of cookies.
- Containers of milk and juice.

Bologna and cheese or ham and cheese are both common, along with small containers of mustard or other condiments. Even feeding the sailors at their general quarters stations requires relaxing GQ requirements slightly, since sailors at GQ may be wearing chem/bio masks.

Collateral Duties

All this Chief Sands can handle. What really drives him nuts are his collateral duties.

Remember, an aircraft carrier is really a small town at sea. There are city council meetings (a department head meeting), cops (the master at arms and NCIS folks), restaurants, municipal services, and everything else you'd find in a small town. (Except for one thing: votes. Not much democracy in the way things are run, although the smart leaders are always listening for good ideas from the crew.)

So in addition to essential services like power, sewer, and electricity, the aircraft carrier also has things like …

- The recreation committee.
- The human relations council.
- The library committee.
- Career counselor committees, for the departmental and division officer career counselors.
- Awards committee (all *sorts* of committees).

There are those who think that perhaps committees and paperwork are occasionally substituted for leadership and responsibility, but I ain't naming no names.

Justice System

There's also a justice system, and the chief probably spends part of his day dealing with it. If one of his sailors is a problem child, the chief will try to handle it at his level by assigned EMI (extra military instruction) or other "administrative" measures. If that doesn't work, he'll involve the division officer and then the department head. As a last resort, he'll put the sailor "on report" and fill out a *report chit*.

The chit makes its way up the chain of command administratively, through the department and on to the executive officer (XO). The XO holds an XOI, or executive officer investigation. If the XO finds that it's probable that an offense has been committed and the individual is responsible, the chit is sent on to the captain for captain's mast.

Captain's mast is an administrative procedure, not a judicial one. However, the administrative actions a captain can impose look pretty much like punishment. The captain can dock the sailor half a month's pay for up to two months, bust the sailor in rank, or (with a number of restrictions) impose confinement, bread and water diet, or restriction to the ship.

Naval Lingo

A **report chit** is a formal document that specifies the offenses that the sailor has committed. The allegations have to be investigated, the facts laid out, the individual counseled.

Every week, Chief Sands will probably have to do something involving the judicial system. He may be assigned to investigate an offense in another department. He may have his own sailors going to XOI and captain's mast, and he'll have to be there as either a witness or a character witness. When he has duty, he'll muster the restricted personnel to make sure they're on the ship (if they're in port) or that they're in their quarters, workspace, or the galley when not on duty.

Duty, ah yes. The chief, of course, is also on a watchbill. He's probably not awake all night walking constantly around the ship—although he will have nights that end up being like that—but he's got a lot more responsibility. If there's a problem, the watch standers will come wake him up. If something goes wrong, the chief will be responsible. If someone needs something from Supply, they'll come wake him up.

The chief has one resource to draw on that Airman Schmuckatelli doesn't: The chief's mess. The khaki ranks, for the most part, try to solve a lot of shipboard problems within the confines of the chief's mess. A conflict between divisions, a difference in opinion over how to handle a disciplinary matter, new ways of maximizing resources—the chiefs figure it all out over dinner.

One of a chief's primary jobs, too, is training the junior officers, and it's not always a whole lot different—if sometimes couched in more polite language—than straightening out someone like Airman Schmuckatelli.

Blow in the Wind

Now we turn to our third hero: Lieutenant Commander Joe Blow, Pilot F/A-18. As an aviator, and particularly a pilot (remember, not all aviators are pilots—some are naval flight officers, the men and women who run the electronic systems of an aircraft), Lieutenant Commander Blow is a veritable king of the realm. Men and women of his ilk command the ship, the air wing, the squadrons, the maintenance activities. They control the flight deck, and their needs dictate the entire rhythm of the ship's operations.

Aviators get to wander around the ship in their flight suits, ignore reveille and other evolutions if they interfere with the flying schedule (and that would include the requirement that they be well-rested before flying), and generally are cut a lot of slack by the rest of the world. They have popcorn makers in their ready rooms, their own movie schedules, and probably a well-stocked bar and lounge somewhere hidden away inside the skin of the ship.

Or, at least, that's the myth.

I mean, think about it. The navy is turning a kid two years out of college loose with a couple of million dollars worth of airframe. Do you really think they're not keeping pretty close tabs on him? If there's an "incident," the paperwork alone is sufficient to sink the skipper's career, and that's assuming no one is seriously hurt.

Flight Schedules (Skeds)

The flight schedule (known as the Sked) on the carrier is normally made up the day before, if Air Ops can swing it, for normal operations. It'll be slipped under every aviator's door sometime in the evening. Flight skeds are built around "cycles," a cycle being sort of a lowest common denominator of time, usually based on the fuel consumption rate of the thirstiest aircraft. If the cycle is defined as one hour, then a normal mission might be two cycles for a fighter aircraft, four for an S-3B, maybe 8 for an E-2 or P-3 (the big land-based fellows).

In addition to cycle time, the crew has to allow time before that to brief the flight, do the preflight inspection of the aircraft and check their own survival gear. After the mission, they're going to debrief, either among themselves in the ready room, with Ops, or with the Intel folks. Now, depending on what's going on, the pre- and post-flight periods can take longer than the mission itself. Or, in an emergency, the pre-flight brief may be a shouted exchange between the pilot and crew as they run for the aircraft, updated by announcements over the 1MC. If the mission has been a bombing run or a surveillance mission, the Intel and Strike folks are going to want to spend some quality time with the crew after they land. If something has been royally screwed up, *everybody*'s going to want to talk to them, probably starting with their captain, who'll be waiting for them on the deck, trying to get the straight story while he's escorting them down to CAG and the admiral.

Flight skeds also take into account an officer's other duties and required crew rest time. If an officer knows ahead of time that he or she has to be somewhere else—say, captain's mast for one of their sailors—they'll "snivel" with Air Ops. Ashore, a training squadron will normally maintain a Snivel Log in the Operations department to allow aviators to post their projected unavailability. Of course, at sea in an emergency, this all goes out the window. Crew rest requirements included.

A Pilot's Reality

Aviation junior officers have just as many collateral duties and watch station requirements to fill their hours as the officers who are qualified in surface warfare, the ones who run the ship. In addition to their flying duties, they'll be responsible for a division or a branch (a subunit of a division) in some department of the squadron. Their qualifications schedule is just as demanding, albeit different since they've spent the last two years in school. They've got to stay current on all their safety quals, swim quals, landing quals, and flying in general while still meeting many of the same shipwide requirements for damage control.

Lieutenant Commander Blow is the safety officer for his squadron. This isn't an SLJ at all. He's a department head and directly responsible for ensuring that every aviator is current on his or her quals, keeping the squadron current on changes—and not only in the air. He's got what happens on the ground (if he's assigned to a squadron based ashore) to worry about, too, everything from whether a piece of tow gear runs into an aircraft to a young sailor forgetting to wear his cranial (helmet) when working on an aircraft.

Flattop Facts

If there's an incident, Lieutenant Commander Joe Blow's records will be so thoroughly examined that the folks working on the Dead Sea Scrolls will look like slackers.

Remember all the personnel issues Chief Sands had to deal with? Lieutenant Commander Blow has fewer of those (because the chief took care of the minor stuff) but the ones that do come across his desk are far more serious. He's also got the junior officers assigned to his department to deal with, and if he's smart, he's listening very carefully to what the chief's mess is saying about his young officers.

T Minus 15 Minutes

And in between all that, he gets to fly. And make sure he's well-rested before the flight. If he were not a department head, he'd probably be pulling alert duty as well when the carrier is in an increased state of readiness.

In alert 15, the aircraft are supposed to be ready to launch in 15 minutes, and the pilots will be hanging around the squadron's ready room waiting to go. In alert 5—5 minutes—the pilots are in their aircraft, engines idling, waiting.

Synchronize Your Watches

Let's look at how the day runs for these three individuals.

0600 Reveille

Airman Schmuckatelli had roving patrol from 0000 to 0200, so he's rolling out of his rack bleary-eyed and fuzzy-headed and heading for the attached shower and bathroom compartment shared with his compartment mates. Lieutenant Commander Blow had squadron duty officer last night and turned in shortly after midnight, after one final check on the maintenance status of the aircraft. Just before he racked out, he heard that gentle swishing sound a piece of paper makes sliding under his door—the daily flight schedule for the next day. He already had a pretty good idea of what's on it, but he rolled out of bed long enough to check. Yep, a CAP mission the next day from 1500 to 1700.

No big surprise, but it will take a chunk of time out of his day anyway. He wakes up, puts on a bathrobe and shower shoes and heads down the passageway to the common head he shares with the rest of the officers on the O3 level. Of course, Chief Sands has already been in the office for two hours.

0700 Quarters

Squadron quarters, department head meeting, division head meeting. As the more senior of the three, Lieutenant Commander Blow has to endure far more meetings than the other two sailors we're following around. Earlier that morning, he attended a department head meeting with his XO and got specific guidance for the day's evolutions (an evolution is any sort of planned event, whether an inspection, a flight, or a drill). He then walks out to the flight deck for squadron quarters, when everyone in the squadrons forms up in ranks to start the day off. His department chief has already taken muster and hands him a chit outlining who's where.

Airman Schmuckatelli is standing in ranks near the back. Chief Sands has gathered his three senior petty officers in his office and is going over the menus, personnel issues, and shipwide evolutions with them.

0800 Muster on Station

Muster on station means "be in your workcenter." For Chief Sands and Lieutenant Commander Blow, this probably means dealing with the accumulated paperwork that has piled up since the previous day. There will be performance evaluations, disciplinary matters, supply chits, maintenance requests and action forms, and everything that the junior officers and petty officers stayed up late the night before generating. Chief Sands is trying to figure out what happened to two pounds of chocolate chips supposedly stored in one of the storage compartments. (Hey, at least it wasn't strawberries.) He's nibbling absentmindedly on a cinnamon roll that's just a few hours old.

With the initial flurry of easy paperwork out of the way, Lieutenant Commander Blow is finally dealing with a task he's been avoiding for a few days—inventorying *equipage*.

In this case, a pair of binoculars is missing from where it should be and just in time for the semiannual equipage inventory. The squadron supply officer needs the forms or an MSLR (missing, stolen, or lost report) tomorrow. Lieutenant Commander Blow is hoping that someone will either uncover it or 'fess up to loaning it to another work center.

Naval Lingo

Equipage consists of those items that are valuable and easy to get lost—for example, binoculars, seven day clocks for aircraft, test equipment.

At the same time, Airman Schmuckatelli is following his chief around with a clipboard, assisting in an inventory of ordnance. Later that day, he'll be UI on a team loading ordnance aviation onto Lieutenant Commander Blow's aircraft, but for now he's getting a taste of what his future holds.

1130 Chow

Airman Schmuckatelli heads immediately for the galley. Unfortunately, the marines have already been through and there are no brownies left. He opts for a burger and fries. As an afterthought, he adds a slice of tomato and some lettuce to the burger in homage to his mother's insistence that he eat his vegetables.

He washes it all down with a couple of glasses of soda, then wanders back by the chow line, wistfully hoping that the cooks have put out some more brownies. He's in luck.

Lieutenant Commander Blow's luncheon experience is much the same, except the cooks haven't sent up more brownies and Blow opts for the turkey burger rather than all beef. He also has a salad. He purposefully skips the bean burritos, since he'll be flying that afternoon. This is a particularly fine point of naval etiquette if the aircraft has a crew of more than one.

Chief Sands takes a plate and has a small portion of everything that is served on the galley line, checking the temperature of the steam lines and the general cleanliness as he does so. After a few nibbles from each dish offered, he heads for the chief's mess, where there is never a shortage of brownies.

1300 Afternoon Muster

Afternoon muster for all is an abbreviated affair, a headcount and progress check more than anything. Lieutenant Commander Blow has managed to sneak in a brief nooner, a short nap in his stateroom, as has the chief.

Airman Schmuckatelli is either too young to need one or has not yet realized the value of the nooner—besides, his handling team musters at 1200 to upload munitions for the afternoon's flight schedule.

There's been a slight change in the requirements, so one team downloads the ammo currently on the hard points of the wings while another stands by to upload. Since Schmuckatelli hasn't finished his PQS yet, he is UI for the evolution, although he'll be allowed to assist in the heavy lifting.

1400 Brief for Upcoming Flight

Lieutenant Commander Blow stops by CVIC (the carrier intelligence center) for an updated briefing on the current tactical scenario. He also checks in with metro—they'll be conducting a briefing later in the ready room, but Blow likes to stay ahead of the power curve. At 1400, all pilots scheduled for missions that afternoon muster in the ready room for a briefing.

This particular day, it's mostly a matter of everyone getting the required traps (landings) to stay current on quals, a matter of great concern to Blow. The evolution is slightly more intense since they're in blue water ops, too far from land to divert to a land airstrip if there are problems. The Operations department briefs both the scheduled evolutions, how many refueling aircraft will be in the air (the tanking availability), and any other forces in the area.

1430 Preflight Aircraft

Blow walks around his aircraft, checking off every item on his NATOPS (Naval Aviation Topics) checklist as he does. He's already been to the paraloft (where his emergency gear is kept) and picked up his ejection harness and chute as well as his emergency radio. He's already looked at the airframe's log book so he knows that a pitot tube (a device on the side of the aircraft that determines speed through air) was recently replaced and he touches it to make sure it's securely affixed.

The log book shows that the safety pins are in the ejection seat, that the ejection seat rockets have been recently inspected, and that the aircraft recently finished a scheduled maintenance inspection with very few discrepancies.

1450 Launch

Airman Schmuckatelli watches from outside the flight line as Lieutenant Commander Blow taxies to the catapult and gets ready for launch (as opposed to lunch, which Chief Sands is still cleaning up after).

Inside his Hornet, Blow has finished another extensive checklist before starting his engines. Once the engines are started, he waits for the signal from the plane captain to taxi forward and take his place on the catapult (also called the cat).

On the cat, he follows the directions of the cat officer, first cycling all of his control surfaces to make one last check and double-checking all gauges and readouts. He's already dialed in his IFF (international friend or foe) code and has all the tactical frequencies and tanker information he'll need scrawled on his knee board, sort of a Dayrunner that straps onto his upper leg so he can see it and write on it while in the cockpit.

One final check, and the cat officer snaps off a salute, turning over control of the aircraft to Lieutenant Commander Blow. Lieutenant Commander Blow returns the salute, braces himself back against the ejection seat, and waits for launch. There's a second of delay and then a small jolt. The Hornet accelerates quickly down the catapult and a few seconds later is airborne.

Schmuckatelli is cornered by his LPO and accused of *skylarking* when there's work to be done. He heads back down below decks to finish the inventory.

Chief Sands is turning over the watch to his relief and thinking longingly of his rack. But there's a meeting of the chief's mess at 1900, a stack of enlisted evaluation forms submitted in rough draft by his senior petty officer, and a training session for those enlisted sailors working on their enlisted warfare specialist (ESWO) quals.

Naval Lingo

Skylarking means goofing off.

As an ESWO himself, Chief Sands is supposed to be giving a lecture on standard conning commands, the standardized orders given to the sailors manning the helm (the wheel) and the lee helm (the device for transmitting orders to the engine room). He finally decides he's got time for another short nap before grabbing some chow and making it to the training set.

Of our three heroes, Lieutenant Commander Blow is having by far the best time. All the paperwork, all the hassles of daily life—all far away right now. He's flying and nothing else matters.

Well, nothing else until he starts getting a master caution warning light. He thumbs the computer through its maintenance routine and sees that his starboard engine is seriously overheating.

He powers back a bit and lets the carrier know, at the same time flipping open his NATOPS manual to the appropriate emergency action page. He's got the bold-faced required actions memorized, of course, but he's still required to follow the checklist.

Fortunately, the first recommended action fixes the problem—most systems on the aircraft are built with triple redundancy. After another 30 minutes of simulating some ACM (air combat maneuvering), the E-2C Hawkeye, a command and control aircraft, vectors him into the holding pattern to wait for his look at the deck, the area called Marshall.

He enters Marshall at the highest altitude and starts flying an oval pattern, descending as aircraft below him break off to head for the deck. Finally, it's his turn. He lands safely, snagging the three wire.

1730 Land

Lieutenant Commander Blow lands, follows the plane captain's directions to a spot on the deck, and runs through his postflight check lists. He then climbs down the accommodation ladder, has a few words with the plane captain, and heads for his squadron maintenance shack to file a report on the overheating engine. If he'd been on a mission other than a training one, he'd also go to the CVIC to be debriefed.

Schmuckatelli has just finished swabbing the deck and is listening to the chief outline his work for the next day. A workcenter inspection by the XO revealed a couple of spots of flaking paint behind one fire extinguisher, and it'll be Schmuckatelli's job to chip the paint off the next day.

 **Flattop Facts** _____

Remember, pilots landing on an aircraft carrier must hit one of usually four wires. These wires are strong enough to stop a 27-ton aircraft traveling at 150 mph in two seconds. Pilots aim at the second or third wire, one of the ones in the middle. If they aim at the first wire, they may come up short and hit the edge of the deck. If they aim at one of the last wires, they might miss all of the wires and be unable to stop.

1800 Gym

Airman Schmuckatelli and Lieutenant Commander Blow head to work out before chow. The airman opts for the weight room near his compartment, while Blow heads for a small compartment—really more of a large landing than anything else—with a few Stairmasters and stationary rowing machines tucked in.

1900 Chow

Much as before, except that Lieutenant Commander Blow opts to shower and change into his khakis and get some face time in the more formal mess.

2000 et seq.

Since Airman Schmuckatelli is not yet PQS-qualified in his billet, no movies for him. He stretches out in his rack, secure in the knowledge that he's not on watch, and delves into a paperback that he picked up from the ship's library. Okay, so he's supposed to be studying, but it's been a long day and he figures no one will notice that he's got the paperback tucked inside his RTM—rate training manual.

Chief Sands finishes up his mess meeting and gives a few other chiefs the lowdown on some young sailors who will soon be released from mess cooking to their home divisions.

Lieutenant Commander Blow watches half of the movie in the ready room but is experiencing that postflight adrenaline depletion—he's yawning and it takes him 15 minutes to realize he's already seen the movie twice. He heads for his rack, intending to get some paperwork done, but knowing he probably won't.

2130 Taps

Taps is piped throughout the ship. Zzzzzzzzz.

The Least You Need to Know

◆ On a carrier, there's always too much work and too few people to do it.

◆ Emergencies and drills are a constant part of life at sea.

◆ An aircraft carrier is really a small town at sea.

◆ No matter what your job on a carrier, chances are you'll be busy from the time you get up until when you go to sleep.

Chapter 10

The Future

In This Chapter

- ◆ Factors that drive military decisions
- ◆ Keeping spending in check
- ◆ Figuring out how the next war will be fought
- ◆ The politics of military planning

In this chapter, I will discuss the future of aircraft carriers. Since I am not a prophet and I don't have a crystal ball stashed away, I am not going to predict what aircraft carriers will look like or what they will do in the years to come.

Instead, I am going to base the information on things that I know. I am going to tell you the reasons why a future carrier will be the way it is: the factors that drive the decisions.

The Vagaries of Military Budgeting

The first thing to remember is that the modern carrier is vastly more complex and sophisticated than the ships we were knocking out so quickly during earlier world wars. Back then, when we were completely geared up, it was less than two months from laying the keel of a new destroyer to launching her. Additionally, during World War II, we were a nation unified against a common enemy. That tends to speed up a lot of things in the procurement process.

Naval Lingo

A **mothball fleet** is a fleet of older ships that have not been used for warfare for some time.

Speculation: Could we again maintain that level of production? I'm not so sure. A lot of procurements procedures would have to be tossed out the window, and so many shipyards have closed that we may not have the capabilities. Sure, there's a *mothball fleet*, both of aircraft and ships, but not only would they require some serious work to activate, you'd also have to find people to operate the gear and the engineering plant. We saw that problem when the battleships took to the seas again.

Moreover, today there's a lot more to launching a ship than building it. First, there's the budgeting process. That alone could fill up 200 pages of probably the most boring stuff you'll ever read. What you really need to know is this: What the navy thinks it needs in carriers isn't necessarily the only factor that drives the decisions.

A Little Uncommon Commonality, Please

Increasingly, Congress is asking that aircraft be interoperable with other services. More than that, as we learned while studying the research-and-development phase of the F/A-18, Congress likes to appropriate and fund money for one aircraft that can do everything each of the services requires.

Sometimes I think they're looking for a common platform that could not only launch from a carrier, conduct bombing runs and surface surveillance, and hunt submarines, but also repair itself and the flight deck and cook nutritious meals for its crew.

The simple fact is that increasing commonality is an incredible engineering challenge. Aircraft that land on carriers need to be able to take a lot more punishment than aircraft that land ashore. The tail hook has to stop the aircraft without ripping the fuselage off or separating from the aircraft, which means reinforcing certain structural bits in the airframe.

Reinforcing translates to more weight. That reduces maximum unrefueled radius of operations for an aircraft unless you increase the capacity of the fuel tanks, and then that changes the aerodynamics of the aircraft and affects the ability of the carrier to launch it.

Heavier aircraft need more speed, which means higher steam pressure behind the catapult, which translates into engineering changes for the steam supply to the catapult.

Sure, there's a lot of flexibility built into systems already, but the point is, you can't change one characteristic without changing everything around it that supports it.

Riding the Global Highway

Additionally, services that operate from the land may have farther to go to reach their targets, and flying a heavier aircraft may impact their missions. It's different with the carrier—it's like having a highway that covers almost the entire world. Barring some problems with shallow water navigation, international treaties, and laws regarding waterways, the carrier can go pretty much wherever she wants to.

Not so with land-based aircraft. There are many more considerations of allied landing fields, refueling places, and that sort of thing. They need the longer range provided by a lighter aircraft.

Ship's Log

Ninety percent of the world's population lives within 100 miles of ocean coastlines.

The Who, What, Where, When, and Why of War

The other factor that affects the contracts awarded for military aircraft and ships is the nature of the war we think we're going to fight. Sometimes, as technology changes, we may change the way we plan to fight a war, too, and that then leads to changes in what the military wants to buy. For instance, the stunning success and usefulness of unmanned aerial reconnaissance vehicles, or UAVs, has led to changes in the way we approach a war.

In theory, the services look at the world, see what threats are emerging, and decide what abilities they need to counter them. They're guided by national decision-makers who provide input on what they want the United States to be able to do.

Is the goal to be able to fight two full-fledged wars on opposite sides of the world at the same time—such as occurred during the Second World War? Or is it to take on two smaller, limited engagements, conducting a holding action in one while winning the first one?

Do we need a large number of smaller task forces to intervene in trouble spots around the world, acting as the world's policeman? Or are we going to sit back and wait until things reach a larger international crisis stage and then intervene, counting on our military-industrial complex to gear up and support any large-scale mission?

Ship's Log

There was no submarine battle or threat to us during Desert Storm and Desert Shield. Does that mean we drop planning for that?

Unfortunately, there are no easy answers to any of those questions. The military knows very well the dangers of thinking in terms of the previous war. It is a subtle, alluring siren, one that has to be resisted.

For instance, the 1991 Persian Gulf operations known as Desert Storm and Desert Shield were quick, decisive, and low-casualty conflicts. The temptation is to think that the next war we will fight will be on those terms as well and let that drive the planning.

Building a Flexible Flattop

As an aside, remember how long it takes to build the carrier. We want to build in enough flexibility so if the world changes radically, the carrier can be refitted to adapt to it, either as is or with modifications.

The carrier, since hulls last a long time, has to be capable of being retrofitted. Imagine how much of a flattop's electronics has changed in the last 50 years, and try to predict what they'll look like even 20 years from now. Not easy, is it?

So, in an ideal world, we first decide what the threat is. Everybody chimes in on this—the war colleges for all the services, geopolitical experts of big think tanks, the State Department, the military, even defense contractors. The military planners try to keep a few basic principles in mind.

First, don't let the conclusion drive the analysis. This is another seductive trap. A defense contractor has just come up with a very nifty piece of gear—perhaps a sensor that is capable of determining whether there is current flowing to telephone lines by looking down from a satellite. Very cool, yes? Absolute top-notch engineering, stability, and performance characteristics.

But the question is: Who cares? Sure, there's some intelligence benefit to be had from knowing how much information is traveling down telephone lines, and if you can listen in on those conversations, so much the better.

But just because you've got this technology available doesn't mean that it is a prime ingredient in military planning. That would be letting the conclusion drive the analysis, the conclusion being that you will need to know what's going on in these telephone lines, just because you can, rather than letting the problem dictate what you need.

Of course, if you could get the enemy—whoever that currently is—to agree to fight the war you want to win, you solve a lot of problems. However, the best planning rarely survives contact with the enemy.

Fear of Casualties

Political conclusions can also drive military analysis in ways that are not productive. Let me give you one example, and it's a difficult subject to discuss: the issue of casualties.

If the mindset is that the U.S. military is so powerful that it is virtually invulnerable, and that the American public will not tolerate nightly news shots of body bags, that's going to impact military planning. Funds are not going to be appropriated for equipment or tactics that don't emphasize minimizing our own casualties.

Certainly, technology has had an impact on this issue as well. With more remote sensing gear, such as the unmanned Predator surveillance aircraft, enhanced satellite imagery, and all sorts of laser technology detection gear, there are plenty of opportunities to reduce casualties. You see the same thing in the civilian world, when small robotic vehicles are used to examine potential bombs instead of two guys clad in *Kevlar*.

Reducing casualties makes sense militarily, too. As equipment grows more and more sophisticated, the training pipeline gets longer and the quality of recruit requirements grows higher and higher. The equipment is more expensive, too—the cost of one fighter aircraft today compared to one even 20 years ago, corrected for inflation, is still stunning.

Flattop Facts

The casualty rate of military tactics and gear is certainly an important consideration. Nobody wants to lose soldiers or sailors—nobody. It's one of those burdens of command, knowing that you might be sending—are sending—people in harm's way and that some of them, maybe a lot of them, are going to die.

Naval Lingo

Kevlar is a bullet- and bomb-proof plastic. That doesn't make you invulnerable—a 500-pound bomb falling on you will still squish you flat. But you'll be flat inside the Kevlar.

Yet in the end, warfare and winning comes back to one primary objective: taking ground away from someone else and holding onto it. There's no real way to avoid that, and it's going to mean men and women on the ground. Predator surveillance craft aren't going to hold ground. Neither are smart bombs. People are.

And people are going to get killed—that's a fact of life in the military. While you must do everything to minimize that, to let a zero-casualties mindset drive military mission and funding as a primary objective is shortsighted.

Off-the-Shelf Technology and Civilian Employees

Another trend in military funding is a requirement to use COTS—commercial off-the-shelf—technology. If a civilian measuring tool or sensor can be easily and quickly modified for military use, do it instead of building a specialized piece of equipment from the ground up.

In simplistic terms, if you can modify an Excel spreadsheet to handle threat data, you use that instead of a top-secret, specially configured kludge of a program.

A corollary is also seen in the increasing use of civilian employees to perform certain functions that normally would be military jobs—base security and maintenance, for instance.

This policy has its own hazards, of course. If positions are filled by civil service employees, it becomes very difficult to change and substandard employees are hard to discharge. If it is delegated to commercial entities, on the notion that competitive bidding will result in a better product at a lower price, one runs into security considerations and the prospect of having every job done by the lowest bidder.

Relevant to an aircraft carrier? Sure. Every carrier deploys with a cadre of civilian technical experts onboard. Usually they're retired military, but not always. Oddly enough, they tend to wear civilian khaki clothes much like their former uniforms and some of them even have a small gold crab—yes, crab—pinned to their collars where their military insignia used to be. (They're sand crabs, civilians are. Get it? Arghh. Well, they think it's funny.)

There are no easy answers to any of these questions (except the one about whether the sand crab insignia is funny). It's a fact of life that politics, national opinion, public sentiment, and a changing world all affect military budgeting and planning.

Let the Gamesmanship Begin!

This all results in some gamesmanship. For instance, suppose the navy wanted an aircraft that was superbly suited to surface surveillance and long-range intelligence missions but those were currently unpopular missions.

The navy might draft the requirements for an aircraft that could do that but also had substantial antisubmarine warfare capabilities, or an additional communications suite, if those were currently "hot" capabilities.

The navy could then "sell" that aircraft to budgeteers as the finest antisubmarine and communications platforms and get the other capabilities thrown in. A similar dance goes on with fighter aircraft, attack and transport helicopters, even ships.

Vets Are in the House!

Another worrisome consideration is the lack of military experience inside Congress. Only a few decades ago, many more of them had served time in one military service or another, or had children who had. This resulted in increased understanding of the realities of warfare and military service.

It also resulted in a cadre of people who had some real-life experience that the military could go to, confident their concerns would be understood. The Marine Corps, in particular, has always had the single strongest military lobby in Congress.

As with anything, when marines make up their minds to do something, it generally gets done. And there's no such thing as an ex-marine. There are former marines who are no longer on active duty, but they are always marines.

A lack of military experience—aside from kissing babies at a base rally or driving around in a tank for a few hours—results in one of three mindsets:

First, they may understand they're ignorant and rely on the advice and insight of the professionals who do have experience.

Second, their naiveté and horror at all things military may lead them to be vocal opponents of military action simply by reflex.

Third—and perhaps most worrisome—it is always those without direct military experience who are the most eager to go to war. And this is really a surprising irony—they're also the least likely to worry about casualties. (At least at first. Until they start hearing from their constituents or their own kid gets drafted.)

They're not the commanders who will have to write letters home to the grieving family. They are not the people who lived and worked with the casualties every day. They're certainly not the ones who will have their butt on the front line.

Experienced military commanders are probably the last ones to advocate the use of military force. They know the difficulties inherent in it, the logistics required, and the *tooth-to-tail ratio* that will be required.

Naval Lingo

The **tooth-to-tail ratio** is the required depth of infrastructure for a military action.

They also understand how easy it is for politicians to change their minds midstream. The temptation to tell the military not only what to do but how to do it can be overwhelming. Although there are certainly national security considerations that have to be factored into any plan, too often these are limiting.

"Take that hill, but don't lose any men doing so."

A Limited Objective War

The 1991 Persian Gulf War was what is called a limited-objective war. That limited objective was: "Defeat the Republican Guard and liberate Kuwait." A lot of trees have died in the discussion of whether this was the right decision at the time, but there can be no doubt that the military executed this limited objective brilliantly.

Criticism has been wrongly leveled at them for failing to go on to Baghdad, but the fact is that that was a national command authority decision. In a limited-objective war, the goal is rarely to reduce the country to a sheet of glass.

Naval Lingo

Smart weapons are those that are guided with precision to their targets, thus minimizing unnecessary damage.

Flattop Facts

Currently, the use of the military inside the United States and the whole doctrine of *posse comitatus*—a post–Civil War ruling which prohibits using the military for law enforcement functions inside the United States—is being reevaluated in light of 9/11. Just as ships were moved off the coast to protect Washington, D.C., so it is entirely possible that carriers could play an increasing role in domestic security.

All Right Already ... Give Us Some Predictions!

So what does all this say about the future of the military and the carrier in particular? More technology—that's a given. More *smart weapons*, more Tomahawks, more unmanned vehicles capable of conducting the necessary surveillance—and perhaps destruction—of enemy radar sites before aircraft go in. There will be higher-tech ships, ones with reduced manning requirements. Increasing interoperability between services.

Interservice Cooperation and Domestic Security

The changes in the last 15 years in interservice cooperation alone have been beyond belief. Increasingly, support equipment such as radio gear, ground equipment, intelligence, and data links will have to be capable of integrating not only between services but with civilian agencies as well.

In the foreseeable future, the goal of limiting casualties will continue to be a major player. However, this may be tested severely in the near future, as we contemplate several areas of the world where things really aren't going to change much unless we have troops on the ground going door-to-door and cleaning out snipers.

"War Is Politics ..."

There is a famous quote: "War is politics continued by other means." In the end, the best solutions and the most permanent ones are not those inflicted by an outside power. Certainly, there are times the United States must act, when atrocities and genocide and national instability affect the rest of the world. There's no doubt about that.

But perhaps one weakness in all military planning is the endgame, the exit strategy. How does the role of the carrier fit in with the goal for stability in a region? When the marines arrive, what happens after they've gotten everything under control? How do you transition to a lasting solution in the area?

The Least You Need to Know

- Congress is asking that aircraft be interoperable with other services but increasing commonality is an incredible engineering challenge.

- Contracts are awarded for military aircraft and ships based on the nature of the war we think we're going to fight.

- Experienced military commanders are probably the last ones to advocate the use of military force.

- One weakness in all military planning is the endgame, the exit strategy.

Part 4

Early History of Aircraft Carriers

When the Wright brothers successfully flew their first "aeroplane" at Kitty Hawk, about a nanosecond or two passed before someone first thought, "Hey, if you could take off and land one of these suckers from a ship, many interesting possibilities might ensue." Well, okay, maybe that's not quite how it happened, but you get the idea. Naval strategists had been using hot-air balloons off of ships for years, so the idea of using fixed-wing aircraft in this fashion came fairly quickly.

In this section we are going to be looking at the early years of the aircraft carrier, those years including all of the firsts—first takeoff, first landing, first carrier, first carrier built from scratch as a carrier, and so on—to the end of World War II, by which time the carrier had already replaced the battleship as the most powerful type of vessel in the fleet.

Chapter 11

Up, Up, and Away

In This Chapter

◆ Combining sea and air power

◆ Launching balloons from ships

◆ How Wilbur and Orville changed the nature of naval warfare

◆ The first takeoff and landing at sea

The concept of using ships to launch airborne vehicles to gain some sort of a military advantage is older than the airplane—almost 100 years older, in fact.

Combining Sea and Air Power

The first naval officer to suggest combining sea and air power was Britain's Rear Admiral Henry Knowles who, in 1803, had a frigate customized so that it could operate a hot-air balloon.

Fifteen years later, Charles Rogier, also from England, did Knowles one better. He had a ship outfitted to operate a fleet of pilotless hot-air balloons, each of which carried bombs that could be dropped on an enemy's ships. These flying weapons were never used, however.

And in 1846, during the Mexican-American War, a man named John Wise proposed that explosives be dropped on the enemy from tethered balloons that could be operated either from land or from a ship. Wise's plan was never carried out, either.

First Air Attack Launched from a Ship

Only three years after Wise's proposal, on July 12, 1849, the first act of war originated from a ship-launched aircraft—but the incident didn't take place in the Mexican-American War as the date might imply. Nor did it take place in North America, for that matter.

> **Ship's Log**
>
> Today, with modern remote-control capabilities, pilotless attacks from the air can be accomplished with stunning accuracy—but that wasn't true 150-odd years ago.

The attack was by the Austrians, who were besieging Venice, Italy. Diminutive pilotless balloons, rigged to drop explosives, were launched from the Austrian steamer *Volcano* in the general direction of the enemy.

The Austrian balloons had no clue when they were and weren't over the enemy. For the most part they dropped their bombs harmlessly. It was clear after this attempt that any balloon attack launched from a ship would need pilots.

Great View

On August 3, 1861, during the American Civil War, the first piloted balloon launched from a ship. The pilot, who was fighting for the Union, was John La Mountain. The ship was a tugboat that had been converted into a transport called *Fanny*, a name that no doubt made it the butt of many jokes.

The Union Army was using enough balloons, mostly for reconnaissance, that a Union Balloon Corps was formed. A larger ship would be needed to operate the sea-based balloon operations, so in August 1861 a coal barge was converted into the first ship configured exclusively for aerial operations. The ship, which came from the Washington Navy Yard, was known as the *George Washington Parke Custis*.

Later in the war, in 1863, the U.S. Army launched reconnaissance balloons from a gunboat named *Mayflower*. The *George Washington Parke Custis* remained the state of the art in what would develop into aircraft carriers until the end of the nineteenth century.

> **Fact Box**
>
> *George Washington Parke Custis* Specifications
>
> Displacement: 120 tons
> Length: 80 feet
> Beam: 14 feet, 6 inches
> Height: 5 feet, 6 inches

The First Aviation Vessel

The first ship to be built specifically for the purpose of launching aerial vehicles was an "aviation vessel," and it belonged to the Royal Swedish Navy. It made its debut in 1904 and was known as *Ballondepotfartyg Nr. 1* or Balloon Depot Ship No. 1.

In 1911, the Italian navy converted the *brigantine Cavalmarino* into a balloon ship. That same year the Italians became the first navy since the American Civil War to use balloons to guide the gunfire of its warships.

Wright Brothers Change Everything

So far, all of the aerial warfare experiments from ships had involved balloons, or the occasional kite. The Wright brothers successfully flew the first airplane at Kitty Hawk on December 17, 1903—120 feet in 12 seconds with Orville at the controls.

After that, the usage of motorized aircraft from oceangoing vessels began almost immediately. In fact, naval interest in using aircraft off of ships increased dramatically the instant the Wright brothers announced their success.

In 1908, a German steam liner company announced that it was making plans to fly planes off of its ships. The announced reason was to speed up cross-Atlantic mail, but the United States feared that the real reason was military—as these were the years leading up to World War I.

Ship's Log

The Swedish aviation vessel displaced 220 tons, so it was much larger than the *George Washington Parke Custis*. The ship was used to patrol the coast for the next quarter of a century when, having seen her day, she was sold.

Naval Lingo

A **brigantine** is a two-masted, square-rigged ship.

Flattop Facts

In 1909 a prophetic book named *L'Aviation Militaire*, written by Clement Ader, was published. It predicted that ships would one day be built so that they were flat on top, their deck serving as a runway for planes to take off from and land upon. He even predicted that these future ships would have "islands" set off to one side.

" " **Ship's Log**

On November 3, 1909, Lieutenant George Sweet became the first officer of the U.S. Navy to fly in an airplane. Lieutenant Sweet was a passenger in a U.S. Army Wright aircraft flown by Lieutenant Frank P. Lahm at College Park, Maryland.

In response to this announcement, the U.S. Navy began making plans to launch an airplane from one of its own ships. The German plans didn't come to fruition, but the plans the United States made in response did.

Glenn Curtiss's Bold Claim

On May 31, 1910, American airplane builder Glenn Curtiss addressed a banquet of army officers, political leaders, and bigwigs in the manufacturing community and made a bold claim. He said that one airplane could sink a battleship. There was some laughter. It seemed preposterous. To prove his point, he began a few experiments. In late June 1910, he dropped several dummy bombs—they were actually lead weights with streamers attached—from a plane at Hammondsport, New York, from heights of 500 and 800 feet.

His target was not a battleship but rather a raft that had been anchored in the center of Lake Keuka. A reporter who had been invited to watch the experiment wrote that the bombs had been quite accurate. Curtiss's comment was that the accuracy was nothing compared to what could be accomplished by a plane with a two-man crew. He had had to both pilot the plane and aim the bombs. If he'd had a copilot to aim the bombs while he flew the plane, they could have achieved precision.

Captain Chambers's Vision

That same year, navy captain Washington Irving Chambers had a vision of the future, and it included naval aviation. In order to convince the admirals that his vision was more than poppycock, he knew that he would have to demonstrate the feasibility of operating airplanes off of ships.

He first asked the Wright brothers whether they would fly a plane off the deck of a ship. They refused. But Glenn Curtiss, the man who "bombed" Lake Keuka earlier in the year, agreed to try—as long as he didn't have to be the pilot. Curtiss's first try didn't go well. Officials of the Hamburg-American Steamship Company offered Curtiss the use of its steamship SS *Pennsylvania*. A large platform was built on the stern of the ship. The *Pennsylvania* was to load a Curtiss plane aboard the platform and then travel 50 miles out to sea. A pilot named McCurdy had volunteered to fly the experimental flight. The plane never got off the ground, however, because an oil can placed carelessly on the wing of the plane fell off and broke the propeller. The experiment was cancelled. But Curtiss tried, tried again, and this time he was successful.

First Takeoff

It happened on November 14, 1910, when Curtiss's latest volunteer, 24-year-old pilot Eugene B. Ely, took off in a 50-horsepower Curtiss plane from a 83-foot by 24-foot wooden platform built atop the bow of the USS *Birmingham* (CL-2), a light cruiser.

Ely was born in 1886. He grew up in Davenport, Iowa, and graduated from Iowa State University. Before he became the seventeenth man in history to receive a pilot's license, he was an expert automobile mechanic and driver. He was an auto salesman when, in 1910, he took a job as an agent for Curtiss Airplanes, where he learned to fly in meets and exhibitions. At the time of Ely's historic first takeoff from a ship, the *Birmingham* was at anchor in Hampton Roads, Virginia. It was not a great day for flying. The experiment was delayed all morning because winds were too strong. In the afternoon a heavy mist came up and limited visibility.

Fact Box
USS *Birmingham* Specifications
Type: Chester-class scout cruiser
Built: Quincy, Massachusetts
Commissioned: April 1908
Weight: 3,750 tons

Eugene B. Ely, the first pilot to take off in an airplane from a ship.

(U.S. Naval Historical Center)

Finally, with the weather getting no better, the pilot decided to take a chance. The flight barely made it. The plane descended after leaving the platform and actually touched the water. A spray came up as the propeller struck the water and the whole plane vibrated just before it began to rise.

Ely flew blind for the next several moments, as the spray from the propeller striking the sea had covered his goggles with saltwater. After a frightening few seconds, he managed to clear his goggles enough so that he could once again see the sky above and the water below.

The short flight ended moments later when Ely—who was a friend of Curtiss—landed on a strip in Willoughby Spit about two and a half miles away.

Finding someone to participate in the experiment hadn't been easy. As it turned out, many established pilots wanted no part of taking off from a ship. But Ely was a stunt pilot who worked in a daredevil show, and looked forward to the opportunity to add to his death-defying resumé.

First Landing

The first man to take off from a ship became the first man to land on a ship when Eugene Ely landed his Curtiss Pusher on a platform built atop the USS *Pennsylvania*, an armored cruiser, during the late morning of January 18, 1911.

Flattop Facts

The landing platform built over the stern of the USS *Pennsylvania* had a downward slope. It was 120 feet long and 29 feet wide.

The ship was at anchor at the time in San Francisco Bay. Ely took off from Camp Selfridge and flew up the coast, over San Francisco, and across the harbor to the Navy Yard. He circled the ship once before making his approach for the landing.

Ely landed with the help of 22 transverse hemp ropes stretched across the platform and held in place with sandbags. Ely's plane was fitted with hooks that hung down from the fuselage.

Ship's Log

It is interesting that the method of "catching" a landing plane on a flight deck remains, in essence, the same today as it was 90 years ago, the very first time it was ever accomplished. The method was adapted from that used by a circus stunt driver, Hugh A. Robinson, who used transverse ropes to stop his car—which would for a moment seem to be about to crash into a crowd of spectators—after performing a loop-de-loop trick.

For this experiment the weather cooperated. It was a calm and clear day. Ely went from touching down to coming to a complete stop in 33 feet. Forty-five minutes after landing, Ely took off again. Though the wheels of his plane almost touched the water before he began to rise, the takeoff was successful and he returned to Selfridge Field in San Francisco.

After the initial experiments with pilot Ely, it was considered a lot easier and safer to launch planes from ships than it was to land planes on them. Therefore Glenn Curtiss built a shipborne seaplane, which was successfully tested in February 1911.

The seaplane could take off from a specially prepared ship. (The *Pennsylvania* was again used for the experiments.) When the plane returned from its reconnaissance mission, however, it would not land on the ship but rather in the water beside it. From there cranes were needed to haul the plane back on board.

First Catapult

The Wright brothers built the first catapult designed to launch an airplane in 1912. It consisted of a heavy weight suspended in a framework tower. A system of pulleys led a rope from the weight to the aircraft.

When the weight was released, the plane was thrown forward. As we learned in Chapter 4, it was Captain Chambers who brought high technology to the catapult, also in 1912, when he designed one that functioned with compressed air.

The value of airplanes as weapons became obvious during the First World War. At first the planes were used for scouting, but by the war's end planes were being used for bombing missions and, of course, the first dogfights were fought. It was during this time that the admirals of the world first began to take Curtiss's idea of using ships as floating airfields seriously.

In Japan an admiral named Isoruku Yamamoto announced that the most effective warships of the future would be those that carried airplanes. His countrymen didn't exactly laugh at him, but it was another decade before anyone agreed with him.

The Least You Need to Know

- The Austrians launched the first ship-based aerial attack, in the form of pilotless balloons, in 1849 against Italy.

- The first ship to be built specifically for the purpose of launching aerial vehicles was a Swedish "aviation vessel" in 1904.

- After the Wright brothers successfully flew the first airplane, the usage of motorized aircraft from oceangoing vessels began almost immediately.

- Eugene B. Ely, at age 24, was the first pilot to both take off from and land upon a ship in an airplane.

- The transverse wire system of catching landing planes was devised from a circus performer's loop-de-loop automobile trick.

Chapter 12

Langley Landings

In This Chapter

- ◆ The U.S Navy's first carrier
- ◆ Building the first aircraft to meet the demands of carrier life
- ◆ Chance Milton Vought's contribution to naval aviation
- ◆ The *Langley*'s brief tenure as a carrier

During the summer of 1919, the Naval Appropriations Act for Fiscal Year 1920 contained a provision that was to change the U.S. Navy forever. The act provided for the conversion of the *Jupiter*, a collier (a ship designed to transport coal), into the first aircraft carrier.

The *Jupiter* Becomes the *Langley*

Plans were drawn up for the new carrier that autumn. The *Jupiter* was reengineered with a flat platform on top that extended its entire length. Catapults were added to both ends of what was called the "flying-off deck." Later, of course, this portion of an aircraft carrier would be known as the flight deck. The ship was renamed the USS *Langley*.

Fact Box
USS _Jupiter_ (AC-3) Specifications Displacement: 19,360 tons Length: 542 feet Beam: 65 feet Draft: 27 feet, 8 inches Maximum Speed: 15 knots Crew: 163

Even before it was converted into a carrier, this was a precedent-setting ship. The _Jupiter_, which launched on August 24, 1912, at the Mare Island Navy Yard in Vallejo, California, was the U.S. Navy's first electronically propelled ship.

Is That a Covered Wagon or an Aircraft Carrier?

The USS _Langley_ (CV-1) was commissioned at Norfolk, Virginia, under the command of Kenneth Whiting. Because the flying-off deck had been placed atop the ship without any consideration for aesthetics, the new carrier quickly picked up a new, and not so complimentary, nickname: the Covered Wagon.

> ### Ship's Log
>
> The _Langley_'s six holds were all converted, the foremost into a tank for AVGAS [aviation fuel], the next two into a hangar, the fourth into a magazine for ordnance and a storeroom, with a lift-well above, and the last two into a second hangar. A total of 55 aircraft were stored in the two hangars, and were hoisted out by a pair of three-ton travelling cranes running on a fore-and-aft girder under the flight deck, and then deposited on a lift which took them to the flight deck. The term "hangar" is misleading, for there is no hangar deck in the conventional sense, merely two pairs of holds into which the aircraft had to be lowered by the crane. There was also a crane for hoisting out seaplanes on either side amidships. The big open space between the flight deck and the tops of the holds was available for working on aircraft.
>
> —Naval historian Antony Preston, describing the _Jupiter_'s conversion to the _Langley_

Flattop Facts

The _Langley_ was named after the pioneer Samuel Pierpont Langley.

The _Langley_'s arresting gear was designed in 1922. According to a U.S. Navy memo that year, "The arresting gear will consist of two or more transverse wires stretched across the fore and aft wires ... [and which] lead around sheaves placed outboard to hydraulic brakes. The plane, after engaging the transverse wire, is guided down the deck by the fore and aft wires and is brought to rest by the action of the transverse wire working with the hydraulic brake."

The *Langley's* arresting gear was known as "fiddle bridges," because the wires resembled those on a violin.

The navy was pleased with the *Langley* and immediately sought more ships with naval aviation capabilities. The U.S. Congress authorized the conversion of the unfinished battle cruisers *Lexington* and *Saratoga* as aircraft carriers on July 1, 1922. All of the pilots assigned to these two new carriers completed their training in taking off and landing on the *Langley*.

An Aeromarine 39-B airplane lands on the flight deck of the USS Langley *in 1922.*

(U.S. Naval Historical Center Photo)

First Takeoff and Landing

The first pilot to take off from the *Langley* was Lieutenant V. C. Griffin, who took off in a Vought VE-7SF while the ship was at anchor in the York River in Virginia on October 17, 1922. (More about the Vought aircraft, and Vought himself, later.)

The first pilot to land a plane on a U.S. Navy aircraft carrier was Lieutenant Commander Godfrey de Courcelles Chevalier, who landed on the USS *Langley* in an Aeromarine plane on October 26, 1922. The ship was underway off Cape Henry, Virginia, at the time. Sadly, Chevalier was killed in a plane crash—not aircraft-carrier related—the following month.

The first catapult launching from the USS *Langley* came on November 18, 1922, when Commander Kenneth Whiting was launched aboard his PT seaplane. The ship was at anchor on the York River in Virginia at the time.

Fact Box
USS *Langley* (CV-1) Specifications Displacement: 11,500 tons Length: 542 feet Beam: 65 feet Width of Flying-Off Deck: 65 feet (flight deck) Draft: 18 feet, 11 inches Maximum Speed: 15 knots Crew: 468 Armament: Four 5-inch guns Aircraft: 55

After six months of flight operations and tests in the Caribbean, in June 1923 the *Langley* sailed to Washington, D.C., where it demonstrated takeoffs and landings for a gathering of dignitaries. From there it went to Norfolk for more tests and alterations, and then it finally made the long trip to San Diego late in 1924 to join the navy's Pacific fleet.

The USS *Langley* officially joined the U.S. Battle Fleet on November 17, 1924. Two weeks later, the ship was named the flagship for Aircraft Squadrons, Battle Fleet—home base for the navy's oceangoing air force. The new carrier remained in the Pacific for the remainder of its life. Based in California and Hawaii, it functioned to train carrier pilots.

Chance Milton Vought

Early aircraft carriers would have been useless without aircraft that could take off and land from them. Although the very first planes to take off from ships were Curtiss planes, the man most responsible for adapting aircraft to the needs of naval aviation was Chance Milton Vought.

Vought was born on February 26, 1890, in New York City. He studied engineering at the Pratt Institute, New York University, and the University of Pennsylvania. After school, at age 20, he went to work for Harold F. McCormick, an aircraft backer.

Flying Lessons from the Wright Brothers

Vought got his flying lessons from the airplane's inventors themselves, the Wright brothers. He was the 156th to receive his pilot's license. In addition to being a pioneer pilot, he also edited a magazine called *Aero & Hydro*.

Vought designed his first plane in 1914, the Mayo-Vought-Simplex. It was used as a training plane by Great Britain's Royal Air Force. Two years later he joined the Wright Co. of Ohio as its chief engineer. Although he only worked there for a brief period, he did develop the Model V Wright flyer.

With partner Birdseye Lewis, Vought formed his own company in 1917, and their aircraft, the VE-7, was considered the state of the art at the time. When the USS *Langley* was ready for launching and receiving aircraft in 1922, it was a Vought VE-7 that accomplished the feat. To accommodate the carrier landing, a regular VE-7 had been equipped with an arresting hook for its flight deck landing.

During the 1920s Vought became involved with the particular problems presented by naval aviation. One problem of land-based aircraft was that they were too heavy and needed to develop momentum over a long runway in order to take off.

Make 'em Lighter

Vought sought to make every part of the plane lighter, including the engine. Pratt and Whitney designed a light engine to satisfy Vought, which he included in his first plane designed especially for naval aviation, the UO-1. Along with having a lighter engine, it was equipped for catapult launches with a bridle around the fuselage in front of the double wings serving as a handle for the catapult to hold when the plane was thrown forward.

Fact Box
Vought UO-1 Specifications
Wingspan: 34 feet
Length: 22 feet
Height: 8 ½ feet
Gross weight: 2,330 pounds
Fuel capacity: 80 gallons
Power plant types: Lawrence J-1 (200 horsepower), Wright E-2 (180 horsepower), and Wright J-3 (190 horsepower)
Maximum speed at sea level: 122 miles per hour
Landing speed at sea level: 53 miles per hour
Initial rate of climb: 880 feet per minute
Range: 395 miles
Service ceiling: 18,200 feet
Crew: 2

During the 1920s, Vought's company was bought out by the United Aircraft and Transportation Corporation, but it continued to function as a separate division.

Vought's next plane designed specifically for carrier use was the O2U-1, the first Corsair, in 1928. More than 500 of them were built and they turned out to be amazingly versatile. Not only could they take off and land on aircraft carriers, but they could even be catapulted off of battleships.

Vought died unexpectedly in 1930 of blood poisoning, but quality naval aircraft continued to be made under his name. These included the following planes:

> **Ship's Log**
>
> The Vought UO-1 made history when it became the first plane to be catapulted from a battleship at night. On November 26, 1924, Lieutenant Dixie Kiefer flew the plane off the USS *California* in San Diego harbor. The only light came from the ship's searchlights trained 1,000 yards ahead.

- The F4U Corsair, the "Bentwing" which became famous during World War II

- The F-8 Crusader

- The A-7 attack aircraft

> **Naval Lingo**
>
> A **seaplane tender** is a seaplane-bearing ship whose job is to attend to other ships, often supplying communication services between a larger ship and shore.

Short Life as a Carrier

The *Langley* remained a carrier for fewer than 20 years. It was mostly an experiment to see if a carrier was feasible, and it passed that test. Once the Navy was confident that aircraft carriers had a future, it immediately created superior vessels—the *Lexington*, *Saratoga*, *Ranger*, *Yorktown*, and others—and the *Langley* was outdated years before the United States became involved in World War II. In January 1937 it was placed in dry dock and was converted into a *seaplane tender*. Its classification was changed from CV-1 to AV-3.

Death of the *Langley*

At the time of the Japanese attack at Pearl Harbor, the *Langley* was anchored off the Philippine Islands, which had also been attacked by the Japanese. The next day, the ship headed for Borneo, and then Australia. In January 1942, the ship began assisting the Australian air force with its antisubmarine patrols.

The following month, while performing these duties, it was attacked by nine twin-engine Japanese bombers and took five hits. The aircraft topside burst into flames, the ship's steering was impaired, and it took a 10° list to port. The *Langley* went dead in the water, and the order was given to abandon ship. The ship that served as America's first aircraft carrier sank about 75 miles south of Tjilatjap, with a loss of 16 lives.

The Least You Need to Know

- A coal transport named *Jupiter* was adapted into the United States's first aircraft carrier, the USS *Langley*.

- Chance Milton Vought was the first to design aircraft specifically for carrier use.

- The first pilot to take off from the *Langley* was Lieutenant V. C. Griffin.

- The first pilot to land a plane on a U.S. Navy aircraft carrier was Lieutenant Commander Godfrey de Courcelles Chevalier.

- The *Langley*, although no longer an aircraft carrier at the time, was sunk by the Japanese during World War II.

Chapter 3

The Next Wave of Carriers

In This Chapter

- ◆ Britain's Royal Navy joints the flattop club
- ◆ Germany's carrier plans are foiled
- ◆ The carrier buildup between the wars
- ◆ Japan's purpose-built aircraft carriers

As soon as the United States proved that planes could be launched from large ships, other countries tried to get into the act. Both during World War I and between the world wars, several other countries got into the business of building aircraft carriers.

In this chapter, we'll take a look at the flattop's early global development, and, in the next chapter, we'll examine how the development of the aircraft carrier was directly related to the gearing up, by both the Allied and the Axis powers, for the Second World War.

First British Carriers

Soon after the airplane was invented in 1903, the British attempted to develop a seaplane—a plane that could land on the ocean—into a military weapon. They didn't get very far, however. The planes that they developed could only land on calm waters, and this simply wouldn't do, as they were expected to function in the choppy waters of the North Atlantic.

So in 1912, with one eye on similar experiments being done by the U.S. Navy, the Royal Navy began to experiment with launching planes from ships. In this case, the launches were conducted from a platform attached to the bow of a battleship.

Converting the *Furious*

Five years later, in 1917, with World War I raging, the Royal Navy constructed a wooden platform, 230 feet long, atop the bow of the battle cruiser *Furious*. This was the first British flight deck. Below the flight deck, the navy built a hangar deck with enough room for eight aircraft—usually four seaplanes and four planes with wheeled landing gear.

The idea was for the wheeled planes to both take off from and land on the *Furious*'s landing deck, but this didn't work out. The superstructure of the original ship, which remained sticking up above the flight deck, caused so much air turbulence that it made it impossible for the planes to safely land.

To remedy this situation, a second deck was built atop the stern of the ship for landing planes. Two narrow ramps were built along the outside of the ship so that planes could be transported from one deck to the other. Even this modification didn't completely eradicate the turbulence problem, so the next step was for the Royal Navy to design an aircraft carrier with a flight deck that covered its entire length.

The *Argus*

The first British aircraft carrier was the HMS *Argus*. The ship was originally going to be an Italian ocean liner built in Great Britain but, because it was wartime, plans were changed and the ship's keel was instead used for the *Argus*.

> **Flattop Facts**
>
> Although work began on the *Argus* in 1917, the same year as the *Furious* experiments, the ship wasn't completed until after the war was over.

The flight deck of the *Argus* was 550 feet long and the ship displaced 14,500 tons. Just below the flight deck was a hangar 65 feet wide and 350 feet long—big enough for 20 aircraft. A single elevator moved planes from the hangar to the flight deck and back again.

The *Argus* had two sets of arresting gear on its flight deck, a set of wires that went across the landing zone, and a second set of wires that went lengthwise down the deck. This second set wasn't designed to stop the plane, but rather to help it continue in a straight path down the flight deck rather than swerving to one side or another.

Ship's Log

Because the adaptation of the ocean liner keel into an aircraft carrier worked so well, the Royal Navy immediately began plans to convert another ship into a carrier.

The *Eagle* and the *Hermes*

The second British carrier, converted from a battleship that was being built by the British for the Chilean navy, was the HMS *Eagle*. It began trials in 1920. The *Eagle* was larger than the *Argus*—it displaced 22,500 tons and there was room on its hanger deck for 21 planes—and it was the first British carrier to have an island with a navigating bridge and a center for controlling flight operations.

The *Eagle* was supposed to have a double-island superstructure with a funnel in each, the funnels being exhaust pipes for the ship's engines. The original intention was also to have a tripod mast. Another early plan was to build a span between the islands that would be 20 feet above the flight deck and sturdy enough to support a navigating position and its own 4-inch antiaircraft guns.

These plans were abandoned after a wind-tunnel test showed that twin islands would cause dangerous wind currents along the flight deck. The *Eagle* was given the standard single island on the starboard side. Although the *Eagle* ended up with only one island, it was a big one—130 feet long with a pair of funnels. The island contained the fire-control and navigation centers, and a large crane—for lifting planes from the hangar deck onto the flight deck—was mounted on the aft end.

The first British carrier to be designed from scratch as a carrier was the HMS *Hermes*, which was commissioned by the Royal Navy in 1924. When built, it had the world's largest flight deck, almost 600 feet long.

Flattop Facts

All three of Great Britain's first aircraft carriers saw action in World War II, but only the *Argus* survived. The *Hermes* was sunk in the Pacific by a Japanese bombing raid on June 1, 1941 (five months before Pearl Harbor), and the *Eagle* was sunk by torpedoes fired from a German submarine on August 10, 1942, in the Mediterranean Sea.

Fact Box
HMS *Hermes* Specifications
Commissioned: 1924
Displacement: 13,000 tons
Length: 600 feet
Beam: 70 feet, 2 inches
Height: 21 feet, 6 inches
Power plant: Twin screw turbines
Maximum speed: 25 knots
Armament: Three 4-inch and six 5½-inch guns
Crew: 664
Air group: 20 planes

Why the Starboard Side?

You might have noticed that it's customary for the island on an aircraft carrier to be on the starboard side of the flight deck. This custom can be traced back to Wing-Captain Clark Hall of the Royal Navy Air Service, who served on the carrier HMS *Furious*.

Hall pointed out that pilots, if they are having difficulty during a landing, will turn to port more often than to starboard. Therefore it was concluded that an island on the starboard side would be hit less frequently by pilots reacting to an emergency during a faulty landing.

Return of the *Furious* (and Friends)

Between 1925 and 1930, the Royal Navy debuted three more aircraft carriers, and one of them was familiar. The *Furious* was remodeled with a full-length flight deck and debuted as a full-fledged aircraft carrier in 1925. The *Furious*'s hangar deck now had room for 48 aircraft. It could achieve a top speed of 30 knots.

The other two new carriers, which were built to similar specifications, were the *Courageous* and the *Glorious*. These latter two ships were both sunk by the Germans during World War II. The *Courageous* was sent to the bottom by a U-boat (submarine) on September 17, 1939. A German cruiser sank the *Glorious* with shots from its big guns on June 8, 1940.

The next British carrier to be built was the *Ark Royal*, and its luck against the German navy was no better than that of the *Courageous* and the *Glorious*. It was the last British carrier to be built before the outbreak of World War II—construction began on the *Ark Royal* in 1935 and was completed in 1938.

Flattop Facts

This was the second British ship named the *Ark Royal*. The first had carried seaplanes during World War I.

The *Ark Royal* had the longest flight deck yet, almost 800 feet. It had a double hangar deck big enough for 60 planes. Three elevators lifted planes from the hangars onto the flight deck. It had a top speed of 31½ knots and displaced 22,000 tons. It was sunk by a U-boat torpedo on November 13, 1941.

Meanwhile, in Germany ...

The German navy showed no interest in aviation until the Germans saw that the British were making advances in this area. The Germans planned to build their first carrier during World War I. It was to be a converted Italian ocean liner with a large flight deck and an island on one side. (The island was their own innovation. The first British carrier with an island on one side didn't make its debut until 1920.)

Plans were to have the carrier capable of carrying 30 planes. However, before work could begin on the ocean liner, the war ended and Germany signed the Versailles Treaty, which banned them from possessing either military aircraft or aircraft carriers.

Plans for a German aircraft carrier were tabled for the next 15 years. It wasn't until the rise of Adolf Hitler and the Third Reich that plans for naval aviation again became active. In 1934, Hitler announced that Germany was going to build its own aircraft carriers. Construction actually began three years later. More about that in the next chapter.

Hosho: The First Japanese Carrier

The Japanese began work on their first aircraft carrier, the *Hosho*, in 1919. Originally, they planned to design the ship along the lines of the British *Hermes*. It was to have three funnels, smaller than their British counterparts, on the starboard side. The funnels were on hinges so they could be lowered. This way, they could be adjusted during flight operations so that smoke from them would not waft across the flight deck restricting visibility. There was room on the ship for 26 aircraft. The ship originally had an island but, after trials, the island was removed in 1923.

Fact Box

Hosho Specifications

Displacement: 10,000 tons

Length: 551 feet, 6 inches

Beam: 70 feet

Height: 20 feet, 3 inches

Power plant: Twin screw turbines

Maximum speed: 25 knots

Armament: Four 5½-inch guns

Air group: 26 airplanes

The Japanese built the *Hosho* from scratch as an aircraft carrier. Although its construction started after that of the *Hermes*, the Japanese ship was rushed into service and thus became the first purpose-built aircraft carrier in the world.

Converting Battle Cruisers

During the 1920s, the Japanese converted two battle cruisers into aircraft carriers. The United States and Great Britain did the same thing, the United States creating the *Saratoga* and the *Lexington*, and Britain creating the *Glorious* and the *Courageous*.

Japan's new carriers were the *Akagi* and the *Amagi*—named after Japanese cities. The latter was never finished, however, because it was damaged beyond repair in a 1923 earthquake. The *Amagi* was replaced by the conversion of a partially completed battleship, the *Kaga*.

Akagi

The *Akagi* was powered by 19 boilers that produced 131,000 horsepower worth of steam for turbines driving four propellers. Originally the ship had room for only 60 planes, but this was later increased to 90. The ship was armed with ten 8-inch guns and twelve 4.7-inch guns. It had a crew of 1,600 and its island was on the port side—on the opposite side from all American islands.

Later the 8-inch guns were taken out and replaced with 14 twin-mounted 25 millimeter antiaircraft guns. The ship displaced 36,500 tons and had a top speed of 31½ knots. Planes in its air group included Mitsubishi A5M fighters, Aichi D1A dive-bombers, and Yokosuka B4Y torpedo bombers.

Kaga

When the conversion of the *Kaga* was complete, its flight deck was 100 feet wide and 560 feet long. The whole ship was 782 feet long with a 97-foot beam. It displaced 29,600 tons and had a power plant that produced 91,000 shaft horsepower.

The *Kaga*'s maximum speed was 27½ knots. It had a range of 8,000 miles at 14 knots. Its air group included Mitsubishi B1M attackers, Nakajima A1N fighters, Aichi D1A fighters, and Mitsubishi A5M fighters.

Albatross: Flattop from Down Under

The first Australian aircraft carrier was the HMAS *Albatross*. The keel was laid for this ship in 1926; it was launched in 1928 and commissioned in 1929. It was designed to carry Fairey IIIF three-seat spotter/reconnaissance seaplanes.

The *Albatross*'s cranes were one of its most unique features. Cranes lifted planes from the sea onto the deck, lowered them from the flight deck to the hangar area, and placed the seaplanes on the ship's catapult so that they could be launched. The hangar was big enough to hold nine seaplanes. The ship was 440 feet long overall with a beam of 61 feet. It had a maximum speed of 22 knots.

The *Albatross* remained in the Australian navy until the onset of World War II, at which time it was transferred to the British navy and operated in the Indian Ocean. It wasn't scrapped until more than 20 years later, in 1964.

Back in the United States ...

Meanwhile, the United States was still busy constructing aircraft carriers, with two more completed in 1927. On November 16, 1927, the USS *Saratoga* (CV 3) was commissioned at Camden, New Jersey, with Captain Harry E. Yarnell commanding. The *Saratoga* was converted from a battle cruiser and, when completed, it had the largest aircraft-carrying capacity in the world, and it was the fastest carrier to boot.

The *Saratoga*'s Air Officer Commander Mark A. Mitscher made the first takeoff and landing aboard the ship in a Vought UO-1 on January 11, 1928.

The ship's original armament, a main battery of eight 8-inch guns in twin mounts forward and abaft (behind) the island, was designed to stand off an attacking cruiser. These arms were upgraded during World War II.

Fact Box

USS *Saratoga* Specifications

Size:

> Displacement: 33,000 tons
>
> Length: 910 feet
>
> Beam: 105 feet
>
> Draft: 35 feet

Armament (during World War II):

> 12 5-inch/38 DP
>
> 2 40mm twins
>
> 23 40mm quads
>
> 16 20mm guns

Propulsion:

> Top speed: 32 knots
>
> Maximum cruising radius: 4,600 miles at 25 knots, or 9,500 miles at 15 knots

Horsepower: 180,000

Drive: Four screws, turbo-electric

Fuel capacity: 9,748 tons of oil

Aircraft:

> 57 F6F Hellcats
>
> 18 TBM Avengers

Flattop Facts _____

During World War II, several changes were made to the *Saratoga*. The height of the foremast and stack structures were cut down and a bulge was added on the port side to compensate for the weight of the island and give the ship better balance.

USS *Lexington*

Less than a month after the *Saratoga* was commissioned, on December 14, 1927, the USS *Lexington* (CV 2) was commissioned at Quincy, Massachusetts, with Captain Albert W. Marshall commanding.

The *Lexington* became the oldest U.S. aircraft carrier to be sunk in warfare when the ship went down at the Battle of the Coral Sea early in 1942.

First War Games

The United States engaged in the first war games that relied heavily on aircraft carriers in January 1929.

The *Lexington* and the *Saratoga*, along with an escorting cruiser, were assigned to launch a surprise "attack" on the Panama Canal. Sixty-nine aircraft took off from the carriers and remained undetected until they were over their target. The carriers' performance impressed naval tacticians.

In a few years, another country would undertake a similarly impressive carrier-launched attack, although this time the attack would be for real, and the target would be Pearl Harbor.

Flattop Facts

Responding to an emergency during January 1930, the USS *Lexington* furnished electricity to the city of Tacoma, Washington, for a 30-day period. To accomplish this, Lady Lex pulled into Tacoma's Baker Dock, where her powerplant was wired to a Tacoma City Light Company power station, and the power was distributed to the residences and businesses of the community. The *Lexington*'s electricity output totaled more than 4.25 million kilowatt-hours.

The Least You Need to Know

◆ The first British aircraft carrier was the HMS *Argus*, which was originally intended to be an Italian ocean liner.

◆ Islands are always on the starboard side of a flight deck so that they are less apt to be hit by a pilot reacting to an emergency during a difficult landing.

◆ Though its construction started after that of the *Hermes*, the Japanese ship *Hosho* was rushed into service and became the first purpose-built aircraft carrier in the world.

◆ In the war games of 1929, two U.S. aircraft carriers launched a simulated surprise attack of the Panama Canal.

Chapter 14

The Pre-War Years

In This Chapter

- The purpose-built USS *Ranger*
- Refueling tankers at sea
- Two new breeds of carriers are developed
- Germany again takes a stab at building a carrier

As the rumblings of war began in Europe, where Germany seemed hell-bent on conquering the continent, and in Asia, where Japan used its military might to spread its control in all directions, the American aircraft carrier came into its own. It developed into a weapon that was ready to combat the Axis powers in a naval war that would erupt both in the Atlantic and the Pacific.

Ranger: First U.S. Carrier from Conception

During the fall of 1931 work began on the first U.S. Navy aircraft carrier that was intended to be an aircraft carrier from its conception. (Remember, the Japanese had built the first purpose-built carrier years before: the *Hosho*.) The United States's previous three carriers had all been converted from existing ships into carriers.

The keel for the USS *Ranger* (CV-4) was laid at the Newport News Shipbuilding and Drydock Company in Newport News, Virginia. It was launched on February 25, 1933, and commissioned on June 4 of that year at the Norfolk Navy Yard, with Captain Arthur L. Bristol in command.

Slow-Moving *Ranger*

The *Ranger* displaced 14,500 tons. She was intended to be larger, but treaty tonnage quotas in effect between the wars kept her size down. For the same reason, the *Ranger*'s top speed of 27 knots was slower than had been originally intended.

Speed wasn't considered essential when the ship was being built because it was intended to carry spotting aircraft for a 21-knot battleship force. By World War II, however, *Ranger*'s slowness had become a deficiency. (By that time, for that matter, treaty tonnage quotas were no longer a concern either.)

Fact Box
USS *Ranger* Specifications

Size:

> Displacement: 14,500 tons
>
> Length: 769 feet
>
> Beam: 80 feet
>
> Draft: 25 feet

Armament:

> 8 5-inch/25 DP
>
> 6 40mm quads
>
> 46 20mm guns

Propulsion:

> Top speed: 27 knots
>
> Maximum cruising radius: 5,800 miles at 25 knots; or 11,500 miles at 15 knots
>
> Horsepower: 53,500
>
> Drive: Two screws, geared turbine

Fuel capacity: 3,675 tons of oil

Aircraft:

> 27 fighters
>
> 24 bombers
>
> 10 torpedo bombers

Setting the Basic Pattern

The design of the *Ranger* set the basic pattern for all American fleet aircraft carriers to follow, in that the flight deck and its supporting elements were *superstructure* rather than part of the hull—as had been the case with the *Saratoga*.

Other design elements on the carrier weren't so trend-setting. Two sets of folding exhaust stacks on either side didn't work very well and were never again seen in future carriers. The *Wasp*, commissioned seven years later, was a much-improved sister ship to the *Ranger* (we'll take a closer look at the *Wasp* later in this chapter).

Naval Lingo

A ship's **superstructure** is everything above the main deck.

1934: First Hydraulic Catapult

During the autumn of 1934 work began on the first hydraulic (that is, water operated) catapult for launching planes from an aircraft carrier. The hydraulic catapult was so successful that it was the chosen method of launching planes from carriers for years to come (although, of course, the system was improved and refined over time).

The first flush-deck hydraulic catapult was known as the Type H Mark I. Manufactured by the Naval Aircraft Factory, in Philadelphia, Pennsylvania, the Type H was the first system to have the entire catapult system enclosed below the flight deck, with only one part protruding up through a slot in the flight deck to attach to the aircraft's nose bridle. The devices were first installed on the *Yorktown* and the *Enterprise* (discussed later in this chapter), with each carrier receiving three catapults.

Meanwhile, in the Land of the Rising Sun ...

As the 1930s dawned, Japan built its second purpose-built aircraft carrier: the IJNS *Ryujo*. It had the same hull design as a Japanese light cruiser. The ship was 590 feet long with a 66-foot beam. Its flight deck was 513 feet long and 75 feet wide. The navigating bridge was under the forward edge of the flight deck. There was no island. It had six oil-fired boilers and two geared turbines. The power plant produced 65,000 shaft horsepower, offering the ship a maximum speed of 29 knots. The *Ryujo*'s range at 14 knots was 10,000 miles. It accommodated a crew of 600.

The *Ryujo* displaced 10,800 tons after several alterations were made to improve stability. Its air group included Mitsubishi A5M fighters, Nakajima B5N torpedo bombers, and Mitsubishi A6M fighter-bombers.

The *Soryu* and *Hiryu*

During the mid-1930s, the Japanese built two more carriers from scratch. These were the *Soryu* and the *Hiryu*. The design of these two ships set the pattern for all of Japan's future carriers until, at the United States's insistence after World War II, Japan ceased to be a naval power.

The *Soryu* had two hangars, one above the other. The lower hangar was 420 feet long and was recessed into the hull. The upper hangar was 520 feet long. The flight deck was 705 feet, 6 inches long and 85 feet, 6 inches wide. Combined, the hangars could accommodate 72 planes. Three elevators transported aircraft from the hangars to the flight deck.

Quad turbines delivered 152,000 shaft horsepower. Maximum speed was 34½ knots. The ship's range, when traveling at 18 knots, was 7,800 miles. Unlike earlier Japanese aircraft carriers, the *Soryu* had its island on the customary starboard side.

The *Soryu*'s armament consisted of 6 twin 5-inch guns and 14 twin 25 millimeter guns. All of the guns had antiaircraft capability. The *Soryu* was launched in December 1935 and commissioned in January 1937.

Ship's Log

As was true the world over, Japan converted from biplanes (planes with double wings) to monoplanes during the 1930s.

The *Hiryu*, which was built next, was different from the *Soryu* in that it, like earlier Japanese carriers, had its island on the port side, opposite of all carriers built by the United States and Britain. It differed from the *Soryu* in other ways as well. It had thicker armor and was 10 feet longer. It displaced 17,300 tons and held 73 planes.

1936: *Yorktown* Commissioned

The fifth U.S. aircraft carrier, the USS *Yorktown*, was placed in commission at the Norfolk Naval Operating Base in Virginia with Captain Ernest D. McWhorter in command. The ship's keel was laid on May 21, 1934, and it was launched on April 4, 1936.

Several years later, during the early stages of World War II, the *Yorktown* would earn the nickname "Waltzing Matilda of the Pacific Fleet" from her sailors. That's because the ship was moving from place to place, dancing from one spot to another on the globe at a hectic pace. And the ship had to dance to get in the way of the still-advancing Japanese navy wherever it could.

The USS *Enterprise*

The USS *Enterprise* (CV 6), not to be confused with the first nuclear-powered aircraft carrier, which came later, was placed in commission on May 12, 1938, at the Newport News Shipbuilding and Drydock Company, Newport News, Virginia, with Captain N. H. White in command. The ship was launched October 3, 1936.

Fact Box

USS *Enterprise* (CV 6) Specifications
Size:
      Displacement: 19,800 tons
      Length: 827 feet
      Beam: 83 feet
      Draft: 31 feet
Armament:
      8 5-inch/38 DP
      8 40mm twins
      6 40mm quads
      50 20mm guns
Propulsion:
      Top speed: 30 knots
      Horsepower: 120,000
      Drive: Four screws, geared turbine
      Fuel capacity: 6,900 tons of oil
Aircraft:
      37 F6F Hellcats
      18 TBM Avengers

The *Enterprise* was a step more sophisticated than the *Ranger;* but it still wasn't very good at defending itself. Its guns could be used against enemy aircraft and light surface ships only.

 Ship's Log

Of the three sister ships *Yorktown, Hornet,* and *Enterprise,* the *Enterprise* would be the only one of the three to survive the war in the Pacific.

Refueling at Sea

One problem facing all early aircraft carriers was refueling. It was impractical for a carrier to return to port each time it ran out of fuel. Therefore, a system was devised whereby carriers could be refueled at sea.

During the late spring of 1939, the aircraft carrier *Saratoga* and the tanker USS *Kanawha* first demonstrated the feasibility of refueling carriers at sea with underway refueling tests off the coast of southern California. By the time the United States entered World War II, all carrier battle groups included tankers designed to keep the carrier's "tank full."

Wasp

On April 25, 1940, the USS *Wasp* (CV 7) was placed in commission at the Army Quartermaster Base in Boston, Massachusetts, with Captain John W. Reeves Jr. in command. The ship's keel was laid April 1, 1936, at Quincy, Massachusetts, by the Bethlehem Shipbuilding Company. The ship was launched on April 4, 1939.

> **Ship's Log**
>
> During the ship's shakedown (testing under operating conditions) on July 9, 1939, one of its planes, a Vought SB2U-2 Vindicator, crashed two miles away. Although the ship and some of its planes rushed to the scene, only some items from the plane's baggage compartment were found. The plane and its two-man crew were lost.

The *Wasp* displaced 14,700 tons and was more than 741 feet long. Its beam at water level was just shy of 81 feet, but its flight deck was much wider: 109 feet. It had a maximum speed of just under 30 knots and accommodated a crew of 2,367.

It had room for 80 planes and was armed with 8 5-inch guns, 16 1.1-inch guns, and 16 .50 caliber machine guns. When the United States entered World War II, the *Wasp* was in the Atlantic Ocean, protecting shipping from German attack.

A Smaller Class of Carriers

It was between the wars that the U.S. Navy first realized that not all aircraft carriers had to be giants of the sea. Just as there are international airports and there are small airstrips, carriers could come in various sizes and provide various functions. The result was the introduction of *light* and *escort carriers*.

The First Light Carriers

During World War II light carriers were used to provide additional air capability to the fleet carriers and the battle fleet, plus provide a fast air-strike capability to smaller operations that didn't warrant the presence of the large (and more expensive) fleet carriers.

The intent of their design was to provide near-fleet-carrier air capability on a smaller hull. Only two classes of light carriers were built:

◆ **Independence class,** which consisted of nine ships (based on and converted from Cincinnati-class light cruiser hulls). Ships of the Independence class were the USS *Independence, Princeton, Belleau Wood, Cowpens, Monterey, Langley, Cabot, Bataan,* and *San Jacinto.*

◆ **Saipan class.** Because of the success of the Independence-class ships, two more ships were built, similar but with enough design changes to warrant designation as a new class of light carrier, the Saipan class. The building of the Saipan-class ships was approved because some of the old ones were apt to be sunk in the war. Their design was based on the hull and machinery of the 13,600-ton Baltimore-class heavy cruisers. This design allowed superior hull subdivision, protection, magazine volume, and a stronger flight deck. They could carry more planes and were slightly faster than the Independence-class ships that had come before.

Fact Box

USS *Monterrey* Specifications
Independence-class light carrier
Size:
   Displacement: 11,000 tons
   Length: 600 feet (at the waterline), 622 feet, 6 inches (overall)
   Beam: 71 feet, 6 inches (at the waterline), 109 feet, 3 inches (extreme)
   Draft: 26 feet
   Crew: 1,560
Propulsion:
   Top speed: 31.6 knots
Horsepower: 100,000
   Drive: Geared turbines
Armament:
   Guns/missiles: 16 40mm antiaircraft guns; 40 20mm antiaircraft guns
Aircraft: 45

One Independence-class carrier, the USS *Princeton* (CVL-28), was sunk by enemy action during World War II. The last surviving Independence-class carrier, the USS *Cabot*, was sold in October 1999 for scrap. Neither Saipan-class ship survives, although both were subsequently converted for other duty prior to decommissioning and scrapping.

The First Escort Carriers

Escort carriers were designed to work in the Atlantic, where it was important to protect merchant convoys. Escorting always remained their primary function, but during the Second World War escort carriers were also used to supplement fleet and light carriers in combat operations, and to transport aircraft from rear areas to the front lines.

Ship's Log

Escort carriers were sometimes called "Jeep Carriers," after the common military ground vehicle. They were also—on occasion, mostly in the newspapers—referred to as "baby flattops."

The first four escort carriers, the Sangamon-class ships, were completed in 1939. The *Sangamon* and her three sister ships, the *Suwanee*, *Chenango*, and *Santee*, were converted from tankers—in fact, they were the only ships in the history of the U.S. Navy to be converted from tankers. During the early stages of World War II, when there was still a shortage of aircraft carriers in the Pacific to combat the Japanese, the Sangamon ships were briefly used.

On June 2, 1941, the USS *Long Island* (AVG 1) became the Navy's first escort carrier to be converted from a cargo ship when it was commissioned at Newport News, Virginia, with Donald B. Duncan in command.

The *Long Island* was originally built as the *Mormacmail*, a cargo ship, by Sun Shipbuilding and Drydock Company, in Chester, Pennsylvania, but was converted in 67 days to a flush-deck carrier.

Ship's Log

The *Long Island* would perform well during World War II, combating German U-boats in the Atlantic Ocean.

The original flight deck, which was built on top of the old cargo ship, stopped well short of the bow, but this was later extended so that the flight deck was as long as the ship itself.

The escort carrier concept worked so well that many more were quickly built, this time from scratch. A sister ship to the *Long Island*, also converted from a cargo ship, was the second escort carrier, but its service was always strictly limited to training.

Fact Box

USS *Long Island* Specifications

Size:

       Displacement: 14,055 tons

       Length: 492 feet

       Beam: 69 feet

       Draft: 26 feet

Armament:

       1 5-inch/51

       2 3-inch/50 DP

       20 20 mm guns

Propulsion:

       Top speed: 17 knots

       Horsepower: 9,000

       Drive: One screw, diesel

       Fuel capacity: 1,295 tons of oil

German Progress

As I noted in the previous chapter, Germany had plans to build its first aircraft carrier during World War I, but those plans were scrapped at the end of the war. In 1937, however, with Germany under the power of Adolf Hitler and his Nazi party and gearing up for war, the country finally began to construct its first two aircraft carriers.

The first was called *Graf Zeppelin* (German for Count Zeppelin), and the second never got past being called "Carrier B." The first was launched on December 8, 1938, whereas the second was never completed.

The *Graf Zeppelin* should have been completed and functional long before it was, but constant battling between the navy and the air force (Luftwaffe) caused numerous delays. By the spring of 1941, the *Graf Zeppelin* was still only 85 percent complete.

As it happened, the Germans fought World War II without an aircraft carrier. In fact, their surface navy wasn't much of a factor in the war. Their U-boats carried the naval load. In 1945,

Ship's Log

In 1947, the war now two years over, the victorious Soviet Union had the *Graf Zeppelin* raised and loaded with loot they had stolen from the Germans. Overloaded as it turned out. While the Soviets were towing the German carrier home it once again sank, this time for good.

with the war almost lost, Hitler ordered that the still-unfinished *Graf Zeppelin* be scuttled (wrecked and sunk) so that it couldn't fall into enemy hands.

The Least You Need to Know

♦ The range of carriers expanded exponentially when a system was developed for them to be refueled from tankers while at sea.

♦ Although the situation was improving, at the beginning of World War II, U.S. aircraft carriers were still not very good at defending themselves.

♦ The development of light and escort carriers proved that flattops could be versatile in their design and purpose.

♦ Because of in-fighting, Germany fought World War II without an aircraft carrier.

Chapter 15

World War II: Part One

In This Chapter

- ◆ The Japanese attack Pearl Harbor
- ◆ The Doolittle Raid on Tokyo
- ◆ Drawing even at the Battle of the Coral Sea
- ◆ The tide turns in favor of the United States at the Battle of Midway

Now we come to by far the most significant period in the history of aircraft carriers: the Second World War. This was the time when the carrier took over from the battleship the lead role when it came to naval power.

So as to not underestimate just how active carriers were in history's largest war, consider this: More aircraft carriers were sunk during World War II (43), than have been built by the United States since (36). (For a complete list of the carriers sunk during the war, see Appendix E.)

Pearl Harbor: Carriers at Sea

On December 7, 1941, the Japanese launched an aircraft carrier-based surprise attack on the U.S. Pacific fleet at Pearl Harbor, in Hawaii, thus beginning American involvement in World War II. Six Japanese carriers were used in the attack, the *Akagi, Kaga, Hiryu, Soryu, Shokaku,* and

Zuikaku. In the first wave of planes from those carriers attacking Pearl Harbor were 132 A6M2 "Zero" fighters, 129 D3A1 "Val" dive-bombers, and 143 B5N2 "Kate" Torpedo Bombers. The Japanese carriers were a key part of the attack, but it was a different story for the American flattops. One key factor of the war was this: All three aircraft carriers of the U.S. Pacific fleet were at sea at the time of the attack and were not damaged.

Aboard a Japanese carrier before Pearl Harbor.

The *Saratoga*, just out of overhaul, was moored at San Diego. The *Lexington* was about 425 miles southeast of Midway, and the *Enterprise* was also at sea, about 200 miles west of Pearl Harbor.

It took the U.S. Navy more than a month to get its act together and launch its first offensive against the Japanese in the Pacific. The first attack was planned for late January 1942. The *Enterprise*—with the commander of the Western Pacific Task Forces, Admiral William F. Halsey, aboard—attacked the Japanese at the Marshall Islands, while the *Yorktown* attacked at the Gilbert Islands.

Neither campaign did much damage, but in the long run, these early campaigns proved to be valuable practice for the pilots, who would carry out far more successful attacks later in the war.

Doolittle Raid

By far the most dramatic attack launched from a U.S. aircraft carrier during the early days of the war occurred on April 18, 1942. On that day 16 B-25 bombers (which we first discussed back in Chapter 6) took off from the USS *Hornet* and flew to Japan, where they bombed a series of Japanese cities, including Tokyo.

The bombers were under the command of Lieutenant Colonel James Doolittle, and the event forever became known as the Doolittle Raid. It proved to be a tremendous morale boost for the United States. Of the 80 men who took off from the *Hornet* that day, 71 survived the mission.

A B-25 takes off from the USS Hornet *to begin the Doolittle Raid.*

The plan had been for Doolittle's planes to land on landing strips in China following their bombing runs, but none of the planes reached the planned landing spots. All but one of the planes crashed, with their crews, for the most part, successfully bailing out. The one plane that did land made it to Vladivostok in Russia.

The raid also had a tremendous effect on Japanese defenses. Forces placed to defend the outer reaches of Japan's conquests were now pulled back to defend the homeland. This made it easier for the United States to "island-hop" its way toward the Japanese mainland—"easier," of course, being a relative term. It wasn't at all easy!

Flattop Facts

The airmen who didn't survive the Doolittle Raid either died when bailing out or were captured and killed by the Japanese.

Battle of the Coral Sea

After Pearl Harbor, for nearly five months, the Japanese had been advancing steadily through the jungle islands of the southwest Pacific toward Australia. In April the Japanese approached the air and sea routes that connected Australia and the United States. If they cut these routes, as they intended to do by invading the islands of New Caledonia, Fiji, and Samoa, they would cut off contact and the vital base of Australia for a buildup of troops.

The Japanese planned to move into Port Moresby, from which they could bomb Australia and control the sea and air routes. The Allies heard of this plan and that the Japanese move was coming in May.

At the end of April 1942 the *Lexington* carrier force and the *Yorktown* carrier force were joined under the command of Rear Admiral Frank Jack Fletcher. The navy sent the two-carrier attack force, supported by its cruisers and destroyers and supplied by its tankers, into the Coral Sea.

 Ship's Log

Battle of the Coral Sea scoreboard:

U.S. losses: One carrier and two other ships sunk; 66 aircraft lost; 543 men killed or wounded.

Japanese losses: One carrier and one other ship sunk; 77 aircraft lost; 1,074 troops killed or wounded.

Early Action

On May 4, the two U.S. carriers launched a surprise attack against another island of the Solomon Islands, Tulagi, which was only 12 miles from Guadalcanal. Several Japanese warships and transports were sunk in the attack. The main portion of the Battle of the Coral Sea, however, began on May 7. In the morning, Japanese planes struck a U.S. oiler and a destroyer, sinking both.

In response, that same morning, planes launched from the *Yorktown* and the *Lexington*. At 11:00 A.M., U.S. planes first located the Japanese carrier *Shoho*. Ninety-three U.S. dive-bombers swarmed over the carrier and sunk her.

Late that afternoon, Japanese planes tried to attack the *Yorktown* and *Lexington*, but their mission was a miserable failure. They couldn't find the ships and turned back to return to their own carrier.

Ship's Log

After bombing the Japanese carrier *Shoho*, Lieutenant Commander R. E. Dixon, a dive-bomber leader, radioed a message back to the *Lexington*: "Scratch one flattop! Dixon to carrier. Scratch one flattop!"

The Japanese planes then accidentally located the *Yorktown*, but mistook it for their own carrier. Six of the Japanese pilots attempted to land on the carrier but were shot down. The others were taken out by American interceptor planes.

Meeting of Enemy Carriers

By May 8, the enemy carrier forces were only 100 miles apart in the Coral Sea, with the *Lexington* and the *Yorktown* groups south of the Japanese carriers.

The United States launched the first salvo with a morning attack upon the *Shokaku*. Dive-bombers managed to hit the Japanese carrier with two bombs, but the ship wasn't dealt a fatal blow. The attack had not been as thorough as planners had hoped it would be because many of the planes from the *Lexington* had gotten lost and had been forced to return to their ship. The *Shokaku* was damaged severely enough, however, that it needed to return to Japan for repairs.

Sinking of the *Lexington*

The Japanese attack on May 8 was more successful. It is good fighter-pilot technique to attack while lined up between your target and the sun. When the enemy tries to see you, they are blinded by the sun directly behind you. Japanese pilots located the *Lexington* and dove out of the sun. They came as low as 50 feet and dropped their torpedo bombs only 1,300 yards from the side of the *Lexington*.

There was a second attack on the *Yorktown*. Bombers and torpedo bombers came after the carrier simultaneously. The *Yorktown* managed to evade several torpedoes. She was dented on both sides by bombs that were near misses. A bomb then struck just behind the island and penetrated five decks down before exploding. Dozens were killed and wounded by the blast and ensuing fire. Crew managed to control the fire and the *Yorktown* continued in the battle. But the ship suffered structural damage and, when the battle was over, it returned to Hawaii for repairs.

The *Lexington* wasn't as lucky. The attack itself had not been enough to finish the *Lexington*, but unfortunately, someone onboard had forgotten to turn off a motor generator, which was standard procedure when damage had been sustained. The motor ignited gasoline vapors deep inside the carrier and the resulting explosion and fire was so severe that "abandon ship" was ordered. Only minutes after the last man had left the ship, the fires reached the ship's torpedoes and the explosions sent her to the bottom.

> **Flattop Facts**
>
> Among the men who had abandoned ship were those who had served on the *Lexington* ever since 1927 when she was first commissioned.

The carrier forces went their separate ways at this point, to lick their respective wounds. But they would meet again the following month in a more decisive battle off the island of Midway.

Essex-Class Carriers

To battle the Axis powers, the United States built a new class of large aircraft carriers. This was the Essex class, and 24 carriers of this class entered the battle between 1942 and 1945. The design was derived from that of the Enterprise-class ships but was much improved.

Fact Box

Essex-Class Aircraft Carrier Specifications

Because specifications changed during the course of the series, a range will be presented in some categories.

Size:

 Displacement: 33,000 tons

 Length: 855–885 feet

 Beam: 93 feet

 Draft: 28 feet

Armament:

 12 5-inch/38

 10–18 40mm quads

 56–62 20mm guns

Propulsion:

 Top speed: 32 knots

 Maximum cruising radius: 10,700 miles at 25 knots or 16,900 miles at 15 knots

 Horsepower: 150,000

 Drive: Four screws; geared turbine

 Fuel capacity: 7,101 tons of oil

They were much larger than the carriers that had come before, and this extra size had been used wisely—to better protect the ship and to enhance the aircraft-operation facilities. The extra protection came in handy against Japanese bombs, torpedoes, and, during the last days of the war, *kamikazes*.

The Essex-class aircraft carriers were equipped to accommodate 37 F6F Hellcats, 36 SB2C Helldivers, and 18 TBM Avengers; or 73 F6F Hellcats (or F4U Corsairs), 15 SB2C Helldivers, and 15 TBM Avengers.

Naval Lingo

Kamikazes were Japanese suicide pilots who flew their planes into U.S. ships during sea battles at the Philippines, Iwo Jima, and Okinawa. The word *kamikaze* means "heavenly wind." It was a term first used in 1570 to describe a typhoon that saved Japan by destroying an invading Chinese fleet. The kamikazes were recruited by Captain Jyo Eiichio, appealing to the pilots' spirit of *bushido*, a concept of martial arts whereby a man is willing to sacrifice his life for a glorious cause.

New to the Essex-class ships was an aircraft elevator and a rectangular flight deck overhang. Both features were built opposite the island.

Bogue Class

New classes of the smaller variety of aircraft carriers were being built as well. The next class of escort carriers, the Bogue class, were completed during 1942 and 1943. There were 10 of them and they, like the Long Island class of ships, were converted from cargo ships. They were built to be very similar to the Long Island class (see Chapter 14) in size and shape. They were better armed, however, with 2 5-inch 38 dual-purpose (DP) guns, 10 40mm quads, and 27 20mm guns.

The other difference was their fuel capacity. The Bogue-class escort carriers could hold 3,420 tons of oil (compared to 1,295 tons capacity on the Long Island class), thus giving these carriers a maximum cruising radius of 22,500 miles when traveling at 17 knots, or 26,300 miles when traveling at 15 knots. They were large enough to accommodate 28 aircraft: 16 FM-2 and 12 TBM.

Casablanca Class

During 1943 and 1944 the Casablanca class of escort carriers was cranked out by shipbuilders in the United States. Never before or since have so many carriers been produced in such a short period of time. Forty-five escort carriers of the Casablanca class were turned out in those crucial two years.

Fact Box

USS *Casablanca* Specifications

Size:

        Displacement: 10,982 tons

        Length: 512 feet

        Beam: 65 feet

        Draft: 22 feet

Armament:

        1 5-inch/38 DP single

        8 40mm twins

        20 20mm guns

Propulsion:

        Top speed: 19 knots

        Maximum cruising radius: 10,200 miles at 15 knots or 7,200 miles at 19 knots

        Horsepower: 9,000

        Drive: Two screws; reciprocating

        Fuel capacity: 2,279 tons of oil

These were the first escort carriers to be built as such from the keel up. They were more streamlined than the escort carriers that had come before. The new ships sported a squared-off stern and two distinctive boiler uptakes at either edge of the flight deck amidships. There was room for 28 planes, usually 12 TBM and 16 FM-2.

Flattop Facts

Five of the Casablanca-class ships were sunk by the enemy during World War II. They were the *Liscome Bay, St. Lô, Gambier Bay, Ommaney Bay,* and *Bismarck Sea.*

Near the end of the war a new class of 19 more escort carriers, the Commencement Bay class, was produced. The first of the line was completed in 1944, but the last were not finished until 1946 when the war was over. These displaced 24,100 tons when carrying a full load. There was now room for 30 planes: 18 F6F and 12 TBM.

Fact Box

INJS *Shokaku* Specifications
Commissioned: 1937
Displacement: 25,000 tons
Length: 844 feet
Width: 100 feet
Aircraft capacity: 84
Armament: 12 triple 25mm antiaircraft guns; 8 twin 5-inch 40 caliber dual-purpose guns

Battle of Midway

The most pivotal battle to ever feature aircraft carriers as the primary weapons was the Battle of Midway, a battle considered by most historians to be the turning point of the Pacific war, the point at which Japanese aggression was first turned back.

The United States was in control of Midway Island when the battle commenced. The Japanese ships arrived from the west, from Tokyo. The U.S. ships were heading west, coming from Pearl Harbor. The two naval forces met just north of Midway Island.

In previous months, the Japanese had had their way. But that was about to change.

U.S. Order of Battle

There were three U.S. aircraft carriers at the battle, which was held between June 3 and June 6, 1942. There was the *Yorktown*, which was heading up Task Force 17, which also included two cruisers and six destroyers. The *Yorktown* had 75 aircraft aboard and was under the command of Rear Admiral Frank Jack Fletcher.

Also at the battle was Task Force 16, which featured two carriers, the *Enterprise* and the *Hornet*. Between them they carried 158 aircraft. There were two squadrons of Wildcat fighters (54 planes), four squadrons of dauntless dive-bombers (75 planes), and two squadrons of Devastator torpedo bombers (29 planes). Task Force 16 was led by Rear Admiral R. Spruance, who was aboard the *Enterprise*. In addition to the two carriers, Task Force 16 included six cruisers, nine destroyers, and four oilers.

Japanese Order of Battle

The Japanese carriers at the battle were split up among four different forces. The main force, Japan's First Fleet, commanded by Admiral I. Yamamoto, featured one light carrier, the *Hosho*, which had eight planes aboard. There were also, in the main fleet, two seaplane carriers, the *Chiyoda* and the *Nisshin*, but neither ship carried any seaplanes. Both had been converted to accommodate midget submarines.

In the First Air Fleet, commanded by Vice Admiral C. Nagumo aboard the fleet carrier *Akagi*, were four carriers. In addition to the *Akagi*, there were the *Kaga*, *Hiryu*, and *Soryu*. This fleet went to battle with 261 aircraft.

The Second Fleet was commanded by Vice Admiral N. Kondo. This fleet featured the light carrier *Zuiho* and its 24 aircraft, as well as two seaplane carriers (the *Chitose* and the *Kamikawa Maru*) which brought 24 float fighters and eight scout planes. The Fifth Fleet, commanded by Vice Admiral M. Hosogoya, contained one carrier, *Junyo*, with 45 aircraft, and a light carrier, *Ryojo*, with 37 planes.

The Japanese fleet had hoped to attack Midway by surprise, much as it had at Pearl Harbor six months before. But, long before Japanese ships neared Midway, their reconnaissance planes spotted U.S. submarines and scout planes in the area, indicating that the element of surprise was lost. They had every reason to believe the United States was waiting for the attack.

On June 2, Nagumo's ships were closing on Midway from the northwest while the American carrier forces had left Pearl Harbor and were headed to a spot 325 miles northeast of Midway to wait for the arrival of the enemy. The fleet was late in arriving at Midway because of bad weather—a long stretch of thick fog had delayed its progress.

The first hostile exchange between the two sides at Midway occurred on June 3, when nine Army Air Force B-17s attacked the Japanese fleet, which at the time was still 570 miles from Midway. No ships were damaged.

June 4 Action

On the morning of June 4, both U.S. task forces were 200 miles north of Midway Island. The first aircraft to be sent aloft were 10 Dauntlesses from Task Force 17 at 4:30 A.M., which went on a search 100 miles to the north. At the same time Admiral Nagumo, his Japanese forces 200 miles south of the island, sent his planes aloft. In all, 171 Japanese planes headed for Midway. There were 36 level bombers from the *Hiryu* and *Soryu*, 99 dive-bombers from the *Akagi* and *Kaga*, and 36 fighters from all of the carriers.

Flattop Facts

On the flight decks of the Japanese carriers, control officers gave the pilots the okay to roll by waving green lanterns.

First contact between the enemy forces came shortly after dawn when a U.S. reconnaissance plane spotted Japanese carriers. Soon thereafter radar picked up the Japanese planes heading for Midway. Within minutes, every U.S. plane available was in the air. The fighters took the lead to engage the incoming Japanese planes. Spruance's Task Force 16 group headed southwest to engage the enemy. Fletcher's Task Force 17 forces picked up their scout planes and headed in the same direction.

From an airstrip on Midway, six new Avenger torpedo bombers and four Marauders took off, heading for the Japanese carriers. As the U.S. bombers approached, antiaircraft guns fired from the Japanese ships below even as Zeroes (Japanese fighter planes) attacked from above. Five Avengers and two Marauders were shot down. One of the Avengers hit the *Akagi* on its way down, but bounced off without doing any damage. None of the U.S. torpedo bombs found their mark. The pilots of American Wildcats and Buffalos tried to intercept the Japanese bombers, but never had the opportunity because they were too busy fighting attacking Zeroes. Seventeen American pilots were shot down that morning.

Things were not going well for U.S. forces down on the island either. The Japanese bombers made it through and successfully dropped their load, destroying the U.S. Marine Corps command post. U.S. antiaircraft fire on the island managed to down only five bombers.

The Japanese attack had been so successful that the commanding pilot radioed back that a second attack should be ordered immediately, that a quick second strike might destroy the Americans' Midway air force. But Japanese military planners didn't take him up on the recommendation. The failure of the earlier bombing raid upon the Japanese fleet had convinced the admirals that no second attack on Midway would be necessary.

U.S. Offensive

Instead it was the United States that went on the offensive. Spruance, his flattops heading west at top speed, decided to attack the Japanese carriers from afar, a dangerous decision since pilots were bound to run extremely low on fuel on their return trips to their carriers. But Spruance hoped that the element of surprise would make up for these risks. He held back only 36 planes to protect his own fleet in case of a counterattack.

At 7:55 A.M. on June 4, 16 U.S. Marine Corps dive-bombers arrived in the skies above the Japanese carriers. But again the Japanese got the best of the situation. Eight of the planes, fully half, were shot down. Of the eight that returned, only two were in good enough shape to ever fly again. One plane made it back to its ship with 259 bullet holes in it.

Minutes after the failed marine raid, 15 air force B-17s dropped their bombs from 20,000 feet up, but they didn't strike any Japanese ships. When the Japanese forces realized that the U.S. ships were approaching as fast as they could, they were startled.

The Japanese leaders now had a problem. Nagumo had dive-bombers and torpedo bombers aboard the *Hiryu*, *Soryu*, *Akagi*, and *Kaga* ready to go. But they had no escorts. The standby and second-wave fighters that might have provided that escort had already been sent into action, to engage U.S. aircraft that were attacking.

As Admiral Nagumo was trying to figure out what to do, a further complication arrived in the form of crippled Japanese planes returning from the Midway bombing. Only after recovering these aircraft did Nagumo again consider his options regarding the advancing U.S. Navy. At 9:18 A.M., feeling like a sitting duck as he headed in a beeline for Midway, Nagumo ordered the First Fleet to change course, an evasive 90°. He hoped that this would at least delay the attack that was coming.

By this time Fletcher's task force had arrived within striking distance of the Japanese ships and launched 35 planes. Eight Wildcats held back and circled above Task Force 17 to look out for attacks. The 35 attacking planes missed their target, however, because of Nagumo's evasive move. Some of the planes managed to refuel on Midway Island but others crashed into the sea.

"Scratch Three Flattops"

The first U.S. planes to reach the Japanese fleet were 16 Devastator torpedo bombers from the USS *Hornet*. These pilots knew that they were virtually on a suicide mission, for they had no margin for error when it came to fuel. They came in at sea level to make a run at the Japanese ships, but Japanese Zeroes attacked them and wiped them out. Only one American pilot survived.

Next, a group of bombers from the *Enterprise* attacked the *Soryu*, but 11 of the 14 were shot down. A third attack from the *Yorktown* was equally disastrous, with 13 of 14 aircraft being lost. Things looked plenty bleak, but then luck turned when a pilot from the *Enterprise*, Lieutenant Commander Clarence McCluskey, spotted four Japanese carriers sailing in a diamond formation. They were the *Hiryu*, *Akagi*, *Kaga*, and *Soryu*. All four had been a part of the Pearl Harbor attack.

At 10:20 A.M., McCluskey and a squadron of Dauntlesses attacked the *Kaga*. The Zeroes protecting the carrier were all far below, still at the proper altitude to wipe out more torpedo bombers. The U.S. bombers dove at the *Kaga* and *Akagi* at a 70° angle. Three bombs hit the *Akagi* and four struck the *Kaga*. Aboard the *Kaga* the captain and most of the officers were killed when a bomb struck the bridge. Eight minutes later Dauntlesses from the *Yorktown* hit the *Soryu* with three bombs. All three Japanese carriers were destined to sink. Admiral Nagumo got off his ship via rope. The captain of the *Soryu* bravely went down with his ship.

Sinking of the *Yorktown*

Admiral Yamamoto, who was nearby aboard the battleship *Yamato*, ordered his Japanese naval forces to continue attacking, despite their huge losses. They still had four light carriers afloat so the battle could continue.

At 11 A.M., 24 planes from the *Hiryu*, the lone remaining Japanese fast carrier, with Rear Admiral Tamon Yamaguchi in command, were launched. These planes attacked the carrier *Yorktown*, and their bombs caused severe damage.

Because of this success, and knowing that there were other U.S. carriers in the area, Yamaguchi launched a second attack at 12:45 P.M. This time the Japanese pilots only had enough fuel remaining for a one-way trip. So this second attack was the last for the Japanese pilots, but it was also enough to finish off the *Yorktown*, the ship known as "Waltzing Matilda." The order to "abandon ship" was given by the captain at 3 P.M.

The attack finished the *Yorktown*, but it had also supplied Spruance with the precise location of the *Hiryu*. The admiral ordered 24 dive-bombers to launch immediately and head toward the *Hiryu* without fighter escort. (Technically, another attack, a submarine torpedo on June 6, actually sunk the *Yorktown*, but it was dead in the water at that point.)

Those bombers arrived in the skies over the *Hiryu* at about 5 P.M. Aboard the *Hiryu* preparations were being made for another attack, another attack that would never occur. Four bombs hit the *Hiryu*.

An hour later, B-17s from Midway tried to dish out the death blow, but their bombs missed. As it turned out, no further blow was necessary. The *Hiryu* was done, the fourth Japanese aircraft carrier to be sunk during the Battle of Midway. Both Admiral Yamaguchi and the ship's captain tied themselves to the bridge of the sinking ship to make sure that they went down with their vessel.

Flattop Facts

The *Hiryu* was scuttled and took 416 men down with her.

As midnight approached on June 4, Admiral Yamamoto ordered Admiral Nagumo to continue to fight, but Nagumo refused. He was instantly replaced. While this was going on, the United States continued to fly planes off its carriers and destroyed a Japanese heavy cruiser.

Final Midway Scoreboard

During the battle the United States lost …

◆ 99 carrier aircraft

◆ 38 land-based aircraft

◆ 1 aircraft carrier (*Yorktown*)

◆ 1 destroyer (*Hammann*)

The Japanese losses included …

◆ 4 fleet carriers

◆ 1 heavy cruiser

◆ 1 oiler

◆ 250 aircraft

And so ended the phase of the war in which the Japanese could be said to be "winning." The tide had turned. In the next chapter, we'll move on to the second phase of the war and consider the aircraft carrier's role in the difficult but systematic destruction of the Axis powers.

The Least You Need to Know

◆ All three of the U.S. carriers based at Pearl Harbor were out at sea at the time of the Japanese sneak attack in 1941.

◆ The Doolittle Raid over Tokyo in 1942 was a carrier-based attack.

◆ Japan and the United States broke even at the Battle of the Coral Sea, in terms of carriers sunk, each losing one flattop.

◆ The U.S. aircraft carrier *Yorktown* was sunk during the battle of Midway, but four Japanese carriers were sunk in return, turning the tide of the war.

Chapter **16**

World War II: Part Two

In This Chapter

◆ Closing in on Japan

◆ Action in the Atlantic

◆ Returning to the Philippines

◆ Fending off kamikaze fighters

◆ Taking Okinawa

After the Battle of Midway, the war in the Pacific took a positive turn for the United States. U.S. forces were now on the offensive, and the Japanese were on the defensive. But that didn't mean that things got any easier. In fact, the battles became larger and bloodier as the U.S. Navy pushed westward—ever farther from Pearl Harbor and closer to Tokyo—and the Japanese became more desperate.

By this time, the United States also had a decided advantage in terms of aircraft carriers. The air power supplied by the U.S. Navy's flattops would be a determining factor in every battle, right up until the Japanese surrender in 1945.

Island Hopping

The U.S. Navy took the Pacific Ocean back from the Japanese, with the help of the other branches of the American military, one island at a time. After Midway, there were only two more true carrier-on-carrier battles in the Pacific. These were the fight for control of the Solomon Islands on August 24, 1942, and the Battle of Santa Cruz on October 26, 1942.

The hero of the Santa Cruz action was the *Enterprise*, which returned to action just in time. The *Enterprise* and the USS *Hornet* took on a quartet of Japanese carriers, the *Shokaku, Zuikaku, Zuiho,* and *Junyo*. The Japanese managed to sink the *Hornet* with a combination attack from torpedo bombers and dive-bombers. The ship was damaged beyond repair and was about to be scuttled to avoid capture when Japanese destroyers sunk her with another salvo of torpedoes. From the Battle of Santa Cruz on, each Pacific battle would be a little farther west than the one before—in other words, a little closer to Japan.

A Japanese bomb astern a U.S. carrier during the Battle of Santa Cruz.

In the Atlantic

The Pacific Ocean wasn't the only theater of action for U.S. aircraft carriers during World War II. There was also a flattop fight going on against the German forces of fascism in the Atlantic Ocean.

The war started out as a battle between the British and German navies for control of the Atlantic Ocean and the Mediterranean Sea. After Pearl Harbor was attacked in the Pacific and the United States joined the war, the U.S. Navy took up the fight against the Germans in the Atlantic as well.

The Ark and the Flood

Key to these battles was the HMS *Ark Royal*, which put up a good fight before it was fatally damaged on November 13, 1941. While sailing in the Mediterranean Sea only 50 miles from Gibraltar, the *Ark Royal* was hit in the starboard side by a single torpedo fired from a German U-boat.

The carrier began to list immediately, but there was still hope that the damage could be contained and she could be towed back to port safely. Unfortunately, flooding in the center boiler rooms washed out the ship's main electrical switchboard. Power was lost, shutting down the pumps that were furiously attempting to control the flooding. She stayed afloat for 14 hours, but finally went down.

Ship's Log

The *Ark Royal* was the third of nine Royal Navy aircraft carriers sunk during the Second World War.

Torch and Leader

For the United States, Air Group 4 led the way, led by the aircraft carrier USS *Ranger*, which was operating in the Atlantic when the United States entered the war. Air Group 4 was involved in Operation Torch and Operation Leader.

In Operation Torch, the USS *Ranger* and her air group supported the invasion of North Africa in 1942. Operation Leader involved attacks on German shipping and port facilities along the Norwegian coast. The *Ranger* Air Group also performed anti-submarine patrol and convoy escort duty in the North Atlantic.

Skipping Truk

Back in the Pacific, the front had now moved 2,400 miles west of Pearl Harbor. Before the U.S. Navy could attack the Marianas, the next step in the island-hopping westward, its forces had to neutralize the Japanese forces on Truk, in the Caroline Islands.

To do this, military planners ordered a bold strike by carrier aircraft. On February 16 and 17, 1944, a U.S. aircraft carrier task force attacked the heavily garrisoned and defended island of Truk. During these intense raids, U.S. carrier aircraft shot down 275 Japanese aircraft and sank 200,000 tons of shipping.

The destruction of Truk from the air was complete. The original plan had been to invade Truk following the bombardment. In Washington, D.C., however, Admiral Ernest King decided to bypass the 100,000 Japanese defenders on Truk and to move on to the Mariana Islands, the capture of which King felt was more important. So the U.S. forces headed on to the Marianas, confident that the remaining Japanese on Truk no longer had the capability to attack them from behind.

To prevent the Japanese from replenishing their supplies and equipment on Truk, the United States regularly reattacked the island, keeping the Japanese at a level of effectiveness considered safe. In April, the United States again bombed Truk, destroying most of the Japanese aircraft on the ground. Still, the Japanese brought in more planes.

> **Ship's Log**
>
> The invasion of the Marianas was called Operation Forger. It included 535 U.S. Navy ships and a land force of 127,751 soldiers and marines.

Even amid U.S. attacks, the Japanese worked furiously to get ready for the battle at the Marianas. New planes and pilots were ferried into position. The new planes worked just fine, but the new Japanese pilots had been hurriedly trained and, as it turned out, they would be no match for their American counterparts.

Philippine Sea

The Battle of the Philippine Sea began on June 19, 1944. The sea battle was fought in preparation for the island invasions of the principal Mariana Islands, those being Saipan, Tinian, and Guam. Those three battles took up much of the summer of 1944 for the soldiers and marines who took part in the land battles.

As the U.S. forces began to invade the Marianas, the Japanese moved its mobile fleet into the vicinity to counterattack. This force included nine carriers, with 473 aircraft. There were also 13 cruisers and 28 destroyers in the fleet. The carriers were kept far apart from one another. They had learned from their mistakes at Midway, where they had their carriers so close to one another that U.S. planes could spot and attack more than one at the same time.

As the war pushed westward the Americans' show of force became increasingly awesome. The navy came to the battle of the Marianas with seven large fleet carriers, eight light carriers, seven battleships, 13 light cruisers, and 69 destroyers. The force was more than one and a half times the size of the Japanese force that showed up.

*U.S. Task Force in the
Philippine Sea.*

U.S. planes on those carriers included …

◆ 475 Grumman F6F Hellcat fighters

◆ 232 Curtiss SB2C Helldiver dive-bombers

◆ 184 Grumman TBF Avenger dive-bombers

Planes from the USS *Hornet* were launched to destroy Japanese planes on the ground
on Saipan. The Japanese response came in four waves, but in what became known as
the "Marianas Turkey Shoot," the Zeroes were confronted by U.S. fighters. The
Americans dominated the dogfight.

Of the 430 Japanese planes that attacked the *Hornet*, all but 35 were shot down. In
addition to dominating the air above the battle, U.S. planes also launched a successful
attack on the Japanese carriers *Shokaku*, *Taiho*, and *Hiyo*, sinking all three.

Only 26 U.S. aircraft were lost in dogfights or to Japanese antiaircraft fire from ships
and on land. Another 80, however, were lost on the evening of June 21, 1944, when,
shot up and low on fuel, they failed to successfully land back on their carriers. Some,
memorably, landed and crashed on the decks of their carriers. Others ditched at sea
and, thankfully, most of these pilots were recovered by rescue parties.

An F6F Hellcat crash lands on the USS Enterprise.

Ship's Log

Some of the most stunning film footage taken during World War II shows planes from U.S. aircraft carriers returning from battle, some of them shot up and on fire from antiaircraft fire or because of dogfights. One of the best places to see this footage is in the documentary *Victory at Sea*. Originally presented as 26 half-hour episodes on NBC-TV, the documentary first aired from October 26, 1952, though April 26, 1953, and is currently available on videocassette in a six-tape pack from New Line Studios. It also has a great soundtrack, written by Richard Rodgers, of Broadway musical fame.

Leyte Gulf: The Greatest Battle

The Battle of Leyte Gulf, which preceded the U.S. invasion of the Philippine Islands and their subsequent liberation from the Japanese, has been called the greatest naval battle in history. A total of 282 ships fought in the battle and 187,000 sailors were involved. It was during this battle that the Japanese ceased to be a naval power. Four Japanese carriers were sunk, along with 22 other ships.

Down Goes the *Princeton*

One of the biggest explosions of the war—it looked like a mushroom cloud—came when the USS *Princeton* was struck by a bomb from a Japanese bomber on October 24, 1944, during the Battle of Leyte Gulf near the Philippines. The plane had emerged from low-hanging clouds and evaded fire from the *Princeton*'s antiaircraft guns.

" " **Ship's Log**

According to historian Edwin P. Hoyt, by the time the U.S. Navy fought in the Battle of Leyte Gulf, its flattops had a phenomenal new weapon: "Radar had been so far improved," he writes, "that night fighters could be sent out from the deck of the carriers on the blackest night, directed to find enemy aircraft, destroy them, and come home, seeing the enemy perhaps only for a moment before opening fire."

The bomber dropped one 500-pound bomb from an altitude of less than 1,200 feet. The bomb struck just forward of the aft elevator. Flames from the explosion shot down to the engineering space and in the hangar and destroyed the ship's firefighting system.

When the flames reached the fuel supply, the resulting explosion caused hundreds of casualties, most on ships that had come alongside to launch a rescue effort, by turning a huge portion of the ship into flying shrapnel. When the *Princeton* had been successfully abandoned, it was sunk by U.S. torpedoes so it couldn't cause any further damage.

Kamikazes: The Aircraft Carrier's Worst Enemy

Kamikazes first struck at Allied ships upon the aftermath of the Battle of Leyte Gulf, in the Philippines, on October 25, 1944. In a span of four hours on that day, kamikazes sank one American aircraft carrier, the *St. Lô*, and damaged four more.

By January 9, 1945, the toll from kamikazes had risen to 8 ships sunk, 7 heavy carriers damaged, and another 20 ships damaged.

Flattop Facts

The Battle of Leyte Gulf featured the only time a super battleship, the Japanese *Musashi*, was sunk entirely by an attack from aircraft—carrier-based aircraft to boot.

Leyte Gulf Scoreboard

The United States fared far better than the Japanese in the Battle of Leyte Gulf, as the following stats indicate.

United States:

◆ One light carrier

◆ Two escort carriers

- Two destroyers
- One destroyer escort

Japan:

- One fleet carrier
- Three light carriers
- Three battleships
- Six heavy cruisers
- Four light cruisers
- Eleven destroyers

Iwo Jima: Marines in Hell

The U.S. Navy also encountered kamikazes at the Battle of Iwo Jima during February 1945. During the battle, one of the bloodiest of the war, fought over the course of a month and won by the U.S. Marines, the fleet was attacked by several kamikaze planes, but nothing like what the fleet would suffer several months later at Okinawa.

The escort carrier *Bismarck Sea* was sunk on February 21 when a suicide pilot slammed his Zero into the ship's flight deck, setting off a series of explosions. During that same attack the *Saratoga* was also badly damaged and forced to return to Pearl Harbor. Another escort carrier, an LST, and a transport were slightly damaged.

Despite this success of the suicide pilots off Iwo Jima, the kamikaze attacks were few as the Japanese decided to gather up what was left of their air force for an all-out kamikaze attack on the U.S. Navy off Okinawa, the site of the war's final battle.

The *Franklin* Gets Too Close

On March 19, 1945, the carrier USS *Franklin* had maneuvered close to the Japanese mainland—only 50 miles offshore. Planes from her flight deck were running predawn bombing attacks on land targets. Then a lone Japanese plane came through the clouds, made a low run on the ship, and dropped two armor-piercing bombs.

One bomb struck the flight deck centerline, penetrating to the hangar deck. The bomb also ignited fires through the second and third decks and knocked out the combat information center and air plot.

The second bomb struck aft and tore through two decks, detonating ammunition, bombs, and rockets. The *Franklin* lay dead in the water, developed a 13° starboard list, and lost all radio communications. Casualties totaled 724 killed and 265 wounded. The ship, amazingly, remained afloat and even made it back to Pearl Harbor for repairs.

Okinawa: Full Wrath of the Kamikazes

By March 1945 only one major Japanese stronghold stood between an experienced and unified U.S. force—sailors, soldiers, airmen, and marines—and the Japanese mainland: the banana-shaped, mountainous, 60-mile-long island of Okinawa, just 350 miles southwest of mainland Japan.

Since the Middle Ages, the island had been a vassal kingdom of both China and Japan. It had been legally part of the Japanese empire since 1879. Now a massive armada approached. One hundred twenty thousand Japanese troops were waiting.

The kamikaze attacks off Okinawa started on March 25, when 26 kamikazes attacked all at once. Eight hit their mark. The battleship *Nevada*, a survivor at Pearl Harbor, took a direct hit. Five days later the cruiser *Indianapolis* was struck and badly damaged.

The next day, the British Pacific Fleet joined the U.S. Fifth Fleet in the attack on Okinawa. The Brit Fleet, under the command of Admiral Sir Bernard Rawlings, featured four carriers, the *Indefatigable*, *Indomitable*, *Victorious*, and *Illustrious*.

> **Flattop Facts**
>
> A kamikaze struck the flight deck of the *Indefatigable*, a direct hit, on April 1, 1945—but a tireless effort by the crew cleared away the rubble and the ship continued to function close to normally for the remainder of the battle.

The True Deluge

On April 6, the true deluge of kamikazes would begin, and the carnage would be the worst the U.S. Navy had ever known. Nine hundred Japanese aircraft, more than two-thirds of which were kamikazes, attacked the U.S fleet that day. During the first 24 hours of the attack it looked like Japan's plan might work, as ship after ship received direct hits. In addition to other damage, three destroyers, two ammunition ships, and an LST were sent to the bottom of the East China Sea.

On April 6, two allied destroyers, one destroyer minesweeper, and two ammunition cargo ships were sunk. On April 7, a kamikaze managed to dive into the USS *Hancock*'s flight deck, causing 800 casualties and crippling the ship.

The *Intrepid* (the same ship that is now a permanent floating museum in New York City—discussed later in this chapter) was hit and damaged by a kamikaze on April 16. The USS *Sangamon* was severely damaged on May 4.

Flattop Facts

There were several other strikes on British carriers by kamikazes during May 1945 but none cost the ships more than a few hours of down time. After the war, the thick armor used in British carriers was given credit for making so many kamikazes "bounce off."

Also on May 4, kamikazes struck two of the British carriers. A kamikaze struck the flight deck of the *Formidable* and exploded, causing 56 casualties and destroying many of the aircraft that had been parked there. Amazingly, the ship was back in action, launching and recovering planes, six hours after the kamikaze struck.

The *Indomitable* was the other British ship struck on May 4, but it got lucky, as the kamikaze bounced off the flight deck and into the ocean without causing any damage.

The Deadliest Kamikaze Attack

But the worst was yet to come. The deadliest single attack to an aircraft carrier came on May 11 when two kamikazes struck the USS *Bunker Hill*, killing 396 crew members and wounding 264. Three days later a multitude of kamikazes attacked the USS *Enterprise*, killing 14 and wounding 34. The *Enterprise* was put out of action for good that day.

Explosion on the USS Bunker Hill, May 1945.

Even with all these successes, the kamikaze offensive was one of diminishing returns. As time went on, through April and May and into June, and the battle at Okinawa grew older, the kamikazes came fewer in number—attrition being the obvious factor here—and fewer got through to their targets due to the increased ability of the navy's antiaircraft gunners to shoot them down before they could do any damage. The sailor gunmen were learning on the job. The final kamikaze to injure an aircraft carrier during World War II struck on June 7, when a Japanese suicide pilot's plane blasted a 30-foot hole in the flight deck of the Casablanca-class escort carrier, the USS *Natoma Bay*, which was at the time about 50 miles east of the southernmost Ryuku Islands, not far from mainland Japan.

Also destroyed in this attack was a plane that had been in the catapult. The plane was catapulted into the sea so its fire would not spread. As was the case on many of the carriers struck by suicide pilots, within hours operations were back to normal.

The Great American Advantage

One thing that the Americans learned was that, in combat, a man who wants to live has a great advantage over an enemy who wants to die. To further reduce the threat of kamikaze disaster, the U.S. fleet repositioned 16 *radar-picket destroyers* to better supply early warnings of kamikaze attacks.

Although the strategy was a sound one from the viewpoint of the entire fleet, it was hell on the men on those destroyers, whose ships now became targets themselves for the kamikazes. The destroyers became such targets for the kamikazes that, after one grueling battle, sailors aboard one battle-weary destroyer placed a huge arrow-shaped sign onboard their ship reading "Carriers this way."

Among the U.S. ships heavily damaged were the aircraft carriers *Enterprise*, *Hancock*, and *Bunker Hill*, flagship of Admiral Raymond A. Spruance, commander of the Fifth Fleet. On the *Bunker Hill* alone, where two kamikazes had made direct hits within the space of one minute on May 11, 396 crewmen were killed.

Naval Lingo

Radar-picket destroyers are the first line of defense that a naval fleet has. They form a perimeter around the fleet, then use their radar to give an early warning of an attack, and their guns to help slow down the attack.

Flattop Facts

The British ships of Task Force 57, also off Okinawa, fared much better than the American ships—in particular the aircraft carriers. Their decks were armored to prevent damage from shellfire, such as a ship might encounter in narrower European waters, and therefore sustained only minor damage, even when suffering a direct hit from a kamikaze.

More than 5,000 American sailors died from kamikaze attacks. Another 4,824 were wounded. Thirty-two U.S. ships were sunk and another 368 were damaged. It was the bloodiest battle in the history of the U.S. Navy. Despite this, the Japanese plan had failed miserably.

The U.S. fleet remained. The invading troops were not stranded, and the Japanese forces on Okinawa were slowly vanquished in blood. The only remaining action of the war was the dropping of atom bombs on the cities of Hiroshima and Nagasaki and the Japanese surrender.

King of the Fleet: Replacing Battleships

When the United States entered World War II, its battleships were considered its most potent naval weapon—but that had changed by the end of the war.

Predominantly because of the increased value of carrier-based aircraft—fighters and bombers, especially—aircraft carriers were the most feared ships on the ocean by war's end. And that has remained the case ever since.

A Floating Museum and War Memorial

The *Intrepid*, which played a key role in World War II and is one of the most successful and battle-tested ships in U.S. Navy history, has since 1982 been one of the top tourist attractions in New York City. The carrier is berthed on the Hudson River along the western shore of the island of Manhattan.

Creative and Interactive

Visitors don't just get an up-close view of an aircraft carrier, which is quite an experience in itself, but they also get to visit a creative and interactive museum with diverse sea, air, and space exhibits.

In addition to the *Intrepid*, visitors to the museum are also able to tour the destroyer USS *Edson* and the guided-missile submarine USS *Growler*, which are docked next door. On the flight deck of the *Intrepid* are more than 25 aircraft, which are arranged so that they tell the story of naval aviation.

It Is the Artifact!

Museum exhibits range from actual artifacts to relevant installations about current events such as "Intrepid Remembers 9/11" and "Defending our Future." Visitors can ride in an A-6 Cockpit Simulator and visit the Virtual Flight Zone.

Most museums are buildings filled with artifacts. The *Intrepid*, however, is the artifact. As the Intrepid website notes, "The decks of this ship are hallowed ground where men fought and died for the ideals of this nation. This, 'it happened here', experience makes every visit to the *Intrepid* an adventure through history."

Flattop Facts

In addition to the exhibits, the museum offers many educational programs, and the flight deck can be rented out for parties and corporate events.

The Least You Need to Know

- After Midway, there were only two more true carrier-on-carrier battles in the Pacific: the battles of the Solomon Islands and Santa Cruz.

- In the Atlantic, Great Britain lost nine aircraft carriers during the Second World War.

- During the Battle of the Marianas, U.S. carrier-based aircraft sunk three Japanese carriers and shot down hundreds of Japanese planes.

- One of the biggest explosions of the war came when the USS *Princeton* was struck by a bomb from a Japanese bomber during the Battle of Leyte Gulf.

- During the last battle of the war, at Okinawa, the Japanese unleashed their most desperate weapon, the kamikaze.

Part 5

The Modern Era

Flattops tend to change to accommodate the changing aircraft they must carry. The biggest change in carrier aircraft since World War II has been from prop planes to jets. We'll examine the early carrier jets and their role during America's participation in a pair of Asian civil wars—in Korea and Vietnam. Then we'll look at the role of carriers during the Falklands War (fought between Great Britain and Argentina), U.S. attacks on Libya following terrorist acts by that nation, the first Persian Gulf War, and the liberation of Kuwait.

Next, we'll look at how carriers helped U.S. forces to a swift victory in Iraq during Operation Iraqi Freedom in the spring of 2003. These carriers include the USS *Abraham Lincoln*, the very ship you toured at the beginning of the book.

Since the United States is not the only country to have flattops in their fleet, we'll look at foreign aircraft carriers of today. Finally, we'll take a tour of the U.S. Navy's newest CVN—the USS *Ronald Reagan*.

The Transformation to Jet Propulsion

In This Chapter

- ◆ The development of the Midway class
- ◆ Jet-propelled planes come into their own
- ◆ The Flying Stovepipe and other failed innovations
- ◆ The *Saratoga* and the *Independence* become guinea pigs for nuclear testers

Because World War II ended during the summer of 1945, the Axis powers never had to face the wrath of the Midway class of large aircraft carriers. They were being built during the war, but were not finished until peacetime had returned.

Bigger and Better Carriers

The ships were the *Midway*, of course, which debuted in the autumn of 1945, the *Franklin D. Roosevelt*, which hit the waves later that year, and the *Coral Sea*, which bowed in 1946. The Midway-class carriers were superior to their predecessors in every way.

The previous largest aircraft carrier had been the *Saratoga*, which displaced 33,000 tons. The Midway-class carriers displaced 45,000 tons. Because this class of ships was so much larger, the antiaircraft guns could be relocated off of the flight deck and onto a continuous protruding platform, called a sponson, along the sides of the superstructure.

Flattop Facts

Another improvement of the Midway class over the Essex class was the positioning of the 5-inch gun batteries. It was no longer necessary to fire across the flight deck when firing to port.

One lesson learned during World War II was that aircraft carriers, when damaged during an attack, were not well-equipped to remain watertight, or to make quick emergency repairs, as were battleships of comparable size. With the Midway class, this inequity was eliminated.

The new class of carriers was equipped to accommodate either 97 F4U Corsairs and 48 SB2C Helldivers; or 73 Corsairs, 27 F8F Bearcats, and 32 F7F Tigercats.

Fact Box

Midway-Class Aircraft Carrier Specifications
Size:
Displacement: 45,000 tons
Length: 968 feet
Beam: 113 feet
Draft: 33 feet
Armament:
18 5-inch/54 DP
21 40mm quads
28 20mm guns
Propulsion:
Top speed: 33 knots
Horsepower: 212,000
Drive: Four screws, geared turbines

After the War: Change in Aircraft

As is customary at the end of a large war, the government and the people became strongly antiwar and preferred to spend their money and attention on other things.

Much of the great U.S. Navy, which had helped defeat the Axis powers, was now dismantled.

Between 1945 and 1950 there were many technological improvements in aircraft carriers, but putting those improvements to practical use cost money, and the U.S. Congress wasn't providing the military with very much of that.

The major change in aircraft carriers between the end of World War II (1945) and the beginning of the United States's participation in the Korean War (1950) was in the aircraft themselves. The familiar prop planes that had been used in the Big One were being replaced by jets and helicopters.

> **Flattop Facts**
>
> By 1950, the United States only had 270 ships commissioned in its navy. Nineteen of those were aircraft carriers, 15 ready for service and four undergoing modifications. At the time of the Pearl Harbor attack in 1941, the U.S. Navy had 233 ships. By the end of World War II the size of the navy peaked at 571 ships.

Phantom Is First

The move from prop planes to jets actually started during World War II. On August 30, 1943, the Navy approved a design by McDonnell Aircraft Corporation of St. Louis, Missouri, for a jet-propelled fighter. The first two prototypes were completed during the fall of 1944.

One prototype passed its initial flight test but crashed on its second flight. The other prototype executed several test flights and was delivered early in 1945. The Navy liked what it saw and, during the spring of 1945, ordered 130 of them. This order was made while World War II raged on and an invasion of Japan seemed inevitable. When the Japanese surrendered, the order for jets by the Navy was cut back to 60.

That first jet ordered into production by the Navy was the FH-1 Phantom. On July 21, 1946, operating from the USS *Franklin D. Roosevelt*, an FH-1 Phantom became the first jet-propelled combat aircraft to operate from an American aircraft carrier. The pilot was Lieutenant Commander James Davidson.

The first carrier-based jet, the Phantom, was also the navy's first airplane to fly faster than 500 mph. McDonnell built 62 Phantoms between 1945 and 1947. By the following year, the USS *Saipan* became the first U.S. carrier to feature an all-jet squadron.

Fact Box

Phantom FH-1 Specifications

First flight: Jan. 26, 1945

Wingspan: 40 feet, 9 inches (wings folded, 16 feet, 3 inches)

Length: 38 feet, 9 inches

Height: 14 feet, 2 inches

Weight: 10,035 lbs.

Speed: 500 mph (max.)

Ceiling: 41,100 feet

Range: 695 miles

Accommodation: One crew

Armament: Four 22mm cannons

Power plant: Two 1,600-pound thrust Westinghouse J30-WE-20 turbojets

Pirates on the Deck—*Not!*

In 1944, while the Phantom was still being designed, the navy also contracted with the Chance Vought Division of United Aircraft, producers of the F4U Corsair, to build a carrier-based lightweight jet-propelled interceptor/fighter.

Naval Lingo

Metalite consisted of balsa wood bonded between two thin sheets of aluminum alloy. Used to cover plane fuselages, Metalite was both lightweight and strong.

The resulting jet, the Vought XF6U-1 Pirate, had several innovations. It was the first navy plane to have wingtip drop tanks and afterburners. It was also the first jet to be built of *Metalite*.

The Pirate had only one engine and a large dorsal fin. Test flights of the first prototypes began in 1946. During initial tests the jet was found to be somewhat underpowered and difficult to handle at slow speeds—not a good trait for a carrier-based jet.

The Pirate was sometimes called a "flying stovepipe" because it had its intake in the nose and exhaust in the tail. It was fitted with straight wings that were mounted on the middle of the body.

To aid the handling problems noted in the experimental model, small "finlets" near the ends of the horizontal tail plane were added. Though the navy was aware that there were bugs in the design that needed to be ironed out, they ordered 65 of them in 1947. The jet was now known as the F6U-1.

Fact Box
F6U-1 Pirate Specifications
Wingspan: 32 feet, 10 inches
Length (with afterburner): 37 feet, 7 inches
Height: 12 feet, 11 inches
Weight empty: 9,200 pounds
Weight gross: 12,571 pounds
Maximum speed: 564 mph at 20,000 feet
Range: 730 miles
Service ceiling: 49,000 feet
Power plant: Westinghouse J34-WE-3 turbojet

The first production model first flew on March 5, 1949. The navy was so unimpressed that it cut the production order in half, and out of the 30 that were eventually built, only one was actually used, and that only for photo-reconnaissance.

The Fury of North America

North American, the F6U-1 manufacturer, had better luck with its design for a jet-propelled, carrier-based aircraft. The result of its research and development was the all-metal construction XFJ-1 Fury, which was first flight-tested in 1946.

Although the cockpit canopy blew off during one flight forcing the pilot to land—safely—while semiconscious, the tests went well overall and the navy ordered 100 of them. The Fury was assigned to the USS *Boxer* in the Pacific beginning in 1947. The Fury was the last navy aircraft to have machine guns.

The Furies didn't stay in service for very long. They really needed a carrier that was bigger than those available. More powerful catapults and arresting gear also needed to be developed. The Furies were used only by the naval reserve after 1949.

Flights of the Banshee

During the spring of 1945, as the war was wrapping up, the navy asked McDonnell to come up with a more powerful version of the Phantom, which had only just begun testing. The new carrier-based jet was called the F2H-1 Banshee, and it first tested at the beginning of 1947.

Fact Box

FJ-1 Fury Specifications

Wingspan: 38 feet, 1 inch

Length: 33 feet, 7 inches

Height: 14 feet, 6 inches

Wing area: 275 square feet

Weight empty: 8,843 pounds

Weight gross: 15,600 pounds

Armament: 6 half-inch caliber machine guns

Power plant: 1 Allison J-35-A-2 turbojet

Top speed: 547 mph at 9,000 feet

Fact Box

F2H-2 Banshee Specifications

Wingspan: 44 feet, 10 inches

Length: 40 feet, 2 inches

Height: 14 feet, 6 inches

Wing area: 294 square feet

Weight empty: 11,146 pounds

Weight gross: 22,312 pounds

Power plant: 2 Westinghouse J34-WE-34 turbojet engines

Top speed: 532 mph at 10,000 feet

Ship's Log

The ejector seat, a staple of jet fighters after World War II, was designed by the Martin Baker company in England. The first American pilot to successfully test the ejector seat in flight was Lieutenant J. L. Furin. His Banshee was traveling faster than 500 mph when he ejected himself on August 9, 1949, and parachuted safely to Earth.

The initial Banshee was still not powerful enough and was quickly replaced by the F2H-2, which could carry more fuel than the original and had the ability to be refueled in the air. Night-flying, all-weather, and reconnaissance versions were also built of the Banshee.

Going to the Bottom at Bikini

During the summer of 1946, the United States decided to test the effect of its new atomic bomb, still the same as those used on Japanese cities, on ships at sea. The tests were conducted near Bikini Atoll in the Marshall Islands. Most of the test ships were those captured from the Japanese during the war, but surplus American ships were also used. Among the latter were the aircraft carriers *Independence* and *Saratoga*.

Flattop Facts

The atomic bomb that sunk the USS *Saratoga* was equivalent in force to 23,000 tons of TNT.

There were two bomb tests, named "Able" and "Baker." For the first test, the bomb was exploded in the air over the water. The *Independence* was placed directly below the explosion, while the *Saratoga* was placed 500 yards away. The *Independence* received severe damage but stayed afloat. The *Saratoga*, in a disappointment, was only superficially damaged. Both were extremely radioactive, however.

For the second test, the Baker, a month later, the atom bomb was exploded below the surface of the water. The *Saratoga* was placed 300 yards from the center of the explosion and the *Independence* was floated 500 yards away.

Ship's Log

During the late 1940s, in Great Britain, designers were experimenting with something called "flexideck carriers." It was thought that planes without landing gear would be much lighter and easier to transport. To accommodate them, new aircraft carriers would be built with soft flight decks. The planes could then just belly flop down onto the springy surface. A couple of brave pilots actually landed their planes on the flexideck, but the whole concept was eventually thought to be impractical and was scrapped. This should not be confused with the term "flex deck" in use today, which means that the flight deck is being used to land and recover aircraft at the same time.

This time the *Saratoga* was damaged so severely that, within eight hours of the explosion, she had sunk. The *Independence* didn't sink on its own, but was so hot with radiation that it had to be sent to the bottom with artillery fire.

The military innovations, development, and testing during peacetime didn't last long. By 1950, the U.S. Navy and its carrier groups once again had a job to do. This time it was in a place called Korea—to be discussed in the next chapter.

The Least You Need to Know

- The first postwar carriers were the Midway-class carriers, which were superior in every way to their predecessors.

♦ The first jet-propelled carrier-based aircraft was the Phantom, built by McDonnell.

♦ The Vought XF6U-1 Pirate was the first navy plane to have wingtip drop tanks and afterburners.

♦ The U.S. carriers *Saratoga* and *Independence* were sunk during and after atomic bomb tests in the Marshall Islands.

Chapter 18

The Korean War

In This Chapter

- ◆ The United States enters another war
- ◆ Carriers play a big role in the Korean "police action"
- ◆ Congress approves the development of new carriers
- ◆ The development of pilotless bombers

When World War II ended in 1945, the American people were exhausted by the war and looked forward to many years of peace. But this was not to be. After only five years of peace, the nation—and its carriers—were once again plunged into war. And, just as was the case in the war against Japan, once again the action was on the other side of the Pacific.

Invasion of South Korea

War came in June 1950, when the North Korean army—which was friendly with Communist China—invaded South Korea—which was friendly with the United States. At the time of the invasion, the U.S. Navy had only one aircraft carrier in the western Pacific: the *Valley Forge*. The carrier immediately headed toward the crisis.

Aboard the *Valley Forge* was a mixture of prop planes and jets, including the following craft:

- 30 F9F-2B fighters
- 28 F4U-4B Corsairs
- 14 AD-4 Skyraiders

The F9F-2B fighters, though jets and therefore much faster than the prop planes on the carrier, still had their limitations. They lacked the endurance of the prop planes and they could carry only a half ton of bombs, an extremely small payload.

Picking Sides

First stop for the *Valley Forge* was Subic Bay—on the west coast of Luzon, the largest of the Philippine Islands, just north of the capital city of Manila—where it picked up supplies and ammunition. From there it moved on to the U.S. base at Okinawa, the island off Japan that was the location of World War II's final battle, and waited to see what would happen in Korea's civil war. Predictably, the Chinese joined the North's forces and the United Nations and its allies agreed to help the South.

Another aircraft carrier, Britain's *Triumph*, was in the Okinawa area and joined the *Valley Forge*. The two carriers then headed what was called Task Force 77 (along with several Allied cruisers and destroyers). On July 1, the carriers attacked North Korea for the first time.

This was not to be an all-out war like World War II. The United States and its allies represented a United Nations force, and their actions were to be limited, designed to even up the sides rather than conquer North Korea.

First Attack

Planes and jets from the *Valley Forge* attacked the North Korean capital, Pyongyang. They destroyed an airport, shot down two North Korean planes, and destroyed nine more planes on the ground. Fireflies and Seafires flew off the *Triumph* and attacked the city of Haeju in North Korea.

> **Ship's Log**
>
> In the United States the war was known euphemistically as a "police action."

Later that same day, both carriers sent planes out to attack North Korean railroad lines. All but one of the planes returned undamaged. The wounded plane was a Skyraider from the *Valley Forge*.

The attempt to land the wounded plane didn't go well. The pilot came in "hot" (at too steep of an angle for a safe recovery), and plowed into other planes parked on the flight deck. One Skyraider and two Corsairs were destroyed in the accident, and another six planes were damaged.

The Evolving Task Force

In later attacks, planes from the carriers of Task Force 77 destroyed a petroleum factory at the North Korean port of Wonsan. The carriers also supported the landing of Allied forces at Pohan. By the end of July, the *Valley Forge* had returned to Okinawa. The *Triumph* was detached from the task force and was sent to become part of a blockade of North Korean coastal waters. The *Valley Forge* would now be joined by the U.S carrier *Philippine Sea*. These two were the largest carriers in the task force, each capable of carrying approximately 80 planes.

By the end of the summer of 1950, two more American carriers, the *Sicily* and the *Badoeng Strait*, would be committed to the efforts in Korea. That made six aircraft carriers in all, five American and one British.

Because, from the U.S. point of view, the war on the land was not going well—the North Koreans were very close to booting the Allies off the continent—the aircraft carriers offshore were kept very busy. Planes from all of the carriers flew missions in close support of troops on the ground, often bombing targets very close to the combat lines.

Dogfight with Russian Aircraft

Carrier pilots from Task Force 77 made their first contact with Russian aircraft flying in support of North Korea on September 4, 1950. The task force at that time was only about 100 miles from Soviet naval and air bases at Port Arthur on the Liaotung Peninsula. The Russian aircraft, in other words, were only 10 minutes flight time away from the Allied ships.

At 1:30 P.M., a task force destroyer reported unidentified aircraft approaching from the direction of the Soviet air base. Two divisions of Corsairs, already in the air on combat air patrol, were ordered to intercept the incoming unidentified craft. They found one plane, a Russian bomber, which took evasive action and headed for Korea when it saw the Corsairs approaching.

The lone bomber and the Corsairs fired at one another. The Soviet bomber was struck, caught fire, and crashed into the ocean. That was the end of the Soviet attack. A destroyer later pulled the Russian pilot's body from the water.

Invasion at Inchon

Task Force 77 was next used in support of General Douglas MacArthur's huge land invasion at Inchon on September 15, 1950. While most of the task force's carriers were offshore near Inchon ready for the invasion, the HMS *Triumph* created a diversion on the other side of Korea and then moved quickly to join the other carriers at the site of the invasion. The *Triumph*'s planes bombed and strafed beach sites far away from the actual invasion site, and helped divert North Korean defenses away from Inchon.

For two days before the invasion, planes from the *Valley Forge* and the *Philippine Sea* bombed and strafed the Inchon area, as well as nearby Seoul.

All of the planes from all of the carriers flew air support on the day of the invasion. The invasion was a success, and the Allied troops took control of the area's airfields within 48 hours of the first landings.

Soon after the Inchon invasion, the task force was joined by two more carriers, the British *Theseus* and the American *Leyte*. By October 1950, Task Force 77 had 350 aircraft onboard its carriers.

Supply Line

The aircraft carriers of Task Force 77 became part of the supply line for troops on the east coast of Korea at Wonsan. Because the waters off Wonsan were mined, the normal supply methods wouldn't work, so planes from the aircraft carriers flew the supplies onto land.

The war had been going well. A North Korean offensive had been pushed back by the United Nations forces, made up predominantly of U.S. and South Korean troops. Negotiations had been held and a cease-fire was called. The United Nations proposed a new, unified Korea with its democratic government in the south. Victory appeared close.

Ship's Log

For fear of escalating the war, carrier pilots from Task Force 77 were not allowed to cross the Yalu River, which served as the border between North Korea and Communist China–controlled Manchuria.

In late October, the U.S. Navy was so confident that all but two escort carriers had exited the waters off Korea. Then everything changed. The Chinese joined the battle with North Korea. The Chinese Communists entered the war *en masse*, and Task Force 77 did a quick about-face and returned to the action.

Bridge Attacks

It was essential to destroy North Korean bridges to inhibit North Korean troop movements. B-29s, flying from air bases in South Korea, were having difficulty bombing with sufficient accuracy to destroy North Korean bridges. Task Force 77 took on the job.

The carrier planes were able to destroy the automobile bridge, but the railroad bridge proved to be more stubborn. Although the carrier planes managed to damage this bridge, they couldn't put it out of commission completely.

Carrier Craft Take on MiGs

At the time it was thought that the Soviet MiG jets were the kings of the sky, but their supremacy in the air first came into question when carrier pilot Lieutenant Commander W. T. Amen, flying an F9F, shot down a MiG on November 9. Nine days later, two more MiGs were shot down by carrier pilots.

Encouraged by these successes, Task Force 77 was again beefed up. Now joining it were the light carrier *Bataan* and the escort carrier *Bairoko*. The latter ship carried F-86as, state-of-the-art fighter jets with swept wings and a top speed of 675 miles per hour. They were said to be better than the Soviet MiG.

Growing Forces, New Carriers

But for all the successes in the air, the ground war remained miserable. Allied troops were forced to make major retreats, movements that needed to be covered by the carriers. Meanwhile, the task force grew steadily.

Thirty-nine U.S. aircraft carriers, of various sizes and ages—would eventually be used in the Korean effort. The Korean conflict impressed upon military planners and funders how important aircraft carriers were for protecting the troops, and new carriers were now on their way.

The keel for the *Forrestal* was laid in 1952. Congress authorized the building of another large carrier, the *Saratoga*, that same year. Congress said that one new large carrier every five years seemed about right.

Copter Carriers?

Carriers were now modified so they could accommodate helicopters. (The hangar-to-flight deck elevators had to have their ceilings raised.) Helicopters, of course, because they took off and landed vertically, were much easier to land on a ship and required a much smaller landing area. Helicopters were used as part of the carrier force not only for land operations, but as an antisubmarine weapon as well.

Flattop Facts

It was soon discovered that helicopters were extremely valuable when it came to minesweeping. Not only could helicopters find a mine from above, but they could hover over them and direct minesweepers to the location.

The first carrier equipped to handle helicopters was the *Siboney*. The helicopters were the 31.5-feet-long HUP-2s. These whirlybirds were soon joined in the carrier fleet by the considerably larger HSS-1s, which were 49 feet long and held a crew of four.

The helicopters ran missions to rescue downed airmen behind the lines. They also picked up and delivered special operatives who were working behind enemy lines.

The War Rages On

During the summer of 1951 the Allies launched Operation *Strangle*, which was a blockade designed to cut off all supply lines to the enemy. The carriers of the Task Force worked in support of the blockade, which lasted from June until September.

During this time the task force carriers—which had now been joined by a modernized *Essex*—launched fighters in support of B-29 bombing raids. Planes took off and landed from the carriers offshore night and day.

The Kapsan Crapshoot

The *Essex* had its biggest influence on the war in October 1951 when it successfully launched a raid to destroy a meeting of high-ranking Chinese and Korean Communists in the city of Kapsan, in the mountains of North Korea.

Eight Skyraiders took off from the *Essex* 100 miles from shore, each carrying two half-ton bombs and a napalm bomb. The Skyraiders approached their target at an extremely low altitude, so that they would be beneath the enemy's radar.

The meeting place was completely destroyed by the bombing raid, and it was later learned that 509 Communist officials had been killed. This earned the American pilots the name of "the butchers of Kapsan" on North Korean radio.

Power Rangers

During June 1952, the Allied forces carried out a number of attacks designed to interrupt North Korea's power supply. The primary target was the Suiho Dam, which had a hydroelectric system responsible for much of the power in North Korea and Manchuria. Other power plants were targets as well.

On June 23, planes from the carriers *Boxer, Princeton,* and *Philippine Sea* launched their attacks. Air force planes joined the naval attack. The attacks went on for three days. The missions were a smashing success, with 11 power plants, including the dam, being destroyed.

Pilotless Bombers

Peace talks began in Korea, and those talks made progress. It began to appear that the war would have a political rather than a military conclusion. Because of this, military strategy was affected. The object was no longer to conquer the opposing army, but to put pressure on the negotiators to agree by doing as much damage to the enemy as possible without putting Allied lives at risk.

Flattop Facts

One of the aircraft carriers operating in support of the UN international police force in Korea was Australia's HMAS *Sydney,* which was the second air-capable ship ever in Australia's navy. It was a Majestic-class carrier. The carrier only began operation in 1949, so it was new as the Korean War began. This ship was also used in the Vietnam War. It was taken out of service in 1973 and scrapped two years later.

Toward this end, a pilotless bomber was devised. Old F6F-5 Hellcats, which had been used during World War II and were now obsolete, were converted into these robot weapons. They were packed with explosives and equipped with a remote control guidance system. They were then catapulted off the aircraft carriers and guided to their target, which, if all went well, they crashed into and destroyed.

During the late summer of 1952 six converted Hellcats were accurately sent to blow up a target.

Last Year

In 1953, the aircraft carriers of Task Force 77 participated in a number of interesting missions. They sent planes to strike an oil refinery at Aoji and a railroad junction surrounded by antiaircraft batteries.

On November 18, 1952, four F9F-5 Panthers from the Allied carriers mixed it up with Soviet MiG-15s. The Panthers shot down two MiGs and damaged a third. One Panther was damaged, but all of them made it back to their carrier, the *Oriskany*.

It was later determined that the Panthers were not as good as the MiGs, but the difference was made up for by the human element. The American pilots were simply superior to the Communist pilots, and that had been the difference in the dogfight.

Ship's Log

The U.S. Navy only had one ace—that is, a pilot who had shot down five or more enemy aircraft—in the Korean War. His name was Lieutenant Guy P. Bordelon, and he accomplished his achievement in three consecutive nights—June 29 and 30, and July 1, 1953. He was a pilot from the carrier *Princeton* flying an F4U-5N Corsair. He shot down two enemy planes on the first night, two on the second, and one on the third night.

And then, in the middle of 1953, the war ended—a tie—with the boundary between North and South Korea left exactly where it had been when hostilities commenced. For the carriers, it had not been as spectacular as World War II had been—the carriers had been used for strategic bombing and strafing, as well as for troop support.

Approximately 280,000 missions were flown off Allied aircraft carriers during the Korean War. Of these, 250,000 were flown by Americans, with the remainder split between Great Britain and Australia. By the time the Korean War was over, the aircraft carrier had reaffirmed itself as the ruler of the seas.

The Least You Need to Know

◆ The first Allied carriers in the Korean fray were Britain's *Triumph* and the USS *Valley Forge*, which were part of what was called Task Force 77.

◆ Allied carriers participated in a blockade of North Korea and attacked locations designed to disrupt North Korea's power supply.

◆ During the last days of the Korean War, old F6F-5 Hellcats that had been used during World War II and were now obsolete were converted into pilotless weapons.

◆ Approximately 280,000 missions were flown off Allied aircraft carriers during the Korean War.

◆ Though the war ended in a "tie," aircraft carriers reestablished themselves as the rulers of the seas.

The Vietnam War

In This Chapter

- ◆ Carriers play a role in yet another civil war
- ◆ Enter the nuclear-powered *Enterprise*
- ◆ Fires do serious damage to carriers
- ◆ Astronauts hitch a lift on aircraft carriers

Ten years after the Korean War ended, the United States found itself involved in another similar conflict in Asia. Just as had been the case in Korea, this war was basically a civil war. Once again, the northern half of the country bordered on China and was controlled by Communists, while the southern half was a democracy that the United States had sworn to protect.

Unfortunately for our cause, South Vietnam's government, though anti-Communist, was corrupt and weak. As it turned out, it didn't make any difference how many troops or equipment we poured into the tiny southeast Asian country, it's impossible to help a country fight that doesn't want to fight for itself.

The Beginning of the Conflict

The first two aircraft carriers to see action in Vietnam were the *Constellation* and the *Ticonderoga*. The Gulf of Tonkin Incident, which officially started U.S. participation in the Vietnam War, occurred on August 2, 1964, when aircraft from the USS *Ticonderoga* drove off North Vietnamese motor torpedo boats attacking the destroyer USS *Maddox*, patrolling international waters in the Gulf of Tonkin. Three days later, on order from President Lyndon B. Johnson, aircraft from the *Constellation* and *Ticonderoga* attacked motor torpedo boats and their supporting facilities at five locations along the North Vietnam coast. Not long after the Gulf of Tonkin incident in 1964, these two aircraft carriers were sending planes to hit targets in Vietnam.

Sixty-four attack sorties were flown, and these aircraft sank or seriously damaged 25 boats. The pilots also destroyed a major part of North Vietnam's petroleum stores and storage facilities. The *Ticonderoga* and *Constellation* were not on their own for long—they were quickly joined by the *Ranger* and the *Kearsarge*. By early 1965, the *Coral Sea* and *Hancock* were also on the scene. The carriers launched attacks on both North Vietnam and enemy strongholds in South Vietnam.

Steady Escalation

The war in Vietnam was one of steady escalation. As the United States steadily increased the number of its troops in Vietnam, it became apparent that the forces from the north were more patient and willing to sacrifice than either the United States—whose boys were fighting a long, long way from home—or the South Vietnamese army. The United States got deeper and deeper into it and never came close to winning.

Anyway, as U.S. involvement increased, so did the involvement of U.S. aircraft carriers. Task Force 77, which you'll recall from the previous chapter, was still around. It now was also known by the name "U.S. Seventh Fleet."

Flattop Facts

In 1965, the United States pretty much had the skies over Vietnam to themselves. The North Vietnamese did have Soviet MiGs, but they were seldom seen. (And when they did show up, the MiGs inevitably lost.)

Daily Strikes

By the spring of 1965, planes from the carriers of the task force were striking targets in North and South Vietnam on a daily basis. Bridges, roads, and even difficult-to-locate trails through the jungle were all targets for the U.S. carrier planes.

In May 1965, two more U.S. carriers, the *Bon Homme Richard* and the *Oriskany*, joined the effort in the waters off Vietnam. Carrier planes had a new worry as the enemy began to fire ground-to-air missiles. Many pilots who were shot down were rescued with U.S. helicopters, but not all of them.

In December 1965, the *Enterprise*, the world's first nuclear-powered aircraft carrier (see Chapter 2), joined the war. The first big attack from the nuclear-powered ship came on December 2, when its planes dropped 167 tons of bombs on enemy positions stretching up and down the entire length of the country.

Ship's Log

By the late summer of 1965, helicopters off of aircraft carriers were being used to transport troops to the scene of the action, about 50 miles south of Danang in South Vietnam, as part of what was known as Operation Starlite. Helicopters working off of aircraft carriers became commonplace for the remainder of the war.

On December 22, 1965, planes from the Big E, as the *Enterprise* was called, along with those from the *Kitty Hawk* and the *Ticonderoga*, knocked out the Yong Bi power plant in North Vietnam, a plant that produced two thirds of the power in North Vietnam's capital, Hanoi.

The *Enterprise* dished out its wrath on the enemy until January 1966, at which time it went back to Subic Bay for rest. It returned to the action in March. And that was how it went. In and out of battle.

The Disasters of 1966 and 1967

Hundreds of men were killed aboard the aircraft carriers *Oriskany* and *Forrestal* during 1966 and 1967, but neither tragedy was caused by enemy action. In both cases fires caused by accidents resulted in many deaths and the destruction of many planes.

Flattop Facts

The *Oriskany* was named after the Revolutionary War's Battle of Oriskany. It was nicknamed "The Mighty O," and was launched on October 13, 1945, at the New York Navy Yard. It was then mothballed for nearly five years and wasn't commissioned until September 25, 1950. Two years later, it became the first carrier to round the southern tip of South America, Cape Horn.

On the morning of October 27, 1966, a fire erupted on the starboard side of the *Oriskany*'s forward hanger bay and raced through five decks, claiming the lives of 44 men. Many who lost their lives were veteran combat pilots who had flown raids over Vietnam a few hours earlier.

The fire started when a magnesium parachute flare exploded in the forward flare locker of Hanger Bay 1, beneath the carrier's flight deck. The crew was heroic, moving heavy bombs as the flames approached and wheeling planes out of danger. Within three hours the fire had been put out and medical assistance was rushed to the carrier from sister aircraft carriers *Constellation* and *Franklin D. Roosevelt*.

The 1966 fire wasn't the first fatal accident aboard the *Oriskany*. In 1953, near the end of the Korean War and in Korean waters, a landing aircraft inadvertently released a bomb onto the carrier, killing two men and wounding 15 others.

> **Ship's Log**
>
> The *Forrestal* was the first U.S. carrier to be built from the keel up with an angled deck.

The *Forrestal* was a newer carrier. On June 6, 1967, the ship left Norfolk, Virginia, for its first combat deployment. The *Forrestal* arrived off the shore of Vietnam on July 25 and began combat operations, its aircraft flying 150 sorties during the next four days, without the loss of a single aircraft. Four days later, tragedy struck.

At 10:52 A.M. on July 29, the second launch of the day was being readied when a Zuni rocket accidentally fired from an F-4 Phantom parked on the starboard side of the flight deck aft of the island. The missile streaked across the deck into a 400-gallon belly fuel tank on a parked A-4D Skyhawk.

Flammable JP-5 fuel spewed onto the deck and ignited, spreading flames over the flight deck under other fully loaded aircraft ready for launch. Ordnance exploded. Rockets ignited. Wind spread the flames, and soon the aft of the ship was one big inferno.

> **Ship's Log**
>
> The two fires during the Vietnam War were not the first fatal infernos aboard aircraft carriers during the decade. On December 22, 1960, fire broke out on the hangar deck of the *Constellation*, which was in the last stages of construction at the New York Naval Shipyard, and 50 civilian workers died in the blaze.
>
> There was one more tragic fire aboard a carrier during the 1960s. On January 14, 1969, a fire aboard the USS *Enterprise*, caused by the detonation of an MK-32 Zuni rocket warhead overheated by exhaust from an aircraft starting unit, took 27 lives, injured 34, and destroyed 15 aircraft.

The final casualty count was 132 dead, 2 missing and presumed dead, and 62 injured. Ironically, the *Oriskany* was called to come to the *Forrestal*'s aid. Fires burned for more than 12 hours. The *Forrestal* was never to serve the navy again.

Still, aircraft carriers and their planes continued to cause major damage to enemy targets, right up until American involvement in that conflict came to an end. But there was nothing an air war over Vietnam could do to change things on the ground, where the war of ideology was far more important than a military war for turf.

Other 1960s Developments

There were many other developments in aircraft carriers during the 1960s besides their involvement in the Vietnam War. The Kitty Hawk class of carriers made their debut in 1961. The first, of course, was the USS *Kitty Hawk*, which was equipped with Terrier antiair missiles.

Splash Down Recovery

Carriers played an important role in the space program. When astronauts came back to Earth and splashed down into the ocean, carrier-based helicopters picked them up. On May 5, 1961, a Marine Corps squadron from the USS *Lake Champlain* recovered Commander Alan B. Shepard, the first American to go into space, as he completed his *Freedom* 7 flight.

Two months later, on July 21, 1961, the USS *Randolph* recovered U.S. Air Force Captain Virgil I. Grissom, the second American in space. On May 24, 1962, a helicopter from the USS *Intrepid* picked up astronaut Lieutenant Commander M. Scott Carpenter after he completed three orbits of Earth in his *Aurora* 7 capsule.

Astronaut Wally M. Schirra is helped from his capsule aboard the USS Kearsarge *on October 3, 1962.*

(Credit: NASA)

Ship's Log

Aircraft carriers continued to participate in the pickup of astronauts who had completed their missions during the Gemini and Apollo programs throughout the remainder of the decade.

Flattop Facts

In 1961, a TV system was first installed on a carrier, so that every takeoff and landing was videotaped. The system was called the Pilot Landing Aid Television (PLAT) system and it was first installed on the USS *Coral Sea*. By 1963, all U.S. carriers were equipped with the system.

On October 3, 1962, the USS *Kearsarge* picked up Commander Walter M. Schirra in the Pacific 275 miles northeast of Midway after six orbits. On May 16, 1963, the *Kearsarge* recovered U.S. Air Force Major L. Gordon Cooper and his *Faith* 7 capsule following his 22-orbit flight. It was the final flight of what NASA called the Mercury program.

Other carrier highlights of the 1960s include the following:

◆ During the Cuban Missile Crisis, in October 1962, the USS *Enterprise*, USS *Independence*, USS *Essex*, and USS *Randolph* took part in the blockade of Cuba, following the discovery of offensive nuclear missiles on the island of Cuba, placed there by the Soviet Union.

◆ Also in 1962, there was a major advancement in catapult systems. An E-2A, piloted by Lieutenant Commander Lee R. Ramsey, was catapulted off the *Enterprise* in the first test of the nose-tow gear designed to replace the catapult bridle. The new system reduced launching intervals and added to flight deck safety.

◆ On October 3, 1964, the USS *Enterprise*, *Long Beach*, and *Bainbridge* completed Operation Sea Orbit. This was the world's first task force composed solely of nuclear-powered ships. The ships circled the globe in 65 days without taking on either fuel or provisions.

◆ On April 27, 1965, a revolt in the Dominican Republic threatened the safety of American nationals, so the USS *Boxer* was sent to the rescue. The carrier began an airlift in which over 1,000 men, women, and children were evacuated to navy ships standing offshore.

Cold War Effect

Even after the war in Vietnam had ended, with the North winning and uniting Vietnam as a Communist state, the United States continued to build many new aircraft carriers. That was because the Soviet Union was building new state-of-the-art carriers. Neither Cold War superpower wanted to fall behind in the arms race.

The Least You Need to Know

- ◆ The first two aircraft carriers to see action in Vietnam were the *Constellation* and the *Ticonderoga*.

- ◆ In December 1965, the first nuclear-powered carrier, the *Enterprise*, joined the war.

- ◆ The worst damage and loss of life aboard carriers during the Vietnam War was caused by accidental fires rather than by enemy action.

- ◆ In addition to their activities off the coast of Vietnam, carriers were also active in the space program, recovering astronauts who had splashed down.

Chapter 20

Other Wars

In This Chapter

- The UK and Argentina in the Falklands
- Saddam, the first go 'round
- Whacking Qadhafi
- Bio of the *JFK*

Between the Vietnam War, the more recent conflicts against Osama bin Laden's Al Qaeda terrorist network in Afghanistan in 2002, and an encore appearance versus Saddam Hussein's Iraq in 2003, aircraft carriers have been busy in the last couple of years.

And in the past couple of decades, Great Britain took their flattops down South America Way, and the United States used carriers to help stifle terrorism of a North African origin. And—of course—we had to kick Iraq out of Kuwait in 1991.

War in the Falklands

The British, if you'll recall, went to war with Argentina briefly during 1982 over possession of the Falkland Islands. The islands had historically

Flattop Facts

The Sea Harrier first saw combat on May 1, 1982, during the Falklands War, operating off of the HMS *Hermes*. The mission was the bombing and strafing of Port Stanley. Four days later the first Sea Harrier was shot down in combat, its pilot killed, by a surface-to-air missile. On May 9, a Sea Harrier sunk its first ship, an Argentine trawler.

belonged to Great Britain but Argentina, thinking that Great Britain had become no more than a paper tiger, took the islands over.

In response, Great Britain sent a fleet of naval ships to retake the islands. The fleet included two carriers, the *Invincible*, which had been commissioned only two years earlier, and the *Hermes*. Both of the British carriers held Sea Harrier planes and helicopters. The ships were off the coast of Norway when war was declared. So war had to wait until the ships could get from Scandinavian waters to the South Atlantic.

Argentina's Lone Carrier

Argentina had a carrier of its own to defend the islands, the *Vienticinco de Mayo*. The Argentine carrier was originally a British ship known as the *Venerable* built after World War II. The British sold it to Argentina without a thought that its guns might one day be turned upon its builder. Aboard this ship were A-4 Skyhawk planes.

The Argentine carrier didn't perform well during the short war. Its one and only catapult broke down and it had no vertical launch aircraft aboard. Argentina's conventional takeoff and landing aircraft were forced to operate exclusively from air bases on land.

Attack on the British Carriers

During the war the British carriers stayed far offshore, an inconvenience because this lessened the length of the missions Britain's Sea Harriers could run. But military planners insisted on keeping the carriers as safe as possible, since the invasion would fall apart if one or both of Great Britain's carriers were sunk.

The Argentines knew that getting to the carriers was a key to the battle. They made their big attempt to sink the British carriers on May 25, using two Super étendard fixed-wing fighters holding Exocet "smart" missiles.

The carriers were located about 70 miles northeast of the Falklands at the time of the attack. Radar from the British fleet picked up the attack in advance. This allowed the British ships to fire into the air chaff radar decoys, which are designed to confuse "smart" missiles such as the Exocet.

Eyewitnesses say that the missiles were heading for the carriers when they suddenly veered off and headed directly into an equipment and supply ship, sinking it. Twelve crew members died, but the carriers were safe.

Britain Dominates

Great Britain dominated the war, and the Falklands (a normally peaceful place that contained more sheep than people) were quickly returned to British rule. The Argentine carrier did get a lick in early, however, when a single missile from a Skyhawk sunk the British frigate *Ardent*.

Flattop Facts

The *Vienticinco de Mayo* was taken out of service in 1985 and was officially stricken during April of 1997. It was sold for scrapping in India on July 8, 1998, and towed away later that year. At the moment there are no aircraft carriers in Argentina's navy.

Strikes Against Libya

Troubles between the United States and Libya started back in 1973 when Libyan leader Muammar Qadhafi claimed that the Gulf of Sidra was within Libyan territorial waters. The United States considered Libya an enemy and routinely patrolled the Gulf of Sidra, a body of water that protruded from the Mediterranean Sea into the northern coast of Libya. The navy wasn't about to stop patrols just because Qadhafi wanted to move the international waters line. The United States said that it would continue to patrol all areas more than 12 nautical miles from the Libyan coast. During the next few years Libyan fighter planes harassed U.S. fighter jets that were flying near their carriers in what the United States considered international waters and airspace.

Then, on August 19, 1973, two F-14 Tomcat fighters off the USS *Nimitz* intercepted two Libyan Su-22 fighter-bombers. While the Tomcats escorted the Libyan fighters out of the area, one of Su-22s shot an air-to-air missile at the Tomcats. The Tomcats successfully evaded the missile, and in response, they blew both Libyan jets out of the sky with Sidewinder missiles. Both Libyan pilots successfully bailed out and were rescued after landing in the sea.

Tensions increased even further during the summer of 1985 when Libya was found to be behind a series of terrorist attacks against American interests. To close the technology gap between the U.S. and Libyan war machines, Libya installed Soviet-built SA-5 missiles to boost their air defense system. The missiles were installed along the Libyan coastline, aimed at U.S. interests, such as the U.S. Coast Guard facility on Lampedusa Island between Sicily and Italy.

In the meantime, U.S. ships continued to disregard Libya's claims regarding their territorial waters. Qadhafi called the line he had drawn in the water a "line of death."

In March 1986, three carrier task forces of the Sixth Fleet (a total of 225 aircraft) maneuvered off the Libyan coast. On March 24, Libya aimed and fired six SA-5 missiles at U.S. jets. No jets were hit, and carrier-based A-6 Intruders responded by firing high-speed antiradiation missiles (HARMs), which destroyed the Libyan missile base. Out on the sea, an A-7 Corsair aircraft launched two Harpoon missiles and struck a Libyan attack vessel. By the next day five Libyan ships had been sunk, including a Soviet-supplied Nanuchka-class missile corvette.

To avenge the sinking of the five Libyan ships, Libya followed with another terrorist attack, exploding a bomb in a Berlin disco. In retaliation, on April 15, the United States struck back at military installations in Benghazi and Tripoli. Featured in this attack were the aircraft carriers *Coral Sea* (yes, the same one that made its debut in 1946) and *America*, which launched 24 A-6 and F/A-18 Hornet strike aircraft against radar and antiaircraft sites at Benghazi.

Flattop Facts

Following the April 15 attacks, all of the carrier-based aircraft successfully returned to their ships.

The planes subsequently hit the Benina military airfield and the Jamahiriya barracks. Libyan transport aircraft, a few MiG-23 fighters, as well as some helicopters, were destroyed on the ground.

A-7 Corsair

One star of the skirmishes against Libya was the A-7 Corsair, which debuted back in 1965. The fighter jet was originally built on the airframe of the F-8U Crusader. The A-7 underwent a number of modifications during its two decades in service.

It was used for close air support attack missions, such as those in Libya during 1986. The A-7E, the final version, had a 20mm gun and could carry payloads of up to 15,000 pounds of bombs and missiles. Eight ordnance stations were available. The A-7 Corsair has since been replaced by the F/A-18 Hornet, with the last of the A-7Es taken out of commission in 1992.

The A-7 was capable of performing a variety of search, surveillance, and attack missions. It could carry four externally wing-mounted 300-gallon fuel tanks, coupled with a variety of ordnance on remaining stations, and could conduct in-flight refueling operations.

Fact Box

A-7 Corsair Specifications

Contractor: Ling-Temco-Vought (Prime, now Northrop Grumman Corp.)

External Dimensions:

> Wing Span: 11.8m
>
> Length: 14.06m
>
> Height: 4.90m
>
> Weight empty: 8,676kg

Power plant: Single Allison/Rolls Royce TF41-A-400 non-afterburning turbofan engine with a static thrust rating of 15,000 pounds

Accommodations: A-7E pilot only; TA-7C two seats

Performance: Maximum speed at 20,000 feet: Mach .94

Range: Greater than 1,900 nautical miles

Armament (A-7E/TA-7C): One internally mounted M61A1 20 mm six-barrel cannon. Six wing pylons (pylons can carry a large single weapon, multiple racks capable of six weapons per rack, or triple racks with three weapons per rack). Two fuselage launch stations.

Could carry 15,000 pounds of payload.

It was capable of transferring more than 12,000 pounds of fuel. It had a fully integrated digital navigation/weapon delivery system. Because it was equipped with the *FLIR* sensory system, the A-7's night-attack accuracy was equivalent to day-attack accuracy.

Naval Lingo

FLIR stands for forward-looking infrared.

Coral Sea: Aged Queen of Flattops

The aged queen of the Libyan attacks was the 45,000-ton Midway-class USS *Coral Sea*, which had been around since the first years of the Cold War. Commissioned on October 1, 1947, the ship remained active until 1993. Its first missions were in the Atlantic.

It trained midshipmen, toured the Mediterranean and Caribbean Seas, and, beginning in 1949, became part of the Sixth Fleet. Its job was to help protect Europe from Soviet aggression.

In 1957, it traveled around the southern tip of South America to the West Coast of the United States where it was modernized. It returned to active service in 1960 with an enlarged flight deck, with a new angled landing area added, three new deck-edge aircraft elevators, and three new powerful steam catapults.

In 1960 it crossed the Pacific for the first of many cruises with the Seventh Fleet. As noted earlier, it was essential to the American war effort in Vietnam, and remained in the area until the bitter end, taking part in the evacuation of Americans from South Vietnam just before that country fell under Communist control in 1975.

During the 1970s and 1980s, the *Coral Sea* covered the Persian Gulf and was in the Mediterranean for its confrontations with Libya. Two more Sixth Fleet deployments took place in the late 1980s. The *Coral Sea* was decommissioned in April 1990, sold for scrapping in May 1993, and broken up at Baltimore, Maryland, over the next several years.

The First Gulf War

In 1990, Saddam Hussein's Iraq invaded neighboring Kuwait, in an attempt to seize that country's rich oil supplies and to gain control of the Persian Gulf, which is key to shipping in the area. Early in 1991 the United States led an international coalition to kick Iraq out of Kuwait, and, of course, aircraft carriers were there.

Biography of a Carrier

Most biographies are about people, but this one is about an aircraft carrier. Below, in timeline form, you'll find the story of the life of the USS *John F. Kennedy*, one of the big heroes of the first Gulf War:

- ◆ **October 22, 1964.** Construction on the *JFK*, named for the thirty-fifth president of the United States, begins at the Newport News Shipbuilding and Drydock Company in Virginia.

- ◆ **May 27, 1967.** The new carrier is christened by President Kennedy's nine-year-old daughter Caroline. The ship enters naval service on September 7, 1968. Ever since its birth, the *JFK* has been stationed in the Middle East. Its maiden voyage was to the Mediterranean because of a deteriorating situation during the days surrounding the Six-Day War between Israel and the United Arab Republic.

- ◆ **1970s.** The ship returns to the Middle East seven more times during this decade.

◆ **1979.** The *JFK* receives its first major overhaul, when it was upgraded to handle the F-14 Tomcat and the S-3 Viking.

◆ **1981.** The CV is back in action, this time traveling to the Indian Ocean. During the 1980s the ship is visited by the ruler of Somalia, the first time a Somali leader had ever been aboard a U.S. Navy vessel, and the carrier went through the Suez Canal, the canal that allows ships to get from the Indian Ocean to the Mediterranean Sea without going around Africa.

◆ **1983.** The *JFK* returns to the Middle East, this time because of a crisis in Beirut.

◆ **1984.** The *Kennedy* goes into dry dock for another overhaul.

◆ **July 1986.** The *JFK* leads an international naval armada during the International Naval Review, which is held in honor of the one hundredth anniversary and rededication of the Statue of Liberty.

◆ **August 1986.** The carrier returns to the Mediterranean, where it stays until March of 1987.

◆ **August 1988.** Departs for its twelfth deployment, again to the Mediterranean Sea.

◆ **January 4, 1989.** The *JFK* makes the headlines when embarked F-14 Tomcats shoot down two Libyan MIG-23s that were approaching the battle group in a hostile manner.

◆ **August 1990.** The crisis in the Gulf begins and the *JFK* is sent to the Persian Gulf on just four days notice.

◆ **September 1990.** The *JFK* enters the Red Sea and becomes the flagship of the Red Sea Battle Force.

◆ **January 16, 1991.** Aircraft from the ship's Carrier Air Wing Three began Operation Desert Storm with attacks on Iraqi forces. The ship launches 114 strikes and 2,895 sorties, with aircrews of CVW-3 flying 11,263 combat hours and delivering more than 3.5 million pounds of ordnance in the conflict.

◆ **March 28, 1991.** The USS *John F. Kennedy* arrives in Norfolk and receives the greatest homecoming celebration since World War II. After the cease-fire in Iraq, the *JFK* once again passes through the Suez Canal and heads home.

◆ **1991–92.** The ship receives some well-deserved rest, and repairs are made to its engineering systems, flight deck systems, and equipment. Changes were also made to ready the ship to handle F/A-18 Hornet aircraft to replace A-7E Corsair IIs.

Flattop Facts _____

The USS *John F. Kennedy* passed an impressive milestone in 1993 when the 250,000th aircraft landed on its flight deck.

◆ **October 7, 1992–April 7, 1993.** In response to turmoil in Bosnia, the ship conducts multiple exercises in the Mediterranean and spends much time in the Adriatic Sea. Following the multiple exercises in the Adriatic, the ship receives a comprehensive overhaul.

◆ **October 1997.** The *JFK* returns to the Mediterranean Sea.

◆ **1998.** The *JFK* rescues a foundered tug during Hurricane Floyd. The ship then plays host to the king of Jordan, before participating in Operation Southern Watch, which includes flying combat missions while enforcing the no-fly zone over Iraq. During its time in the Persian Gulf, 10,302 aircraft landed safely atop the *Kennedy*. The aircraft of the ship also set a record during the Gulf War for bombing accuracy.

◆ **January 1, 2000.** The *JFK* earns the title "Carrier of the New Millennium." It was the only carrier underway as the year 2000 arrived. Since then the ship has been a test bed for *cooperative engagement capability* (CEC).

Naval Lingo _____

Cooperative engagement capability (CEC) enables battle group ships and aircraft to share sensor data and provide a single, integrated picture to all.

◆ **February 7, 2002.** The *JFK* deploys to support Operation Enduring Freedom, the war on terrorism in Afghanistan, from the North Arabian Sea. (We will be discussing the terrorist attacks of September 11, 2001 and its aftermath more in our next chapter.) After its stint in the Arabian Sea, the *JFK* returns home for a well-deserved facelift.

The first war against Iraq went smoothly, but—as we now know—the U.S. military's work there went unfinished. The next chapter looks at the role of aircraft carriers in the war on terrorism, which began soon after the September 11, 2001, attacks on New York City and Washington, D.C., and in Operation Iraqi Freedom, the final attack on Baghdad.

Fact Box

USS *John F. Kennedy* Specifications

Built by Newport News, the *JFK* had her keel laid on October 22, 1964, she was christened May 27, 1967, and commissioned on September 7, 1968. The ship is 1,052 feet long and, from keel to mast top, 23 stories tall. Its standard displacement is more than 80,000 tons. The ship has 18 decks, 8 boilers, 4 aircraft elevators, 4 steam-powered catapults, 4 wires of arresting gear, 4 gear-turbine engines, and a top speed of 30 knots. The flight deck is 4.56 acres in size.

There are two anchors, at 30 tons each. There's room for more than 80 aircraft. There is more than an acre and a half of hangar space. The JFK is a city of 4,642 people. There are 6 physicians and surgeons, 4 dentists, 2 stores, and 1 barber shop.

And the cooks are busy. Almost 10,000 eggs are served every day. Eight hundred loaves of bread are baked every day, and almost 1,000 gallons of milk consumed. A ton of mail goes through the ship's post office daily. Quite a neighborhood.

The Least You Need to Know

◆ Keeping Great Britain's carriers safe was considered top priority in the UK's quick and one-sided battle with Argentina for the Falkland Islands in 1982.

◆ In 1986, the United States used their carriers to help stifle Libyan terrorism.

◆ One of the big heroes of the first Gulf War was the carrier USS *John F. Kennedy*.

◆ The *JFK* earned the title "Carrier of the New Millennium" because it was the only carrier underway as the year 2000 arrived.

Chapter 21

Return to the Gulf

In This Chapter

- ◆ The September 11, 2001, terrorist attacks
- ◆ Operation Enduring Freedom
- ◆ Operation Southern Watch
- ◆ Operation Iraqi Freedom

On September 11, 2001, the United States was attacked by the Al Qaeda terrorist network, led by Osama bin Laden and headquartered in Afghanistan. The network was protected by Afghanistan's ruling government, a band of thugs known as the Taliban.

Within weeks, the United States responded by sending forces to Afghanistan to decimate the Taliban and Al Qaeda, and—with a little luck—capture Osama bin Laden dead or alive. The operation in Afghanistan was known as Operation Enduring Freedom.

Enterprise Executes an About-Face

On September 11, 2001, the USS *Enterprise* had just been relieved from being on station in support of the patrolling of the "no-fly zone" over southern Iraq. These patrols had been taking place steadily since the end of the first Iraqi War in 1991.

The *Enterprise* was heading south in the Indian Ocean, beginning its trip back to homeport in Norfolk, Virginia, when, on TV, crewmembers saw the live coverage of the attacks.

> **Ship's Log**
>
> The patrolling of the no-fly zone over Iraq began in 1991 at the conclusion of the first Gulf War, and was called *Operation Southern Watch*.

Without an order from the chain of command, the *Enterprise* executed a 180-degree course change and headed back to the waters off Southwest Asia, 600 miles from Afghanistan. The carrier then remained on station in support of Operation Enduring Freedom, launching air attacks against al Qaeda terrorist training camps and Taliban military installations in Afghanistan.

For the next 21 days, aircraft from the *Enterprise*, including F-14 Tomcats and F-18 Hornets, flew nearly 700 missions in Afghanistan, dropping hundreds of thousands of pounds of ordnance.

New Carriers in Town

Three carriers arrived in the Arabian Sea to relieve the *Enterprise* and continue the attack. These were the USS *Carl Vinson*, USS *Theodore Roosevelt*, and the USS *Kitty Hawk*. They arrived on the scene in October 2001. Then, slightly more than two months after the attacks on the twin towers of the World Trade Center and the Pentagon, the nuclear-powered carrier USS *John C. Stennis* left San Diego, heading toward the Arabian Sea as part of Operation Enduring Freedom. It took the carrier and its battle group six weeks to get to the Arabian Sea.

> **Flattop Facts**
>
> The *Stennis* battle group included 10 U.S. and Canadian ships and submarines, plus more than 80 tactical aircraft and a total of 8,500 sailors and marines.

The *Stennis, Vinson,* and *Roosevelt* each carried some 50 strike planes plus about 25 other aircraft such as airborne battle management planes, refueling planes, and search and rescue helicopters.

The USS *Abraham Lincoln* arrived on the scene later, and its jets began running bombing missions. The navy jets pretty much had their way in the skies over Afghanistan.

Gulf Deployment

U.S. armed forces had not yet completed their task in Afghanistan when the focus of U.S. foreign policy shifted to Iraq, where Saddam Hussein remained in power, more than a decade after the first Gulf War had kicked Saddam's army out of neighboring Kuwait. President George W. Bush took his case against Iraq's madman leader to the people, and the U.S. Congress gave the president permission to use force to topple Saddam's regime.

Flattop Facts

For the first anniversary of the 9/11 attacks, members of the crew of the 820-foot Tarawa-class amphibious assault ship USS *Belleau Wood* assembled on the flight deck so that, for aerial photographs, they spelled out "9-11 LET'S ROLL." Later that month the ship—which held 18 helicopters and six AV-8B Harrier jump jets—was used to support the War on Terrorism in Yemen. The ship patrolled the narrow Bab el Mandeb Strait that separates Djibouti and Yemen.

The *George Washington* was deployed on June 20, 2002, for the region and was in or near the Mediterranean. The *Lincoln*, which got underway on July 24, arrived in the Gulf in October. The *Harry S. Truman* and its battle group left Virginia for the Persian Gulf area on December 5, 2002. The *Constellation* arrived in the region soon thereafter.

Flattop Facts

The four aircraft carriers and their battle groups brought to the Persian Gulf 250 precision-strike aircraft and more than 2,000 Tomahawk Cruise missiles.

Four carriers wasn't the limit, either. A fifth carrier, the San Diego–based *Nimitz*, was also sent to the Gulf region by late December. A sixth, the *Kitty Hawk* (based in Yokosuka, Japan) was sent early in 2003.

The *Nimitz* attacked targets inside Iraq during Operation Iraqi Freedom with Carrier Air Wing Eleven. "The Black Aces" of Strike Fighter Squadron 41 flew their Super Hornets from the deck of the *Nimitz*.

Having multiple carriers in the region before the war began was particularly important since the United States was unsure if it would be able to use airfields in neighboring countries.

Flattop Facts

Six carrier battle groups took part in Desert Storm, but no more than four carriers were engaged in that battle at any one time.

The *Abraham Lincoln* Is in the House

By Halloween 2002 the USS *Abraham Lincoln* had left its position in support of the war on terrorism in Afghanistan and was in the Persian Gulf.

> **Ship's Log**
>
> One U.S. carrier, taken all by itself, would be the seventh-largest air force in the world.

> **Naval Lingo**
>
> **No-fly zones** in southern and northern Iraq were established after the 1991 Persian Gulf war to prevent Iraq from carrying out air strikes against Shiites in southern Iraq and Kurdish forces in the north of the country. The zones were patrolled by the United States Air Force and Navy and by the British.

Its warplanes were busy taking off and landing from its flight deck. The missions of these pilots were twofold. They were performing patrol missions over Iraq's southern *no-fly zone* and practicing bombing runs over potential Iraqi targets should the United States go to war with Iraq.

Practice bombing runs from the *Abraham Lincoln* were carried out over airfields, towers, and military targets of all descriptions in south Iraq. (Airfields because they are easy to find and towers because, often, they are not.)

A "Low-Grade War"

Between Operation Desert Storm and Operation Iraqi Freedom, the aerial patrols and practice missions over Iraq's no-fly zones became routine. They developed, according to the *New York Times*, into a "low-grade war." As the second war with Iraq grew closer, hostilities in the air over Iraq increased. Allied planes were being fired upon, on an average, more than once a day by the autumn of 2002. Speaking at that time, Captain Kevin C. Albright, commander of the ship's air wing, explained, "It gives us the opportunity to train in the same environment that we may possibly go to war in. We are looking at target sets and practicing."

According to Rear Admiral John M. Kelly, commander of the *Abraham Lincoln* Battle Group, the Iraqis were determined to shoot a plane down during the no-fly zone skirmishes. The Allied planes bombed the defense sites in retaliation, but with minimal effect. U.S. retaliatory efforts were hampered by the Iraqis' sparing use of weapons radar, which diminished our smart weapons' ability to find them. Because of this, the Pentagon allowed a broader range of targets when Allied planes ran their retaliatory missions. The list of targets grew to include command and control centers, communications relay stations, military radars, and other stationary targets—sites that were difficult to hide and repair.

Super Hornets in Action

In 2003, the USS *Abraham Lincoln* was more powerful than ever. The ship contained the VFA-115 strike fighter squadron, the first squadron to fly the new F/A-18E Super Hornet, which was bigger than the old Hornets, had a greater range, and could carry more bombs (see Chapter 4). The pilots called the F/A-18E "Rhino."

The bombing missions over Iraq were well-choreographed and featured combinations of pilots from the U.S. Air Force and Navy and Britain's Royal Air Force. Many of those same pilots had recently participated in the war in Afghanistan. The only difference was, over Afghanistan they didn't get shot at.

Things were very different over Iraq. To help protect the pilots, the United States used an air force U-2 reconnaissance plane and an air force RC-135 Rivet Joint electronic surveillance plane to keep tabs on Iraqi defenses.

Ship's Log

She's 98,000 tons of diplomacy we can put anywhere in the world.

—Captain Michael Groothousen, commander of the USS *Harry S. Truman,* regarding his charge.

Orders to Strike

If pilots were given orders to "strike," this meant that, if they were fired upon, they were allowed to bomb targets on the potential target list. A typical target was a command and control center, which was attacked by a concrete-penetrating, bunker-busting bomb that could be guided to its target from a satellite. To carry out an attack with a laser-guided bomb, the pilot needed to keep a laser focused on a target for up to 30 seconds as he maneuvered his aircraft.

These practices helped the navy get used to Iraqi terrain, winds, and weather, all of which affected their infrared targeting systems. This also gave the pilots a chance to practice their *knobology*. Practices were videotaped so they could be reviewed later. Missions over Iraq averaged 3½ hours. About 90 minutes of that was actually spent over Iraq.

Flattop Facts

Since getting the guys who are down there shooting up is very important to pilots, favorite targets in Iraq always included SAM (surface-to-air missiles) sites.

Naval Lingo

Knobology is what navy pilots call the series of steps necessary to target a precision-guided bomb.

Waiting in the Wings

As a second Gulf War approached, waiting in the wings—the wings being the docks at Norfolk, Virginia—ready to move into the Persian Gulf, was the USS *Harry S. Truman*. This carrier contained 5,500 sailors and air-wing personnel, 40 attack aircraft, and more than 30 radar jammers, refuelers, and surveillance planes.

Taken all by itself, the *Truman* is the seventh-largest air force in the world. It is the flagship of Battle Group 2, which also includes three destroyers, one frigate, and a cruiser.

> **Ship's Log**
>
> Anyone who reads the newspapers knows that, starting in 2002, many cruise ships had big problems with illness. Someone would come onboard with a bug and pretty soon, because everyone was living in enclosed spaces close together, everyone was sick.
>
> Well, the same is true of naval vessels, even ships as large as aircraft carriers. In December 2002, hundreds of sailors aboard the USS *Theodore Roosevelt* came down with influenza. The illnesses occurred during exercises in the Atlantic. At the peak of the epidemic, 300 of the more than 5,000 crew members stationed aboard the ship were sick.
>
> Navy officials were puzzled—and more than a little concerned—at first as to the cause of the widespread sickness. They flew blood samples to the U.S. naval base in Norfolk, Virginia, for testing and were relieved to discover that the sick sailors were suffering from a common form of influenza.
>
> Doctors and other medical personnel aboard the carrier treated the cases in the standard fashion: advising plenty of fluids. Crew members who were still healthy were told to wash their hands regularly to prevent spreading the outbreak.

Operation Iraqi Freedom

On March 18, 2003, President Bush gave Iraqi leader Saddam Hussein 48 hours to leave Iraq, or to face the consequences. The following day, warplanes from the *Abraham Lincoln* were fired upon four times while over-flying the no-fly zone. In response, jets from the *Lincoln* fired in the general direction from which the antiaircraft fire came.

On the eve of the war, Vice Admiral Timothy Keating, commander of the Fifth Fleet, addressed the crew of the *Abraham Lincoln*:

We can achieve surprise by going about this particular conflict … in a way that is very unpredictable and unprecedented in history—with remarkable speed, breathtaking speed, agility, precision, and persistence.

The plans we have are unlike anything anyone has seen before. Hopefully [the war] will be quick, [though] we are prepared for it to take however long it takes. You are the muscle that will make it all work. It's going to be a tough time for you. When it's all done, and they rewrite history, because that is what you are going to do, your names will be written in gold on those pages. You will have contributed in a magnificent way to the re-entry of Iraq into the league of nations. You should know that you go with the unqualified support of millions of Americans and hundreds of millions of freedom-loving people around the world.

He went on to tell the crew and the pilots that their goal was to "reduce to an absolute minimum, if not eliminate, non-combatant casualties."

When President Bush's 48-hour deadline came and went with no movement from Saddam, the war was on. The United States dropped its first bomb on an area where Saddam Hussein was thought to be. Whether Saddam survived these attacks remains a mystery.

Iraq was surrounded by U.S. aircraft carriers as the war began. The *Constellation* and the *Kitty Hawk* were in the Persian Gulf. The *Harry S. Truman* and the *Theodore Roosevelt* were in the western end of the Mediterranean Sea. The *Abraham Lincoln* was in the Arabian Sea, but it later joined the others in the Persian Gulf.

The First Day

Each carrier carried 75 aircraft and was accompanied by 30 warships. During the first 24 hours of the war, F-14 Tomcats and F/A-18C Hornets—loaded with 500-pound, 1,000-pound, and 2,000-pound bombs fitted with laser and global positioning system guidance systems—from the *Kitty Hawk* attacked the city of Basra and Iraqi military strong points on the al-Faw Peninsula.

The *Kitty Hawk* also launched radar jamming EA-6B Prowlers over Baghdad, to retard the enemy's ability to see U.S. planes coming. From the *Abraham Lincoln*, that same day, Hornets, Super Hornets, Tomcats, and Prowlers flew over Baghdad. Part of their mission was to drop precision-guided bombs on an Iraqi air base west of Baghdad. Despite less-than-perfect-weather, with cloud cover and rain, the mission was successful.

Ship's Log

During the first three days of the war, the three carriers in the Persian Gulf flew 550 sorties.

Meanwhile, in the Mediterranean, Tomcats and Hornets were launched from the *Theodore Roosevelt* armed with missiles and bombs, headed for undisclosed locations.

Changing on the Fly

The bombing missions were pretty much set in stone that first day, but pilots had to learn to be more flexible as the war progressed and the situation on the ground often called for sudden shifts in where air support was most needed.

> **Flattop Facts**
>
> Before a mission was flown, pilots set preprogrammed coordinates into their jet's computers. The computer then directed the satellite-guided bombs to the targets in Iraq.

> **Naval Lingo**
>
> To a pilot, the **walk** is the preparatory walk he takes to his jet before a mission to make sure everything is in good order.

On March 25, 2003—still during the first week of the war—planes took off from the *Abraham Lincoln* and headed to an established destination.

However, Captain Kevin C. Albright, the commander of the nine squadrons in the *Lincoln*'s air wing, received a request from a ground commander to provide air support for his troops in south central Iraq. The planes' missions were changed at the last moment to accommodate the request.

According to Captain Albright, "Early on, we knew our targets when we *walked*. Now it's a pickup game. You have no idea who you are talking to, what your coordinates will be. From the ground, they have to talk your eyes (guide a pilot in the air with verbal instructions) to the bad guys."

Converted to Tankers

Not all of the Super Hornets on the *Lincoln* were used as bombers during the first week of the war. Four of the twelve in the carrier's air wing were converted to tankers. Instead of dropping bombs, they were in charge of refueling other jets while in the air. The Super Hornets, as it turned out, made excellent tankers.

The jets that were designed as tankers had no defensive capabilities and therefore had to stay away from the combat zone. Because the Super Hornets could better defend themselves against enemy antiaircraft fire, those that had been converted to tankers could refuel bombers close to, or even directly over, potential targets.

> **Ship's Log**
>
> The computer systems used in the second Iraqi War were many times more sophisti-
> cated than those used in 1991. During the first Gulf War, for example, the air force
> and the navy each had its own computer systems. They were not linked together in any
> way. The only communication between the two air groups was to make sure they
> stayed out of each other's way.
>
> Things were very different in 2003. One giant computer network covered the U.S. air
> attack. The navy and air force were in constant communication, coordinating joint mis-
> sions, with each force bringing elements to the table that the other didn't have.

Life During Wartime

The strangest thing about a carrier during war operations isn't how much things
change, but how much things stay the same. For many on the ship, life goes on
unchanged by the fact that bombers and surveillance jets are taking off and landing
on the flight deck. The laundry still needs to be done. Paper work still needs to be
written and filed. The food still needs to be prepared.

Even life on the flight deck isn't that different. There is more coming and going than
during times of peace, but it isn't like the launching and recovering of a jet on a carrier's flight deck is anything unusual. The only people who really are affected by the
war are the pilots and those who are loading up the jets with bombs and missiles. For
them, the adrenaline is pumping.

Of course, one reason for the normalcy is the general feeling that the enemy has no
way to directly attack the carriers. The air and the sea belong to the United States
and the coalition. Things, as you'll recall, were quite different during World War II,
when an attack from the sea or the air could come at any time.

Even though carriers are well protected, there is always a chance that an enemy can
slip through the security barriers and do some damage. The enemy could launch a
missile at one of the carriers or attack in a boat—just as al Qaeda attacked the USS
Cole. Since the carriers are in interna-
tional waters, they do not have the right
to order the fishermen and other vessels
to not come too close. If there were ever
an attack on a carrier, however, the crew
would be ready. Drills are held frequently
so everyone will know what to do if an
attack does come, however.

Flattop Facts

Although there are more than
5,000 sailors aboard an aircraft carrier, only seven of them
are authorized to fire the ship's
weapons.

Aboard the *Kitty Hawk*, if a whistle blows an alert over the shipwide intercom, the carrier can activate its defense systems of missiles, automatic cannon, and machine guns in a matter of seconds. The ship remains locked, loaded, and ready to go at all times. Such preparedness was justified when, during the first week of the war, two tugboats were seized carrying 68 mines.

Lookouts keep a close eye on the many fishing boats that continue to sail around the many warships in both the Mediterranean Sea and the Persian Gulf. Each of the carriers in the region has onboard defense systems that include Sea Sparrow and Rolling Airframe missiles, radar-directed Gatling guns, and .50-caliber and M-60 machine guns.

Flattop Facts

When journalists are invited aboard one of the U.S. carriers near Iraq, the ship needs to be "sanitized" (all classified material removed or covered up), so that the press, even inadvertently, does not report or transmit anything that might jeopardize the carrier's security.

This is especially true when reporters are allowed to visit the commands directions center, a series of compartments that comprise the nerve center of the carrier. The center is behind a door that only opens when the person entering punches the correct code into a keypad. Inside, the file cabinets all have combination locks on them.

When the press visits, the crew covers all radar and computer screens and switch sensory equipment to an unclassified signal. Reporters are not allowed to use tape recorders. The navy reviews all press photos before they are released to the public.

This Is Not a Drill

An aircraft carrier during an actual battle is a picture of organized determination. Pilots, mechanics, ordnance makers, and cleaning crews busily go about their duties. The hours of training and drilling have made their activities routine.

Flattop Facts

What do pilots say to themselves while in the air, heading toward their targets? The most common answer is: "I say to myself, 'Please God, don't let me screw this up.'"

One by one the fighter jets rise on their elevator from the hangar bay to the flight deck. Once up top they taxi to their takeoff positions and are attached to the steam-operated catapult. It is during this time that their wings unfold.

When all of the pilots and their jets have departed for their missions there is a new tension aboard the ship. The prayers now are for all of them to come back. When the jets do begin returning to the ship, both their landing gear and their tail hook dropping, everyone counts, and no one relaxes until the same number of jets has returned as took off.

Into the Drink

Not all went perfectly as American troops inched their way toward Baghdad. On March 31, an S-3B Viking airplane veered off the USS *Constellation*'s flight deck while taxiing after landing. It turned left instead of right to get out of the way for the next landing and slipped into the water. The two pilots ejected into the water and were rescued by a search-and-rescue swimmer and lifted into a helicopter. The plane sank in 200 feet of water and is considered lost.

All carrier-based aircraft returned from their sorties on every carrier until April 2, when an F/A-18 from the *Kitty Hawk* did not come back. It had been shot down over Iraq, and a search-and-rescue operation began looking for the pilot. Twelve days later it was announced that the pilot, 30-year-old Nathan D. White, had been killed in action.

Price tag department: During the war against Iraq in the Spring of 2003, five aircraft carrier battle groups were used in a "Heavy Air Option" against Iraq costing about $9 billion—that is, $9 billion above that budgeted for routine operations. The force also included two and one third army divisions, ten air force tactical air wings, and about one third of a marine expeditionary force.

President Lands on the *Abraham Lincoln*

On May 1, 2003, 43 days after the beginning of Operation Iraqi Freedom, President Bush announced to the nation that "major combat operations in Iraq have ended." To further establish the aircraft carrier as the king of the navy, he made his announcement to a national TV audience from the deck of the USS *Abraham Lincoln*. The ship, which was in the Pacific heading toward California at the time, was going home for the first time in 10 months. During that time, in operations in Afghanistan and Iraq, the ship's air wing had dropped 1.6 million pounds of munitions, including 116 Tomahawk missiles.

The carrier had sailed 103,000 miles. More than 12,700 aircraft had launched and been recovered without a mishap. Also of note: There were 150 new dads aboard who had yet to see their newborn sons and daughters.

Ship's Log

President Bush landed on the *Abraham Lincoln* in the copilot seat of an S-3B Viking. The president had been a fighter pilot during the 1970s, having flown in an F-102 Delta Dagger during his stint in the Texas Air National Guard. He was asked if he had flown the Viking and admitted that the pilot had briefly turned over the controls to him. "Yes, I flew it," President Bush said, "Really exciting. I miss flying."

The Least You Need to Know

◆ During the latter half of 2002, U.S. military focus shifted from Afghanistan to Iraq.

◆ Aboard the *Kitty Hawk*, if a whistle blows an alert over the shipwide intercom, the carrier can activate its defense systems of missiles, automatic cannon, and machine guns in a matter of seconds.

◆ Many pilots viewed the bombing campaigns over the no-fly-zone in southern Iraq as a practice run for the war against Iraq.

◆ By the time Operation Iraqi Freedom began in March 2003, the United States had Iraq surrounded with carriers—with flattops ready to go in the Mediterranean Sea, the Persian Gulf, and the Arabian Sea.

Chapter 22

Carriers Around the World

In This Chapter

- ◆ Spanning the globe alphabetically
- ◆ Building new flattops
- ◆ Purchasing used carriers

Except for the occasional reference to a British carrier, we have pretty much limited our look at modern aircraft carriers to those in the U.S. Navy fleet. But many countries around the world have flattops as part of their naval defense. In this chapter, we will take a look at all the world's carriers.

You might be surprised to learn which countries have them—there's even an aircraft carrier in Thailand's navy! So as not to show favoritism, we'll take the countries in alphabetical order.

Brazil

Brazil has one World War II–era British-built Colossus-class light fleet carrier, called the *Minas Gerais*. After it was built—60 years ago—it spent some time in the Royal Navy. When it was a British ship, it was named the HMS *Vengeance*. It was built by Swan Hunter in Wallsend-on-Tyne.

The skip was laid down in 1942, launched in 1944, and it has been in service since 1945. It displaces 15,890 tons.

Brazil purchased the ship from Great Britain in December 1956 and had it refitted in Rotterdam. The refitting was completed in 1960. During the refitting, the ship received all new weapons, a steam-powered catapult, an angled flight deck, mirror optical landing equipment, new radar, and two new elevators.

The *Minas Gerais* underwent another refit between 1991 and 1993. At that time the ship received new navigational and landing control radars and a Brazilian-developed tactical data handling system incorporating data links for escorting vessels.

Although the ship is prepared to handle state-of-the-art fighter jets, at the moment its air group consists only of the following helicopters:

- SH-3A Sea King
- UH-13 Esquilo-II
- UH-14 Super Puma choppers

France

France has two aircraft carriers in its navy—one nuclear-powered and one conventionally powered. The nuke carrier is the *Charles de Gaulle*. It was laid down in 1989, launched in 1994, and has been in service since 2000.

The *Charles de Gaulle*

The *Charles de Gaulle* usually accommodates 35 to 40 aircraft. These include the following:

- 24 Rafale-M and Super étendard fixed-wing fighters
- 2 E-2C Hawkeye radar aircraft
- 14 Panther SAR helicopters

The crew consists of 1,950 people. Because of the small size of the flight deck—261 meters long with a 195-meter angled-deck portion—aircraft cannot take off and land at the same time. The ship has two 75-millimeter steam catapults. The catapults can launch aircraft up to 25 tons in weight.

The hangar deck has a lower ceiling than some, about 20 feet high, but—to make up for this—it is larger in area and better protected. The hangar is big enough to accommodate 23 fixed-wing aircraft and two helicopters at once.

The *Foch*

France's conventionally powered aircraft carrier is the *Foch*. Built in France, the ship was laid down in 1957, launched in 1960, and has been in service since July 1963.

Plans are for the *Foch* to be taken out of service and discarded in the near future. This ship is noted for being well-armored. The ship's thick layer of protection includes a reinforced flight deck, armored bulkheads in the engine room and in the magazines, and a reinforced-steel bridge superstructure.

Flattop Facts

Foch's older sister ship, the *Clemenceau*, was retired in 1997.

The hanger on the *Foch* usually accommodates 14 Super Étendard fighter-bombers, two Panther SAR helo, and two Super Frelon logistics helicopters. The machinery spaces and boilers are enclosed in an armored *redoubt*. Living spaces are air-conditioned. There are three bridges in the island, one each for flag, navigation, and aviation. The flight deck is 257 meters long.

Naval Lingo

A **redoubt** is an enclosed and defended space.

The two elevators are each capable of raising a 15-ton aircraft from the hangar deck to the flight deck in nine seconds. Two steam-powered catapults were installed during the 1980s. A small retractable ski-jump structure was added in 1994 to aid in the launching of a small French-built, single-seat fighter jet called the Rafale-M.

India

India's only aircraft carrier was the former HMS *Hermes*, which was laid down in 1944, launched in 1953, and placed in service in 1959. The British had stopped using the ship in 1985 and sold it to India the following year. India changed the name to the *Viraat*, which means "mighty." The ship displaces 23,900 tons and has the following aircraft onboard:

◆ Twelve Sea Harrier Mk 51

◆ Six Sea King Mk 42B ASW helicopters

◆ Three Sea King Mk 42C logistics helicopters

Flattop Facts

The *Viraat* suffered severe engine room flooding in 1993 when a main seawater induction valve failed in port during repairs.

During the 1970s the *Viraat* was converted from a standard aircraft carrier into a helicopter commando carrier. In 1981 it was adapted again to accommodate the Sea Harrier. This adaptation included the construction of a ski-jump takeoff ramp. The Sea King helicopters aboard the *Viraat* are equipped to launch Sea Eagle antiship missiles.

There are two aircraft elevators, one on the angled deck on the port side and one aft on the centerline. The ship has 25–50-millimeter armor over its magazines and machinery spaces.

The flight deck is approximately 20 millimeters thick. The ship has British computerized combat data systems. It also carries up to 80 torpedoes for its helicopters. The most recent refit, in 2000, incorporated a new long-range radar, a new and improved communications suite, a shipboard damage control alarm system, fire curtains in the hangar space, and new, faster elevators.

Plans are currently underway to add two aircraft carriers to the currently existing Indian navy. One is currently being built and is expected to be in service by 2010. The other is to be purchased from the Russian navy.

India's first carrier, recently deactivated, was adapted from a British carrier. India purchased the Majestic-class HMS *Hercules* from Britain in 1957 and transformed it into the INS *Vikrant*. Among its features were a single hangar, angled flight deck, electric elevators, a steam catapult, and air conditioning in all living spaces.

Two geared steam turbine units producing 20,000-shaft horsepower provided the *Vikrant*'s power plant and allowed it to travel at a maximum speed of 24.5 knots. The flight deck measured 680 by 128 feet. Displacement with a full load was 19,500 tons. Total crew was 1,345.

The air group consisted of Hawker Sea Hawks—known as White Tigers in the Indian navy—and Dassault Breguet Alizes—which are known as Cobras in India. In 1971, the *Vikrant* saw action in the India-Pakistan War. The ship and her air group proved to be a very important part of this conflict as these planes demolished five major Pakistani ports.

Italy

Italy has one aircraft carrier in its navy and a second, designed for V/STOL aircraft only, currently under construction. The existing carrier is the *Giuseppe Garibaldi*. This ship was laid down in 1981, launched in 1983, and has been in service since 1985. It is the flagship of the Italian fleet.

When holding a full load, the *Giuseppe Garibaldi* displaces 13,370 tons. It is 591 feet long with a beam at the waterline of 77 feet. It has a ski jump at the end of a flight deck that is 570 feet long and 100 feet wide. Maximum speed is 30 knots. Its range, when traveling at 20 knots, is 9,000 miles. The power plant, all 80,000-shaft horse-power of it, consists of four gas turbines. The ship has five decks.

When this ship first hit the seas, its air group was made up of 18 Sea King helicopters. There was room for 12 of them in the hangar, which measured 39 by 360 feet. Now the air group consists of anywhere from 6 to 20 Harriers.

Because this is a carrier geared toward helicopters, which under emergency conditions might have to take off and land in rough seas, the ship has two pairs of fin stabilizers.

The ship is armed to defend itself from three types of attack:

- From the air
- From surface vessels
- From submarines

The ship combats surface ships with four double missile launchers—that is, four launchers, each capable of launching two missiles simultaneously. Two launchers are located on either side of the hull, just forward of the transom. These launchers fire Otomat Mk.2 surface-skimming missiles.

To combat aircraft, the ship uses two Albatross system 8-cell SAM launchers that fire Aspide missiles. These launchers are located just forward and aft of the island. The fixed antisubmarine armament is made up of two triple-torpedo launchers. The ship also has two 105mm rocket launchers for short-range antiaircraft defense. Total crew: 825.

Russia

We learned earlier about a Russian aircraft carrier that had been retired from duty and is now serving as a theme park. But Russia, the former Soviet Union, still operates flattops. Today's Russian navy has two aircraft carriers, one for conventional take-off and landing aircraft and one for helicopters. Both ships are capable of fighting with more than their air power—both are equipped to fire guided missiles.

Kuznetsov

The longer of the two, the one for jets, is called the (take a deep breath) *Admiral Flota Sovetskogo Soyuza Kuznetsov*—but we'll call it *Kuznetsov* for short. It was built in the Ukraine, laid down in 1983, launched in 1985, and placed in service in 1991—just in time for the end of the Cold War.

The Kuznetsov displaces 55,000 tons when fully loaded. Its total length is 307 meters.

The Kuznetsov's air group consists of …

- Twenty-four Su-27K Flanker-D interceptors.
- Sixteen Ka-27PL Helix-A ASW helicopters.
- Three Ka-29RLD AEW helicopters.
- Two Ka-27PS Helix-C SAR helicopters.

Ship's Log

Admiral Flota Sovetskogo Soyuza Kuznetsov is the ship's third name. It was originally the *Leonid Brezhnev*, then the *Tbilisi*. It has had its current moniker since 1990.

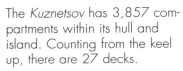

Flattop Facts

The *Kuznetsov* has 3,857 compartments within its hull and island. Counting from the keel up, there are 27 decks.

The ship also has 44 missile launchers, which can shoot Shipwreck, Gauntlet, and Grison missiles.

The original plan was for this ship to have a sister, the *Varyag*. It was laid down in 1985 and launched in 1988, but then the Soviet Union dissolved and, out of money, the Ukraine had the ship stricken in 1993. The *Varyag* was stripped of just about everything but the superstructure, which was sold by the Ukraine, and towed to Macao where it currently serves as a floating hotel and pleasure palace.

Admiral Gorshkov

Russia's helicopter carrier is called the *Admiral Gorshkov*. It was originally known as the *Baku*. Although I'm still counting this as a active member of the Russian navy, the truth is that it has not been out to sea under its own power since 1991, or, in other words, since the breakup of the Soviet Union.

I'm not just being kind. The ship is still officially commissioned and has a crew (skeletal though it is). It has had some tough times over the past decade, including two damaging fires, one in 1993 and another the following year. The reason that the ship is still commissioned, yet inactive, is that Russia is trying to sell it. It has had a prospective customer in India, but negotiations have dragged on for some time.

Admiral Gorshkov functions as a heli-coptertoting carrier now—it carries 24 choppers— but it was originally intended to accommodate V/TOL fighters as well. The original plans were for the ship's air group to consist of 14 Yak-41M Freehand and eight Yak-38 Forger VTOL fighters and sixteen Ka-27-series helicopters.

The ship's flight deck is 195 meters long. To improve airflow over the flight deck, there is a single, movable air-deflector plate. The hangar is 130 meters long and 25 meters wide. The ceiling is 6.6 meters high.

Ship's Log

All three of the Soviet Kiev-class carriers (the country's Cold War carriers) are out of action. The *Kiev* was scrapped in 1999. *Novorossiysk* was sold to India, while the stripped hulk of the *Minsk* was sold to an entertainment company in 1998 (price tag: $5 million) and is now being used as a gambling casino near Hong Kong.

Look Out Disney! Welcome to Flattop World!

Decommissioned Cold War–era Russian carriers are being used for something most unexpected: fun.

According to a Chinese newspaper, the Chinese port city of Tianjin is planning to spend the equivalent of $602 million to create a huge military-themed amusement park centered around a decommissioned Russian aircraft carrier.

Final Resting Place for the *Kiev*

The park is planned to be seven-square-kilometers and will feature a weapons display along with sightseeing and defense education areas. There will also be a 3.3-million-square-meter marine area.

If all goes as planned, the park will be the final resting place for the *Kiev*, a 30-year-old carrier that was decommissioned in 1995. A Tianjin company bought the carrier, which had been stripped of engines, weapons, and communications equipment for the equivalent of $8.4 million. The new owner had originally planned to cut the vessel up for scrap.

The *Minsk* Was First

The most amazing thing about this story is that, if the Chinese do manage to turn the *Kiev* into a theme park, it won't be the first foreign aircraft carrier to be transformed into a theme park in China.

The first was in South China, in the city of Shenzhen, near Hong Kong. The first aircraft carrier theme park opened in 2000. It is called Minsk World and uses another decommissioned aircraft carrier from the former Soviet Union, the *Minsk*. More than three million people have visited the park.

Spain

Spain's lone aircraft carrier is a modified U.S. Sea Control design and is currently named the *Príncipe de Asturias*. Since it went into service in 1988, it has had two other names as well—it was originally called the *Canarias* and then the name was changed to *Almirante Carrero*. The ship is currently based at Rota, where it is the flagship of the Spanish fleet. This ship's most noteworthy trait is that, like many of the new breed of carriers, it isn't really a flattop at all. It is a curved-top, with a 12° ski-jump on the bow. The takeoff pattern from the ski-jump is angled to starboard.

Its design includes two pairs of fin stabilizers, and its propeller system is designed to be quiet. Because the Spanish navy is now coed, the ship was recently modified to accommodate both sexes.

Príncipe de Asturias's air group consists of the following:

- ◆ Eight EAV-8B Harrier V/STOL fighters
- ◆ Two SH-60Bs
- ◆ Ten SH-3D/G
- ◆ Four AB-212

Flattop Facts

The *Príncipe de Asturias* was built at Ferrol in Spain by E. N. Bazán. The other aircraft carrier built by Bazán is currently the pride and joy of the Thai navy.

The flight deck is 175.3 meters long and 29 meters wide. There are two elevators, one at the extreme aft and the other to starboard of the flight path, forward of the island. It has a range of 6,500 miles when traveling at an average of 20 knots. The weapons system is fully computerized.

Thailand

Thailand's aircraft carrier is one of a kind, built by the same company that built Spain's carrier, E. N. Bazán of Ferrol, Spain. It is called the *Chakri Naruebet*, and with a ski jump on the bow, it greatly resembles its cousin, *Príncipe de Asturias* of Spain.

Chakri Naruebet's flight deck is 174 meters long. Its armament includes provisions for three Mistral missile launchers, although those systems are not currently operative. It has a range of 10,000 miles at an average speed of 12 knots.

Naval Lingo

Chakri Naruebet means "In Honor of the Chakri Dynasty."

Its air group consists of the following:

- Six AV-8S Matador V/STOL fighters

- Four S-70B-7 Seahawk helicopters

- Up to 14 other assorted helicopters (usually a combination of Sea King-sized choppers and CH-47 Chinook-sized helicopters)

The only problem with Thailand purchasing an aircraft carrier from Spain is that Thailand's navy really couldn't afford it. The ship—which accommodates a crew of 62 officers, 393 enlisted, and up to 146 air-crew personnel—is currently operating only one day each month, just to keep it from getting rusty, and it never leaves its naval base harbor at Sattahip.

Ship's Log

Thailand's aircraft carrier has special, ultraluxurious quarters for the Thai royal family.

The hull has 14 watertight compartments. It has two pairs of fin stabilizers. The hull form includes a wedge at the stern to improve speed and economy.

United Kingdom

The Royal Navy currently operates three Invincible-class carriers, with no plans to replace them until 2012. They are the *Invincible*, the *Illustrious*, and the *Ark Royal*, which were placed in service in 1980, 1982, and 1985, respectively.

The ships are rotated so that only two are active at any given time while the third undergoes repairs and maintenance. All the ships have a special hull and propeller system to make them hard to hear on enemy sensor systems.

They originally had 7° ski jumps on their bows, but these have been increased to 12° to help the Sea Harrier take off. The flight deck is 183 meters long and has been slightly angled to port to minimize the chances that an errant aircraft might strike the ship's Sea Dart SAM launcher.

The ships displace 20,710 tons when fully loaded. Each ship has a range of 7,000 miles at 18 knots. Each can accommodate a crew of 60 officers, 625 enlisted, plus 366 air group personnel, which includes another 80 officers.

Each ship has an air group consisting of ...

- Eight Sea Harrier FA.2 V/STOL fighter-bombers.

- Eight Sea King HAS.5 ASW helicopters.

- Three Sea King AEW.2A helicopters.

Although Great Britain might once have been the ruler of the sea, as you can see by the limited number of aircraft carriers it has today, that crown clearly belongs today to the United States.

The Least You Need to Know

- Some countries, like Russia and Thailand, have aircraft carriers that they cannot afford to operate.

- In 1971, the Indian carrier *Vikrant* saw action in the India-Pakistan War, and her air group demolished five major Pakistani ports.

- All three of the Soviet Union's Cold War–era carriers are out of action.

- Great Britain currently operates three Invincible-class carriers, with no plans to replace them until 2012.

Chapter 23

The Navy's Newest Carrier: The USS *Ronald Reagan*

In This Chapter

- ◆ Commissioning the USS *Ronald Reagan*
- ◆ Making modifications and updates
- ◆ CVN-76's specifications
- ◆ Looking ahead to the next new carrier

On Saturday, July 12, 2003, the U.S. Navy's newest nuclear aircraft carrier, the USS *Ronald Reagan*, stood as tall in the water as a 20-story building as it was commissioned into the navy. It was the first aircraft carrier to be named after a living president.

The ceremony took place under a cloudless sky at the Norfolk Naval Station in Norfolk, Virginia. Former First Lady Nancy Reagan shook hands with members of the crew and then officially brought the ship to life with the words, "Man the ship and bring her to life." The crowd of thousands cheered.

Ninth Nimitz-Class Carrier

Mrs. Reagan had also been present at the christening of the ship. She broke the bottle of champagne across the *Ronald Reagan*'s bow in 2001. Design work on the ship began in 1995, and the keel was laid in 1998. The ship is the ninth Nimitz-class carrier built for the navy since 1975.

> **Ship's Log**
>
> The USS *Ronald Reagan* replaces the 41-year-old USS *Constellation*, which left service after the Iraq war and, when this book went to press, was scheduled to be decommissioned in August 2003.

After Mrs. Reagan spoke the words, the crew of the ship was allowed to board, which they did on the run, sending a stream of sailors up the gangplank and onto the four-and-a-half-acre deck.

At that precise moment two F-14 Tomcats and two F-18 Hornets flew overhead in formation, and the carrier's whistle gave a long and loud toot.

Fifty-Year Lifespan

The ship is expected to serve the navy for the first half of the twenty-first century. It will be a part of the U.S. Navy's Pacific fleet, and will be based in San Diego, California. It will carry an airwing of more than 80 planes. From now on it will be the home of 6,000-plus sailors.

Like the other supercarriers in the navy, it will be able to move through the sea at a speed greater than 30 knots, and, because it is powered by a nuclear reactor, it will be able to go for more than 20 years—the full stint of a career sailor—without needing to be refueled.

A Celebration of the Gipper

Ronald Reagan, 92 at the time of the commissioning ceremony, could not attend because he suffers from Alzheimer's disease. Before the commissioning, many speakers talked about the former president. So even though the "Gipper" was not there physically, his presence was certainly felt.

The ship's commanding officer, Captain Bill Goodwin, said, "Quite frankly, there's not a better name for an aircraft carrier than *Ronald Reagan*."

United States senator John Warner of Virginia said, "Ronald Reagan had a classic optimism and rugged spirit. It is most fitting that this carrier should bear a name that reflects audacity, decisiveness, as well as the respect that our adversaries will hold for it and the great nation it represents."

Ship's Log

At the ceremony to commission the USS *Ronald Reagan*, Vice President Dick Cheney said, "This is a great American ship bearing a great American name. Today's navy is, in many ways, a monument to Reagan's vision. He came to the presidency with a clear understanding of the tools our navy would need to protect the American people. If the purpose of naming an aircraft carrier is to convey the strength and seriousness of this country and our military, then we have certainly accomplished that. Something tells me that any potential adversary of the United States will take notice when word arrives that the USS *Ronald Reagan* has been sighted offshore."

Warner, chairman of the Senate Armed Services Committee and a former navy secretary, continued, "Nothing could shake Ronald Reagan's determination to rebuild the strength and the morale of every branch of the United States military. Nothing could shake his deep moral confidence and sense of purpose. And because of these qualities, Ronald Reagan changed the course of history as few men have ever done. He has seen the cause he stood for vindicated in his own lifetime, and the free peoples of the world will honor his name for generations to come."

Flattop Facts

The carrier was built by a division of Northrop Grumman in Newport News, Virginia, The contract to build the ship was awarded December 6, 1994.

A Thoroughly Modern Ship

The USS *Ronald Reagan* (CVN-76) was built using more than one billion parts from over three thousand suppliers in 47 states and the District of Columbia. Although it is a Nimitz-class ship, it uses laser, electronic, satellite, and computer technologies that were unavailable when the USS *Nimitz* was delivered to the navy in 1975.

A New Bow

The bow was lowered onto the ship in March 2000. *Ronald Reagan* is the first Nimitz-class carrier to have a new bulbous bow design, which outweighs bows erected on previous carriers by about 120 tons. The new bow increases propulsion efficiency and provides more buoyancy to the forward end of the ship.

The new bow will be incorporated into the next scheduled aircraft carrier, the USS *George H. W. Bush* (CVN-77) and may become a retrofitted design-change for all Nimitz-class carriers during future refueling and overhaul.

Fact Box

USS *Ronald Reagan* Specifications

Class: Nimitz

Builder: Newport News Shipbuilding Company, Newport News, Virginia

Keel laid: 1998

Christened: 2001

Commissioned: July 12, 2003

Length: 1,092 feet

Waterline beam: 134 feet

Flight deck width: 252 feet

Displacement: 97,000 tons

Top Speed: 34.5 miles per hour

Aircraft: 85

Elevators: 4

Catapults: 4

Power plant: Two A4W nuclear reactors, four steam turbines, four screws, producing more than 260,000 shaft horsepower

Endurance: 1.5 million nautical miles

Cost: About $4.5 billion

Naval Lingo

CMWDS stands for countermeasure wash-down systems.

Flattop Facts

The ship's motto is "Peace Through Strength," a phrase coined by President Reagan. The phrase was taken from a September 24, 1988, radio address to the nation on foreign policy, in which President Reagan uttered the words, "If we have learned anything these last eight years, it's that peace through strength works."

As part of what is called the ship's *CMWDS*, the *Ronald Reagan* has a series of sprinklers in vital areas throughout the ship. In case of emergency, these would help contain the spread of fire or chemical, biological, or radiological attacks.

Modified Island

The island was installed on November 11, 2000. The *Ronald Reagan* has a significantly modified island, with a new mainmast and radar and communications antennas completely rearranged. The height of the island is unchanged from previous Nimitz-class islands, but there is one fewer deck, and each remaining deck has become taller to compensate.

In May 2003, the ship went out to sea for the first time for its Builders' Sea Trials off the coast of

Virginia. Sailors assigned to the ship worked in conjunction with shipbuilders Northrop Grumman and Newport News to make sure that all the state-of-the-art systems aboard the vessel worked properly. The ship passed every test with flying colors.

Mission: Defend Freedom

According to the U.S. Navy, the mission of the USS *Ronald Reagan* is …

> … to provide sea-based tactical air power for defense of America's right to freedom of the seas as well as the protection of United States sovereignty.
>
> USS *Ronald Reagan* will be capable of projecting tactical air power over the sea and inland, as well as providing sea-based air defense and anti-submarine warfare capabilities.
>
> [It] will execute response options ranging from peacetime presence to general war. The air wing embarked will be able to destroy enemy aircraft, ships, submarines, and land targets, or lay mines hundreds of miles from the ship.
>
> USS *Ronald Reagan's* aircraft will be used to conduct strikes, support land battles, protect the battle group or other friendly shipping, and implement a sea or air blockade. The air wing will provide a visible presence to demonstrate American power and resolve in a crisis.

The new ship has plenty of punch in addition to its airwing. The ship is armed with three Mk.29 eight-cell NATO Sea Sparrow launchers, four Phalanx CIWS, and a classified number of 21-cell RAM launchers.

Also aboard the *Ronald Reagan* is a bronze piece of artwork, a profile of the fortieth president affixed to a small portion of the Berlin Wall. The artist, Chas Fagan, a former Soviet Studies major, has said, "The events [since 9-11] have called on us to apply a bit of Reagan-like resolve in facing down those who would do us harm. The name 'Ronald Reagan' is a bold reminder of the strength that comes from character and steadfastness …. The USS *Ronald Reagan* will sail with the memory of the president."

Next in Line

As noted previously, the next aircraft carrier to enter service with the U.S. Navy will be CVN-77, named the USS *George H. W. Bush*, after the naval aviator and former president of the United States, George Herbert Walker Bush.

The ship was named after the elder President Bush in a ceremony held December 9, 2002, at the Pentagon in Washington, D.C. Like the *Ronald Reagan,* the ship is being built in Newport News. It is scheduled to join the fleet in 2009.

So with the commissioning of the *Ronald Reagan,* and the building of the next CV, the *George H. W. Bush*, aircraft carriers will remain the most powerful thing that floats well into the future.

The Least You Need to Know

- The USS *Ronald Reagan* is the newest American aircraft carrier and the first to be named after a living president.

- The USS *Ronald Reagan* stands as tall in the water as a 20-story building.

- The ship is expected to serve the navy for more than 50 years.

- The ship has a brand new bulbous bow design that increases propulsion efficiency and provides more buoyancy to the forward end of the ship.

- With its classified number of missile launchers, the ship packs a punch above and beyond that of its airwing.

Appendix A

Acronyms

AAA   Antiaircraft artillery, also known as triple-A or flak

AAM   Air-to-air missile

AAW   Antiaircraft warfare

ACV   Auxiliary aircraft carrier

AEW   Airborne early warning

AEWC   Airborne early warning and control

AFCS   Automatic flight control system

AIM   Air intercept missile

AMRAAM   Advanced middle-range air-to-air missile

ASM   Antiship missile

ASR   Air-sea rescue

ASUW   Antisurface warfare

ASW   Antisubmarine warfare

ATACO   Air tactical control officer

ATARS   Advanced tactical air reconnaissance system

ATO   Airborne tactical officer

AVG   Aircraft escort vessel

AVT   Auxiliary aircraft transport

AWACS   Airborne warning and control system

BMEWS   Ballistic missile early warning system

BPDMS   Basic point defense missile system

CAM   Catapult aircraft merchant

CAP   Combat air patrol

CAS   Close air support

CATCC   Carrier air traffic control center

CATG   Commander amphibious task group

CCA   Carrier controlled approach

CIC   Combat information center

CINC   Commander-in-chief

CIWS   Close-in weapon system

COD   Carrier onboard delivery

CTOL   Conventional takeoff and landing

CV   U.S. Navy designation for aircraft carrier

CVA   U.S. Navy designation for attack aircraft carrier

CVAN   Nuclear-powered attack aircraft carrier

CVB   Battle aircraft carrier

CVBG   Aircraft carrier battle group

CVE   Escort aircraft carrier

CVHE   Helicopter escort aircraft carrier

CVL   Light aircraft carrier

CVN   Nuclear-powered aircraft carrier

CVS   Support aircraft carrier

CVU   Utility aircraft carrier

DDG   Guided missile destroyer

DIANE   Digital integrated attack and navigation equipment

DLCO   British abbreviation for deck landing control officer

DP   Dual-purpose

ECM   Electronic countermeasures

ESM   Electronics surveillance measures

ESMO   Electronic support measures operator

EWO   Electronic warfare operator

FAA   Fleet air arm; British term

FAADS   Forward area air defense system

FAC   Forward air controller

FFG   Guided missile frigate

FLIR   A type of radar known as forward-looking infrared

FOD   Foreign object damage

GCI   Ground control intercept

HARM   High-speed antiradiation missile

HOTAS   Hands on throttle and stick

HUD   Heads-up display

IADS   Integrated air defense system

ICBM   Intercontinental ballistic missile

IFF   Identification friend or foe

IR   Infrared

JBD   Jet blast deflectors

LFC   Landing force commander

LSO   Landing signal officer

MAC   Merchant aircraft carriers (Great Britain)

MAD   Magnetic anomaly detector

MAG   Marine aircraft wing

Navair   Naval air systems command

NFO   Naval flight officer

OTH   Over the horizon

Remro   Remote radar operator

RIO   Radar intercept officer

SAC   Supporting arms coordinator

SAG   Surface action group

SAM   Surface to air missile

SAR   Search and Rescue

SCS   Sea control ship

Senso   Sensor operator

SLOC   Sea lines of communication

SSM   Surface to surface missile

STO   Short takeoff

STOL   Short takeoff and landing

STO/VL   Short takeoff/vertical landing

TAC   Tactical air coordinator

TACAN   Tactical airborne navigation

Tacco   Tactical coordinator

TAC-TAS   Tactical towed array sonar system

TARPS   Tactical air reconnaissance pod system

TASM   Tactical air to surface missile

VDS   Variable depth sonar

VFR   Visual flight rules

VIFF   Vectoring in forward flight

VOD   Vertical onboard delivery

V/STOL   Vertical/short takeoff and landing

VTOL   Vertical takeoff and landing

WOD   Wind over deck

U.S. Navy Aircraft Carriers

Hull No.	Ship	Commissioned	Decommissioned (or loss)	Disposition
1	*Langley*	March 20, 1922	February 27, 1942	Converted to AV 3; sunk by enemy action about 75 miles south of Tjilatjap
2	*Lexington*	December 14, 1927	May 8, 1942	Sunk during the Battle of the Coral Sea
3	*Saratoga*	November 16, 1927	July 26, 1946	Sunk during atom bomb test at Bikini Atoll
4	*Ranger*	June 4, 1934	October 18, 1946	Sold for scrap to Sun Shipbuilding & Drydock Company
5	*Yorktown*	September 30, 1937	June 7, 1942	Sunk at the Battle of Midway
6	*Enterprise*	May 12, 1938	February 17, 1947	Sold
7	*Wasp*	April 25, 1941	September 15, 1942	Sunk by enemy action off San Cristobel Island
8	*Hornet*	October 20, 1941	October 26, 1942	Sunk by enemy action at the Battle of the Santa Cruz Islands
9	*Essex*	December 31, 1942	June 30, 1969	Stricken 1973; sold for scrapping 1975.
10	*Yorktown*	April 15, 1943	June 27, 1970	Stricken 1973; became a museum in Charleston, South Carolina, 1975
11	*Intrepid*	August 16, 1943	March 15, 1974	Became a floating museum in New York City in 1982
12	*Hornet*	November 29, 1943	May 26, 1970	Stricken, 1989; turned into a museum, 1998
13	*Franklin*	January 31, 1944	February 17, 1947	Stricken, 1964

Hull No.	Ship	Commissioned	Decommissioned (or loss)	Disposition
14	*Ticonderoga*	May 8, 1944	September 1, 1973	Stricken, 1973; sold for scrap, 1975
15	*Randolph*	October 9, 1944	February 13, 1969	Stricken, 1973; sold for scrap, 1975
16	*Lexington*	February 17, 1943	November 8, 1991	Stricken, 1991; now a museum in Corpus Christi, Texas
17	*Bunker Hill*	May 25, 1943	July 9, 1947	Stricken, 1966; retained as test ship until 1972; scrapped, 1973
18	*Wasp*	November 24, 1943	July 1, 1972	Sold for scrap, 1973
19	*Hancock*	April 15, 1944	January 30, 1976	Stricken and sold for scrap, 1976
20	*Bennington*	August 6, 1944	January 15, 1970	Stricken, 1989; scrapped 1994
21	*Boxer*	April 16, 1945	December 1, 1969	Stricken, 1969; scrapped 1971
22	*Independence*	January 14, 1943	August 28, 1946	Sunk as target, 1951.
23	*Princeton*	February 25, 1943	October 24, 1944	Sunk by enemy in the Sibuyan Sea
24	*Belleau Wood*	March 31, 1943	January 13, 1947	Transferred to France, 1953–1960; returned; stricken and scrapped, 1960
25	*Cowpens*	May 28, 1943	January 13, 1947	Stricken and scrapped, 1959
26	*Monterey*	June 17, 1943	January 16, 1956	Stricken, 1970; scrapped, 1971
27	*Langley*	August 31, 1943	February 11, 1947	Transferred to France, 1951–1963; sold 1964

continues

continues

Hull No.	Ship	Commissioned	Decommissioned (or loss)	Disposition
28	*Cabot*	July 24, 1943	January 21, 1955	Transferred to Spain, 1967; returned to private U.S. organization, 1989; auctioned by U.S. Marshals Service to Sabe Marine Salvage, 1999
29	*Bataan*	November 17, 1943	April 9, 1954	Stricken, 1959; scrapped 1961
30	*San Jacinto*	December 15, 1943	March 1, 1947	Stricken, 1970; scrapped 1971
31	*Bon Homme Richard*	November 26, 1944	July 2, 1971	Stricken, 1989; scrapped, 1992
32	*Leyte*	April 11, 1946	May 15, 1959	Stricken, 1969
33	*Kearsarge*	May 2, 1946	January 15, 1970	Stricken, 1973; scrapped, 1974
34	*Oriskany*	September 25, 1950	September 20, 1979	Stricken, 1989
35	*Reprisal*	Never completed		Hull scrapped 1949
36	*Antietam*	January 28, 1945	May 8, 1963	Stricken and scrapped, 1973
37	*Princeton*	November 18, 1945	January 30, 1970	Stricken, 1970
38	*Shangri-La*	September 15, 1944	July 30, 1971	Stricken, 1982
39	*Lake Champlain*	June 3, 1945	May 2, 1966	Stricken, 1969; scrapped 1972
40	*Tarawa*	December 8, 1945	May 13, 1960	Stricken, 1967
41	*Midway*	September 10, 1945	April 11, 1992	Stricken, 1997; may be used as museum
42	*Franklin D. Roosevelt*	October 27, 1945	October 1, 1977	Stricken, 1977; scrapped, 1978
43	*Coral Sea*	October 1, 1947	April 26, 1990	Scrapped, 1993
45	*Valley Forge*	November 3, 1946	January 15, 1970	Stricken, 1970; scrapped 1971
47	*Philippine Sea*	May 11, 1946	December 28, 1958	Stricken, 1969

Hull No.	Ship	Commissioned	Decommissioned (or loss)	Disposition
48	*Saipan*	July 14, 1946	January 14, 1970	Name changed to *Arlington*, 1965; scrapped 1976
49	*Wright*	February 9, 1947	May 27, 1970	Scrapped, 1980
59	*Forrestal*	October 1, 1955	September 30, 1993	Stricken, 1993; may be converted into a museum
60	*Saratoga*	April 14, 1956	August 20, 1994	Stricken, 1994
61	*Ranger*	August 10, 1957	July 10, 1993	In inactive reserve
62	*Independence*	January 10, 1959	September 30, 1998	In inactive reserve
63	*Kitty Hawk*	April 29, 1961	Active	
64	*Constellation*	October 27, 1961	Active	
65	*Enterprise*	November 25, 1961	Active	
66	*America*	January 23, 1965	August 9, 1996	Stricken, to be scrapped
67	*John F. Kennedy*	September 7, 1968	Active	
68	*Nimitz*	May 3, 1975	Active	
69	*Dwight D. Eisenhower*	October 18, 1977	Active	
70	*Carl Vinson*	March 13, 1982	Active	
71	*Theodore Roosevelt*	October 25, 1986	Active	
72	*Abraham Lincoln*	November 11, 1989	Active	
73	*George Washington*	July 4, 1992	Active	
74	*John C. Stennis*	December 9, 1995	Active	
75	*Harry S. Truman*	July 25, 1998	Active	
76	*Ronald Reagan*	Under construction		

Foreign Aircraft Carrier and Carrier Aircraft Specifications

Aircraft Carriers

Brazil

British Colossus Class

Number: A11

Name: *Minas Gerais*

Homeport: Rio de Janeiro

Status: Active

Boilers: 4

Airwing:

    4 SH-3A Sea Kings

    2 UH-13 Esquilo-IIs

    2 UH-14 Super Pumas

Range: 12,000 miles at 14 knots

China

Shichang Multirole Support Ship

Number: 82

Name: *Shichang*

Homeport: Unavailable

Status: Active

France

Charles De Gaulle Nuclear-Powered, Light Multirole Aircraft Carrier

Number: R91

Name: *Charles De Gaulle*

Homeport: Brest

Status: Active

Power: Nuclear

Laid down: 1989

Launched: 1994

Commissioned: 2000

Airwing:

   24 Rafale-M and/or Super étenard fixed-wing fighters

   2 E-2C Hawkeye radar aircraft

   A fluctuating number of Panther SAR helicopters

Aircraft cannot take off and land at the same time.

Clemenceau Light Multirole Aircraft Carrier

Number: R98

Name: *Clemenceau*

Homeport: Toulon

Status: Decommissioned, September 1997

Power: Conventional

Laid down: 1957

Launched: 1960

Commissioned: 1963

Builder: Ch. De l'Atlantique, St.-Nazaire

Airwing:

    14 Super Étenard fighter-bombers

    2 Panther SAR helicopters

    2 Super-Frelon logistics helicopters

India

Viraat VSTOL Aircraft Carrier (United Kingdom Hermes Class)

Number: R22

Name: *Viraat*

Homeport: Bombay

Status: Active

Power: Conventional

Laid down: 1944

Launched: 1953

Commissioned: 1959

Airwing:

    12 Sea Harrier Mk 51

    6 Sea King Mk 42B ASW helicopters

    3 Sea King Mk 42C logistics helicopters

Range: 6,500 miles at 14 knots

Crew: 143 officers, 1,207 enlisted

Italy

Luigi Einaudi VSTOL Aircraft Carrier

Number: C552

Name: *Luigi Einaudi*

Homeport: None

Status: Planned

Builder: Fincantieri, Muggiano (La Spezio)

Laid down: 2001

Launching (scheduled): 2005

Commission (scheduled): 2007

Airwing:

   8 AV-8B-plus Harriers, or

   12 EH.101 helicopters (usually a mix of the two aircraft)

Range: 7,000 miles at 20 knots

Crew: 430 ship's company, 203 air group, 140 flag staff, 620 troops, 1,390 total

Giuseppe Garibaldi VSTOL Aircraft Carrier

Number: C551

Name: *Giuseppe Garibaldi*

Homeport: Taranto

Status: Active

Builder: Italcantieri, Monfalcone

Laid down: 1981

Launched: 1983

Commissioned: 1985

Airwing:

   16 SH-3D Sea King helicopters, or

   10 AV-8B-plus Harriers

Japan

Osumi-Class Amphibious Assault Ships

Number: LST 4001

Name: *Osumi*

Homeport: Kure

Status: Active

Builder: Mitsui, Tamano

Laid down: 1995

Launched: 1996

Commissioned: 1998

Crew: 135 (also carries 330 troops; can accommodate as many as 1,000 troops in emergency)

Number: LST 4003

Name: (none)

Homeport: (none)

Status: Under construction

Number: LST 4002

Name: *Shimokita*

Homeport: (none)

Status: Under construction

Russia

Kuznetsov Multirole Aircraft Carrier

Number: 11435

Name: *Admiral Flota Sovetskogo Soyuza*

Homeport: (none)

Status: Active

Builder: Chernomorskiy (Nosenko); Nikolayev, Ukraine

Laid down: 1983

Launched: 1985

Commissioned: 1991

Airwing:

    18 Su-27K/Su-33

    4 Su-26UTG

    17 Ka-27

    2 Ka-31

Range: 3,850 miles at 29 knots

Endurance: 45 days

Crew: 510 officers, 1,442 enlisted ship's company, 626 air group, 40 flag staff

Ship was formerly known as the *Tbilisi*, *Leonid Brezhnev*, and *Riga*.

Modified Kiev Class

Number: 11434

Name: *Admiral Gorshkov*

Homeport: (none)

Status: non-operational

Builder: Chernomorskiy (Nosenko), Nikolayev, Ukraine

Laid down: 1978

Launched: 1982

Commissioned: 1987

Airwing:

    19 Ka-27PL Helix-A ASW helicopters

    2 Ka-27PS Helix-D SAR utility helicopters

Range: 4,050 miles at 29 knots

Endurance: 30 days

Crew: 383 officers, 1,229 enlisted, 430 air group, 50 flag staff

Ship was formerly known as the *Baku*.

Spain

Príncipe De Asturias VSTOL Aircraft Carrier

Number: R11

Name: *Príncipe De Asturias*

Homeport: Rota

Status: Active

Power: Conventional

Laid down: 1979

Launched: 1982

Commissioned: 1988

Airwing:

    6–12 EAV-8B Harrier

    6–10 SH-3 helicopters

    2–4 AB-212EW helicopters

    2 SH-60B helicopters

Range: 6,500 miles at 20 knots

Crew: 90 officers, 465 enlisted, 201 air group, 7 flag staff

Ship was formerly named the *Canarias*, and the *Almirante Carrero*.

Thailand

Chakri Naruebet VSTOL Aircraft Carrier

Number: 911

Name: *Chakri Naruebet*

Homeport: Sattahip

Status: Reduced operating status

Power: Conventional

Builder: E. N. Bazan, Ferrol, Spain

Laid down: 1994

Launched: 1996

Commissioned: 1997

Airwing:

    14 AV-SS Matador VSTOL fighters

    4 S-70B-7 Seahawk helicopters

Range: 7,150 miles at 16.5 knots

Crew: 62 officers, 393 enlisted, 146 air group, 675 troops

United Kingdom

Invincible-Class VSTOL Aircraft Carriers

Number: R05

Name: *Invincible*

Homeport: Portsmouth

Status: Active

Power: Conventional

Builder: Vickers, Barrow

Laid down: 1973

Launched: 1977

Commissioned: 1980

Airwing:

    8 Sea Harrier FA.2 VSTOL fighter-bombers

    8 Sea King HAS.5 ASW helicopters

    3 Sea King AEW.2A helicopters

Range: 7,000 miles at 18 knots

Crew: 60 officers and 625 enlisted plus air group

Number: R06

Name: *Illustrious*

Homeport: Portsmouth

Status: Active

Power: Conventional

Builder: Swan Hunter, Wallsend

Laid down: 1976

Launched: 1978

Commissioned: 1982

Airwing:

    8 Sea Harrier FA.2 VSTOL fighter-bombers

    8 Sea King HAS.5 ASW helicopters

    3 Sea King AEW.2A helicopters

Range: 7,000 miles at 18 knots

Crew: 60 officers and 625 enlisted plus air group

Number: R07

Name: *Ark Royal*

Homeport: Portsmouth

Status: Active

Power: Conventional

Builder: Swan Hunter, Wallsend

Laid down: 1978

Launched: 1981

Commissioned: 1985

Airwing:

    8 Sea Harrier FA.2 VSTOL fighter-bombers

    8 Sea King HAS.5 ASW helicopters

    3 Sea King AEW.2A helicopters

Range: 7,000 miles at 18 knots

Crew: 60 officers and 625 enlisted plus air group

Carrier Aircraft

Brazil

SH-3A Sea King

Contractor: Sikorsky Aircraft, Division of United Technologies

Mission: Helicopter with antisubmarine warfare, search and rescue, and miscellaneous utility roles, including limited external cargo capability

Weight: 14,000 lbs. dry; 21,000 lbs. maximum operating

Dimensions:

    Main rotor diameter: 62 feet

    Main rotor disc area: 3,019 square feet

    Length: 72 feet, 7.5 inches

Power plant: Two General Electric T-58-GE-402 turbo-shaft engines producing 3,000 horse-power

Armament:

    Two MK-46/44 antisubmarine torpedoes

    Various sonobuoys and pyrotechnic devices

Endurance: 5 hours

Range: 500-plus miles

Internal capacity: 10

Rescue hoist lifting capacity: 600 lbs.

UH-13 Esquilo-II

Contractor: Bell Helicopter

Mission: Transport

Weight: 2,800 lbs. loaded

Dimensions:

> Height: 9 feet, 4 inches
>
> Main rotor diameter: 37 feet, 2 inches
>
> Tail rotor diameter: 5 feet, 10 inches
>
> Overall length: 43 feet, 4 inches

Power plant: Lycoming O-435 of 240 horsepower

Armament: None

Cost: $65,000

Maximum speed: 105 mph

Cruising speed: 100 mph

Range: 300 miles

Service ceiling: 17,000 feet

UH-14 Super Puma

Builder: Aerospatiale

Origin: France

Mission: Transport helicopter

Weight: 9,832 lbs. empty; 19,841 lbs. maximum takeoff

Dimensions:

> Maximum speed: 163 mph
>
> Maximum range: 523 miles
>
> Main rotor diameter: 51 feet, 2.2 inches
>
> Length: 61 feet, 4.2 inches
>
> Height: 16 feet, 1.7 inches

Power plant: 2 1400-kW (1,877-shp) Turbomeca Makila turbo-shafts

Armament:

  Optional cannon

  Machine-guns or rocket-launcher pods

User countries: Argentina, Brazil, Chile, Republic of the Congo, Finland, France, Gabon, Germany, Indonesia, Japan, Jordan, Kuwait, Mexico, Nepal, Netherlands, Oman, Saudi Arabia, Singapore, South Korea, Spain, Sweden, Switzerland, Thailand, Togo, Turkey, United Arab Emirates, Venezuela, Zimbabwe

France

Rafale-M

Builder/contractor: Dassault Aviation

Mission: Fighter jet

Weight: 21,319 lbs. empty; 47,399 lbs. maximum takeoff

Dimensions:

  Length: 50 feet, 2.5 inches

  Height: 17 feet, 6.25 inches

  Wing span: 35 feet, 9.25 inches

Power plant: SNECMA M88-3 afterburning turbofans

Armament:

  1 internal DEFA 791 B 30mm cannon

  Up to 13,228 lbs. of ordnance carried on up to 13 external hard points

Maximum level speed at 36,069 feet: Mach 2.0

Service ceiling: 54,000 feet

E-2C Hawkeye Radar Plane

Builder: Grumman Aerospace Corp.

Mission: An early warning, command, and control platform, whose task is to provide airborne radar coverage around a carrier battle group

Weight: 40,600 lbs. empty; 53,000 lbs. maximum takeoff

Dimensions:

  Wingspan: 80 feet, 7 inches

  Length: 57 feet, 9 inches

Height: 18 feet, 4 inches

Wing area: 700 square feet

Power plant: Two Allison T56-A-425 turboprop engines (9,200 horsepower)

Armament: None

Crew: 5

Service Ceiling: 37,000 feet

Panther Search-and-Rescue Helicopter

Builder: Aerospatiale

Mission: Search and rescue

Weight: 5,071 lbs. empty; 9,460 lbs. maximum with external load

Dimensions:

Rotor diameter: 39.17 feet

Fenestron tail rotor diameter: 3.6 feet

Power plant: 2 Turbomeca Arriel IMI turbo-shafts

Speed: 177 mph maximum

Endurance: Over 4 hours with standard tanks

Range: 509 miles maximum with standard tanks

Capacity: 2 pilots; 10 equipped troops

Super Frelon Logistics Helicopter

Builder: Aerospatiale

Mission: Search and rescue; antisubmarine warfare

Weight: 15,130 lbs. empty; 228,660 lbs. maximum takeoff

Dimensions:

Main rotor diameter: 62 feet

Length (rotors turning): 75 feet, 6.7 inches

Height: 22 feet, 2.1 inches

Power plant: three 1,171-kW (1,570-shp) Turbomeca Turmo IIIC6 turbo-shafts

Armament:

Four homing torpedoes in the ASW role, or

Two Exocet missiles

Speed: 154 mph maximum

Range: 4 hours maximum

User countries: People's Republic of China, Democratic Republic of the Congo, France, Iraq, Israel, Libya

Italy

AV-8B Harrier VSTOL Fighter Jet

Builder: McDonnell Douglas

Mission: Attack and destroy surface targets under day and night visual conditions

Dimensions:

Length: 46.3 feet

Wing span: 30.3 feet

Power plant: One Rolls Royce F402-RR-408 turbofan engine

Armament:

MK-82 series 500-lb. bombs

MK-83 series 1,000-lb. bombs

GBU-12 500-lb. laser-guided bombs

GBU-16 1,000-lb. laser-guided bombs

AGM-65F IR Maverick missiles

AGM-65E Laser Maverick missiles

CBU-99 cluster munitions

AIM-9M sidewinders

Lightning II targeting POD to deliver GBU-12 and GBU-16 bombs with pinpoint accuracy

Thrust: F402-44-408: 23,400 pounds

Crew: 1

Cost per aircraft: $23,700,000

EH-101 Helicopter

Builder: EH Industries

Mission: Shipborne and land-based multirole naval helicopter

Weight: 15,667 lbs. empty; 29,766 lbs. maximum takeoff

Dimensions:

    Rotor diameter: 60.4 feet

    Length: 74.1 feet

    Height: 21.6 feet

Power plant: Three Rolls-Royce/Turbomeca RTM 322 turbo-shafts

Armament: External provision for up to 2,112 lbs. of weapons, such as four lightweight homing torpedoes

Crew: Four

User countries: Canada, Italy, United Kingdom

Sea King helicopter

(See Brazil)

Russia

Su-27K Fighter Jet

Country of origin: Russia

Mission: Interceptor, establishment of air superiority

Weight: 66,000 lbs. maximum

Dimensions:

    Length: 69 feet

    Wing span: 47 feet, 6 inches

Power plant: Two 12,550kg thrust Lyulka AL-31F

Armament:

    One 30mm GSh-301 cannon

    Up to 6,000 kg payload of missiles and bombs including

        Alamo air-to-air missiles

        Archer air-to-air missiles

Speed: Mach 2.35 maximum

Crew: 1

Ceiling: 49,530–58,500 feet

Payload: 13,200 lbs.

User countries: Belarus, Russia, People's Republic of China, Ukraine

Ka-27 Helix Helicopter

Country of origin: Russia

Builder: Kamov

Mission: Shipborne antisubmarine helicopter

Weight: 24,251 lbs. normal takeoff; 27,778 lbs. maximum takeoff

Dimensions:

    Rotor diameter: 52 feet, 2 inches each

    Length: 37 feet, 0.9 inches

    Height: 17 feet, 8.6 inches

Power plant: Two 1660-kW (2.225-shp) Isotov TVS-117V turbo-shafts

Armament:

    Under-fuselage weapons bay for torpedoes and other stores

    Stowage for sonobuoys and wire-guided torpedoes

Speed: 155 mph maximum

Range: 497 miles maximum

User countries: India, Russia, South Korea, Ukraine, Vietnam

Spain

AV-8B Harrier

(See Italy)

SH-3A Sea King

(See Brazil)

SH-60B Sea Hawk

Builders: Sikorsky Aircraft Corporation (airframe); General Electric Company (engines); IBM Corporation (avionics components)

Country of origin: United States

Mission: Used for antisubmarine warfare, search and rescue, drug interdiction, antiship warfare, cargo lift, and special operations

Weight: Varies; 21,000 lbs.

Dimensions:

    Length: 64 feet, 10 inches

    Height: 13 feet

    Rotor diameter: 53 feet, 8 inches

Power plant: Two General Electric T700-GE-700 or T700-GE-701C engines

Armament:

    Two 7.62mm machine guns mounted in the windows

    AGM-114 Hellfire or AGM-119 Penguin missiles

    Three Mk46 or Mk 50 torpedoes, or additional .50-caliber machine guns mounted in the doors

Speed: 180 knots maximum

Range: 380 nautical miles, range becomes unlimited with air refueling capability.

Crew: 3

Thrust: Up to 1,940 shaft horsepower

Thailand

AV-8S Matador V/TOL Fighter

Specifications are similar to AV-8B Harrier (See Italy)

United Kingdom

AV-8B Harrier

(See Italy)

SH-3A Sea King

(See Brazil)

Aircraft Carriers Sunk During World War II

American

Lexington, May 8, 1942
Yorktown, June 7, 1942
Wasp, September 15, 1942
Hornet, October 26, 1942
Liscombe Bay, November 24, 1943
Block Island, May 29, 1944
Princeton, October 24, 1944
St. Lô, October 25, 1944
Gambier Bay, October 25, 1944
Ommaney Bay, January 4, 1945
Bismarck Sea, February 21, 1945

British

Courageous, September 17, 1939
Glorious, June 8, 1940
Ark Royal, November 14, 1941
Hermes, April 9, 1942
Eagle, August 11, 1942

Avenger, November 15, 1942
Dasher, March 27, 1943
Nabob, August 22, 1944
Thane, January 15, 1945

Japanese

Shoho, May 8, 1942
Akagi, June 4, 1942
Kaga, June 4, 1942
Hiryu, June 4, 1942
Soryu, June 4, 1942
Ryujo, August 24, 1942
Chuyo, December 4, 1943
Shokaku, June 19, 1944
Taiho, June 19, 1944
Hiyo, June 20, 1944
Taiyo, August 18, 1944
Unyo, September 16, 1944
Zuikaku, October 25, 1944
Zuiho, October 25, 1944
Chitose, October 25, 1944
Chiyoda, October 25, 1944
Shinyo, November 17, 1944
Shinano, November 29, 1944
Unryu, December 19, 1944
Yamashio Maru, February 17, 1945
Amagi, July 24, 1945
Shimane Maru, July 24, 1945
Otakisan Maru, August 25, 1945 (sunk by mine after war)

Glossary

abaft   Toward or at the stern of a boat or ship; behind.

air boss   Officer in charge of launching and recovering aircraft—on the hangar deck and flight deck.

airdale   Flight deck crewman.

air wing   All the aircraft on a single aircraft carrier.

beam   Width of a ship at its widest point.

blue on blue   Friendly fire.

bolter   An aborted landing on an aircraft carrier.

bow   Front of the ship.

brigantine   A two-masted, square-rigged ship.

chaff   Strips of aluminum foil fired into the air to confuse enemy radar.

chit   Signed voucher for either money or the answer to a request for something, e.g., to change watches with another person, to go to the front of the line during chow. As good as money for whatever commodity the chit specifies.

conn   Control. Can be used either as a noun or a verb.

displacement   The volume or weight of water moved by the entrance into a body of water of a floating ship.

draft   The depth of water a ship requires to operate without running aground. Normally, how deep the ship is below the water plus a few feet so it's not sucking up mud.

drop line   Strip of vertically arranged lights on the center of the transom of an aircraft carrier used by pilots to align themselves for landing.

equipage   Those items that are valuable and easy to lose, such as binoculars, seven-day clocks for aircraft, test equipment.

flak   Antiaircraft fire (comes from German *flieger abwehr kanonen*).

focsle   Raised portion of a ship's bow, short for forecastle.

fouled deck   A flight deck that is not ready to receive incoming planes.

glide path   Angle of descent for a landing plane.

hard points   Locations on an aircraft's wings where weapons can be mounted.

island   Superstructure of an aircraft carrier that rises above the flight deck and contains the navigating bridge, radio room, and other operational facilities. The island usually is put at the far starboard side of the flight deck.

jet blast deflector   Barrier at the aft end of the catapult designed to deflect the hot blast of launching jets. The jet blast deflector is made of steel and is water-cooled.

kamikazes   Japanese suicide pilots who flew their planes into U.S. ships during sea battles at the Philippines, Iwo Jima, and Okinawa. The word *kamikaze* means "heavenly wind."

Kevlar   A bullet- and bomb-proof plastic.

kill ratio   The number of enemy aircraft shot down compared to the number of its own type shot down by the enemy.

knot   A nautical mile per hour.

mothball fleet   A fleet of older ships that have not been used for warfare for some time.

port   Left.

PriFly   Primary flight control.

repair eight   The damage control team responsible for the flight deck.

shakedown   Testing under operating conditions.

smart weapons   Weapons that are guided with precision to their targets, thus minimizing unnecessary damage.

sonobuoys   Underwater listening devices.

starboard   Right.

stern   Back of the ship.

tender   An auxiliary ship, normally a repair ship or supply ship. In older fleets, the ship whose job it is to attend to other ships, often supplying communication services between a larger ship and shore.

tooth-to-tail ratio   The required depth of infrastructure for a military action.

waveoff   Order from the LSO to the pilot to abort the landing.

Bibliography

Books

Adcock, Al. *Escort Carriers in Action*. Carrollton, Tex.: Squadron/Signal Publications, 1996.

Alexander, Joseph H., and Merrill L. Bartlett. *Sea Soldiers in the Cold War*. Annapolis, Md.: Naval Institute Press, 1995.

Atkinson, Scott R. *Civilian-Military Differences on Soviet Aircraft Carrier Deployment*. Alexandria, Va.: Center for Naval Analyses, 1990.

Baker, A. D., III. *The Naval Institute Guide to Combat Fleets of the World*. Annapolis, Md.: Naval Institute Press, 2000.

Baldwin, Sherman. *Ironclaw: A Navy Carrier Pilot's Gulf War Experience*. New York: William Morrow and Company.

Beaver, Paul. *Carrier Air Operations since 1945*. Harrisburg, Pa.: Arms and Armour Press, 1983.

Belote, James H., and William M. Belote. *Titans of the Sea for 1941–1944: The Development and Operations of Japanese and American Carrier Task Force During World War II*. New York: Harper & Row, 1975.

Bennett, Christopher. *Supercarrier*. Osceola, Wis.: Motorbooks, 1996.

Bergaust, Erik. *Aircraft Carrier in Action*. New York: Putnam, 1968.

Bonds, Ray. *Modern Carriers*. New York: Prentice Hall Press, 1988.

Bradshaw, Thomas I. *Carrier Down: The Story of the Sinking of the USS* Princeton *(CVL-23)*. Austin, Tex.: Eakin Press, 1990.

Brown, David. *Aircraft Carriers*. New York: Harcourt, Brace and Company, 1944.

————. *Carrier Operations in World War II*. Annapolis, Md.: Naval Institute Press, 1974.

Bryan, J., and Philip G. Reed. *Mission Beyond Darkness*. New York: Duell, Sloan and Pearce, 1945.

Bryan, James T. *The Unknown Memorial: The Fighting Lady, the National Memorial to Carrier Aviation USS* Yorktown *CV-10*. New York: James T. Bryan, 1991.

Burns, Eugene. *Then There Was One*. New York: Harcourt, Brace and Company, 1944.

Carlin, Michael. *Trial, Ordeal of the USS* Enterprise, *14 January 1969*. West Grove, Pa.: Tuscarora Press, 1993.

Castillo, Edmund L. *Flat-Tops: The Story of Aircraft Carriers*. New York: Random House, 1969.

Chesneau, Roger. *Aircraft Carriers of the World, 1914-Present*. Annapolis, Md.: Naval Institute Press, 1984.

Condon, John Pomeroy. *Corsairs and Flattops: Marine Carrier Air Warfare, 1944-1945*. Annapolis, Md.: Naval Institute Press, 1997.

Couhat, Jean Labayle, and Bernard Prezelin. *Combat Fleets of the World, 1988-89: Their Ships, Aircraft and Armament*. Annapolis, Md.: Naval Institute Press, 1988.

Cracknell, W. H. *Profile War Ship 15: USS Enterprise/(CVa.N-65)*. Berkshire, England: Profile Publications Ltd., 1972.

Cressman, Robert. *That Gallant Ship USS* Yorktown *(CV-5)*. Missoula, Mont.: Pictorial Histories Publishing Company, 1985.

Cressman, Robert, and Michael J. Wenger. *Steady Nerves and Stout Hearts: The Enterprise (CV-6) Air Group and Pearl Harbor,* 7 December 1941. Missoula, Mont.: Pictorial Histories Publishing Company, 1990.

Davis, Jacquelyn K. *Aircraft Carriers and the Role of Naval Power in the Twenty-first Century.* Cambridge, Mass.: Institute for Foreign Policy Analysis, 1993.

Dresser, James. *Escort Carriers and their Air Unit Markings during World War II in the Pacific.* Ames, Iowa: J. Dresser, 1980.

Dunn, Patrick T. *The Advent of Carrier Warfare.* Ann Arbor, Mich.: UMich., 1991.

Fahey, James C. *Ships and Aircraft of the US Fleet.* (Eighth Edition) Annapolis, Md.: Naval Institute Press, 1980.

Faltum, Andrew. *The Essex Class Carriers.* Baltimore, Md.: Nautical and Aviation Publishing Co. of America, 1996.

Francillon, Rene J. *Tonkin Gulf Yacht Club: US Carrier Operations Off Vietnam.* London: Conway Maritime Press Ltd., 1988.

Friederich, Rudolf J. *Aircraft Carriers (United States Navy): An Operational History of the 60 United States Fleet Aircraft Carriers, 1922 to 1991.* Knoxville, Tenn.: Rudolf J. Friederich, 1991.

Friedman, Norman. *Carrier Air Power.* Greenwich, Conn.: Conway Maritime, 1981.

———. *US Aircraft Carriers: An Illustrated Design History.* Annapolis, Md.: Naval Institute Press, 1983.

Fry, John. *USS Saratoga CV-3: An Illustrated History of the Legendary Aircraft Carrier, 1927-1946.* Atglen, Pa.: Schiffer Pub., 1996.

Garrison, Peter, and George Hall. *CV: Carrier Aviation, Airpower No. 1001.* Novato, Calif.: Presidio Press, 1987.

Gillcrist, Paul T. *Feet Wet: Reflections of a Carrier Pilot.* Atglen, Pa.: Schiffer Publishing Ltd., 1997.

Grant, Zalin. *Over the Beach: The Air War in Vietnam.* New York: W. W. Norton Co., 1986.

Grove, Eric. *Sea Battles in Close Up: WW II, Volume 2*. Annapolis, Md.: Naval Institute Press, 1993.

Halliday, Jon. *Korea, the Unknown War*. New York: Pantheon Books, 1988.

Hammel, Eric. *Guadalcanal: The Carrier Battles*. New York: Orion Books, Crown Publishers Inc., 1987.

———. *Guadalcanal: Decision at Sea*. New York: Crown Publishers, 1988.

Hanson, Norman. *Carrier Pilot*. Bar Hill, Cambridge, England: Patrick Stephens Ltd., 1979.

Hezlet, Sir Arthur Richard R. *Aircraft and Sea Power*. New York: Stein and Day, 1970.

Hines, Eugene G. *The "Fighting Hannah": A War History of the USS* Hancock *(CV-19)*. Nashville, Tenn.: Battery Press, 1989.

Holmes, Tony. *Carriers: United States Naval Air Power in Action*. New York: Military Press: Distributed by Crown, 1990.

———. *Seventh Fleet Super Carriers: US Naval Air Power in the Pacific*. London: Osprey Publishing Ltd., 1987.

Holmes, Tony, and Jean-Pierre Montbazet. *World Super Carriers, Naval Air Power Today*. London: Osprey Publishing Co., 1988.

Hooper, Edwin Bickford, Dean Allard, et al., "The United States Navy and the Vietnam Conflict." Washington, D.C.: U.S. Government Printing Office, 1976.

Hoyt, Edwin P. *Carrier Wars*. New York: Paragon House, 1992.

Humble, Richard. *United States Fleet Carriers of World War II in Action*. New York: Blandford Press, 1984.

Jensen, Oliver. *Carrier War*. New York: Simon & Schuster, 1945.

Johnston, Stanley P. *Queen of the Flattops: The USS* Lexington *and Coral Sea Battle*. New York: E. P. Dutton & Company, 1942.

Jordon, John. *Illustrated Guide to Modern Naval Aviation and Aircraft Carriers*. New York: Arco, 1983.

Jones, Thomas D., and Michael Benson. *The Complete Idiot's Guide to NASA*. Indianapolis: Alpha Books, 2002.

Jordan, John. *Modern Naval Aviation and Aircraft Carriers*. London: Salamander Books Ltd., 1983.

Kasulka, Duane. *USN Aircraft Carrier Air Units, Vol. I 1946-1956*. Carrollton, Tex.: Squadron/Signal Publications, 1985.

———. *USN Aircraft Carrier Air Units, Vol. II 1957–1963*. Carrollton, Tex.: Squadron/Signal Publications, 1985.

———. *USN Aircraft Carrier Air Units, Vol. III 1964-1973*. Carrollton, Tex.: Squadron/Signal Publications, 1988.

Kaufman, Yogi. *City at Sea*. Annapolis, Md.: Naval Institute Press, 1995.

Kenney, Douglas, and William Butler. *No Easy Days: The Incredible Drama of Naval Aviation*. Louisville, Ky.: Butler, Kenney, Farmer, 1995.

Kernan, Alvin. *Crossing the Line: A Bluejacket's World War II Odyssey*. Annapolis, Md.: Naval Institute Press, 1994.

Kilduff, Peter. *U.S. Carriers at War*. Harrisburg, Pa.: Stackpole Books, 1981.

Kinzey, Bert. *USS America in Detail & Scale*. Blue Ridge Summit, Pa.: Tab Books, 1989.

———. *The USS Enterprise CVa.(N)-65 to CV(N)-65*. Blue Ridge Summit, Pa.: Tab Books, 1991.

———. *USS Forrestal in Detail and Scale*. Waukesha, Wis.: Kalmbach Books, 1993.

———. *USS Lexington*. Blue Ridge Summit, Pa.: Tab Books, 1988.

Lawson, Robert L. *Carrier Air War in Original WWI Color*. Osceola, Wis.: Motorbooks International, 1996.

Layman, R. D. *Before the Aircraft Carrier: The Development of Aviation Vessels (1849-1922).* Annapolis, Md.: Naval Institute Press, 1989.

———. *To Ascend from a Floating Base: Shipboard Aeronautics and Aviation, 1783-1914.* Rutherford, N.J.: Fairleigh Dickinson Univ. Press, 1979.

Lehman, John F. *Aircraft Carriers.* Calif.: Sage Publications, 1978.

———. *Command of the Seas: Building the 600 Ship Navy.* New York: Charles Scribner's Sons, 1988.

Lindley, John M. *Carrier Victory: The Air War in the Pacific.* New York: Elsevier-Dutton, 1978.

MacDonald, Scot. *Evolution of Aircraft Carriers.* Washington, D.C.: GPO, 1964.

MacGlashing, John W. *Batmen: Night Air Group 90 in World War II.* St. Paul, Minn.: Phalanx Publishing Company Ltd., 1995.

MacIntyre, Donald G. F. W. *Aircraft Carrier.* New York: Ballantine Books, 1968.

Markey, Morris. *Well Done!* New York: D. Appleton-Century Co., 1945.

McCracken, Kenneth. *Baby Flat-Top.* New York: Farrar & Rinehart, 1944.

Mears, Frederick. *Carrier Combat.* Garden City, N.Y.: Doubleday, Doran and Company, 1944.

Melhorn, Charles M. *Two-Black Fox, The Rise of the Aircraft Carrier, 1911-1929.* Annapolis, Md.: Naval Institute Press, 1974.

Messimer, Dwight R. *Pawns of War: The Loss of the USS* Langley *and the USS* Pecos. Annapolis, Md.: Naval Institute Press, 1983.

Miller, Max. *Daybreak for Our Carrier.* New York: McGraw-Hill Book Company, 1944.

Mizrahi, J. V. *Carrier Fighters.* Calif.: Sentry Books, 1969.

Morrison, Wilbur H. *Above and Beyond, 1941-1945.* New York: St. Martin's Press, 1983.

Musciano, Walter A. *Warbirds of the Sea.* Atglen, Pa.: Schiffer Publishing Ltd., 1994.

Norman, C. J. *Aircraft Carriers*. New York: F. Watts, 1986.

Polmar, Norman. *Aggressors, Vol. 2, Carrier Power vs. Fighting Ship*. Charlottesville, Va.: Howell Press, 1990.

———. *Aircraft Carriers: A Graphic History of Carrier Aviation and Its Influence on World Events*. Garden City, N.Y.: Doubleday, 1969.

———. *The Naval Institute Guide to the Ships and Aircraft of the US Fleet*. Annapolis, Md.: Naval Institute Press, 1996.

———. *The Ships and Aircraft of the US Fleet*. Annapolis, Md.: Naval Institute Press, 1987.

Poolman, Kenneth. *Allied Escort Carriers of WW II in Action*. Annapolis, Md.: Naval Institute Press, 1988.

———. *Escort Carrier*. London: Leo Cooper, 1988.

———. *Escort Carriers of World War II*. New York: Sterling Pub., 1989.

Power, Hugh Irvin. *Carrier* Lexington. College Station, Tex.: Texas A&M University Press, 1996.

Preston, Antony. *Aircraft Carriers*. London: Hamlyn, 1979.

———. *The World's Great Aircraft Carriers*, San Diego, Calif.: Thunder Bay Press, 2000.

Raven, Alan. *Essex-Class Carriers*. Annapolis, Md.: Naval Institute Press, 1988.

Reese, Lee Fleming, ed. *Men of the Blue Ghost (USS* Lexington *CV-16) 1943-1946*. Lexington, Mass.: Lexington Book Company, 1980.

Reynolds, Clark G. *The Carrier War: The Epic of Flight*. Alexandria, Va.: Time-Life Books, 1982.

———. *The Fast Carriers*. Melbourne, Fla.: Krieger, 1978.

———. *The Fighting Lady, The New* Yorktown *in the Pacific War*. Missoula, Mont.: Pictorial Histories Publishing Company, 1986.

Roberts, John. *The Aircraft Carrier* Intrepid. Annapolis, Md.: Naval Institute Press, 1982.

Rose, Lisle Abbott. *The Ship that Held the Line: The USS* Hornet *and the First Year of the Pacific War*. Annapolis, Md.: Naval Institute Press, 1996.

Rowe, John S., and Samuel L. Morison. *The Ships and Aircraft of the U.S. Fleet*. Annapolis, Md.: Naval Institute Press, 1972.

Self, Chuck. *The USS* Hornet *CV-12, CVa.-12, CVS-12*. Shreveport, La.: Chuck Self, 1995.

Skiera, Joseph A., ed. *Aircraft Carriers in Peace and War*. New York: F. Watts, 1965.

St. John, Philip A. *USS* Yorktown: *CV-10, CVa.-10, CVS-10: The Fighting Lady*. Paducah, Ky.: Turner Pub., 1993.

Stafford, Edward P. *The Big E: The Story of the USS* Enterprise. New York: Random House, 1962; Annapolis, Md.: Naval Institute Press, 1988.

Steichen, Edward. *The Blue Ghost: A Photographic Log and Personal Narrative of the Aircraft Carrier USS* Lexington *in Combat Operation*. New York: Harcourt, Brace & Co., 1947.

Stern, Robert C. *The Lexington-Class Carriers*. Annapolis, Md.: Naval Institute Press, 1993.

Sumrall, Robert F., ed. *USS* Hornet *(CV-8): Lost in Action in the Battle of Santa Cruz, 27 October 1942*. Missoula, Mont.: Pictorial Histories Publishing Co., 1985.

Sweetman, Bill. U.S. Naval Air Power: *Supercarrier in Action*. Osceola, Wis.: Motorbooks International, 1987.

Tanner, Jane. *The USS* Saratoga: *Remembering One of America's Great Aircraft Carriers, 1956-1994*. Atlanta, Ga.: Longstreet Press, 1994.

Terzibaschitsch, Stefan. *Aircraft Carriers of the U.S. Navy*. Annapolis, Md.: Naval Institute Press, 1989.

———. *Escort Carriers and Aviation Support Ships of the U.S. Navy*. Annapolis, Md.: Naval Institute Press, 1989.

Thomas, Geoff. *U.S. Navy Carrier Colors: Units, Colors and Markings of U.S. Navy Carrier-Borne Aircraft during the Second World War*. Surrey, England: Air Research Publications, 1989.

United States Naval Vessels: The Official United States Navy Reference Manual Prepared by the Division of the Naval Intelligence 1 September 1945. Atglen, Pa.: Schiffer Military History, 1996.

Wilson, George C. *Supercarrier: An Inside Account of Life Aboard the World's Most Powerful Ship, the USS* John F. Kennedy. New York: Macmillan, 1986.

Winston, Robert A. *Aircraft Carrier.* New York: Harper & Brothers, 1942.

Winton, John. *Air Power at Sea, 1945 to Present.* New York: Carroll and Graf, 1987.

Wooldridge, E. T., ed. *Carrier Warfare in the Pacific, An Oral History Collection.* Washington, D.C.: Smithsonian Institute Press, 1993.

Newspapers and Magazines

"Armada gets set to sail for Iraq face-off." *New York Post*, December 28, 2002, 2.

Clemetson, Lynette. "As a War Finally Erupts, Sailors Still Do the Wash." *New York Times*, March 21, 2003, A17.

———. "For Squadron in the Gulf, a Mission Filled With Miracles Is a Pilot's Dream Come True." *New York Times*, March 22, 2003, A5.

———. "Pilots Learn to Overhaul Flight Plans." *New York Times*, March 25, 2003, A9.

Defrank, Thomas M. "Smart Blitz rocks Baghdad: 1,500 targets hit in hi-tech raid." *Daily News*, March 22, 2003, 8.

Gordon, Michael R. "U.S. Pilots in Gulf Use Southern Iraq for Practice Runs." *New York Times*, November 3, 2002, A3.

Highfill, Mitch. "F/A-18E/F Hornet: Latest Upgrade Features." *Military Technical Journal*, April 1996, 78–79.

Horstmanshoff, K. V. "The Car Turns 25: Grumman F-14D," *Military Technical Journal*, October 1996, 56–58.

"The Largest Manmade Moving Structure: USS *Enterprise*, First Nuclear Aircraft Carrier." *Military Technical Journal*, October 1995, 67–70.

Larson, Lt. Col. George A. (Ret.). "Operation Forger: Seizure of the Marianas." *Military Technical Journal*, August 1997, 54-59.

"Shower of cruise missiles pummels the enemy." *New York Post*, March 22, 2003, 7.

Sisk, Richard. "U.S. flexing gulf strength." *Daily News*, December 28, 2002, 8.

Sujo, Aly. "Allies pound Iraq sites: U.S. Brits destroy command centers." *New York Post*, December 27, 2002, 4.

"U.S. Planes Bomb West Iraq After Being Fired On." *New York Times*, March 19, 2003, A1.

"USS *Kitty Hawk* Ready to Handle Threats." *New York Times*, March 23, 2003, A11.

Website

Walton, Marsha, "Carrier group departs for Arabian Sea." CNN.com, posted November 12, 2001.

Index

W

walks, 250
war, nature of, 133-134
  casualties, 135-136
  COTS technology, 136
  flexible carriers, 134-135
  gamesmanship, 136-137
  lack of veterans in Congress,
    137-138
  limited objective war, 138
war games, 167
war memorials, *Intrepid*, 204
  artifacts, 204-205
  interactive museum, 204
Warner, Senator John, christening USS *Ronald Reagan*,
  266
wars
  forward presence, 6
  life on carrier, 251-252
    missions, 252-253
Wasp-class ships, 38-39
watch-standing, hours, 91
watchbills, 115-116
wave offs, 48-49
weather, 93
"Whistling Death" (Chance-
  Vought F4U Corsair), 73
White, Captain N. H., USS
  Enterprise, 173
White, Nathan D., Operation
  Iraqi Freedom, 253
Whiting, Commander
  Kenneth, USS *Langley*, first
  catapult, 152-153
Wildcats, 71-72
wings, fold-back, 50-51
Wise, John, 144
World War II
  aircraft carrier uses, 7
  amphibious attacks by
    marines, 36-37
  Atlantic battles, 194-195
    Ark Royal sinking, 195
    Operation Leader, 195

Battle of the Coral Sea, 182
  early action, 182-183
  enemy carriers, 183
  USS *Lexington* sinking,
    183-184
Battle of Iwo Jima,
  kamikazes, 200
Battle of Leyte Gulf, 198
  final score, 199-200
  kamikazes, 199
  USS *Princeton* sinking,
    198-199
Battle of Midway, 187
  final score, 192
  Japanese battle order,
    187-188
  June 4 action, 188-189
  sinking of Japanese carri-
    ers, 190-191
  U.S. battle order, 187
  U.S. offensive, 189-190
  Yorktown sinking, 191
Battle of Santa Cruz, 194
Battle of the Philippine Sea,
  196-198
Bogue-class carriers, 185
Casablanca-class carriers,
  185-187
"Doolittle Raid," 65,
  180-181
end of war, 204
  change in aircraft,
    210-211
Essex-class carriers, 184-185
film footage, 198
Intrepid war memorial, 204
  artifacts, 204-205
  interactive museum, 204
Okinawa kamikaze attacks,
  201
  Bunker Hill and *Enterprise*
    attacks, 202-203
  radar-picket destroyers,
    203-204
  true deluge, 201-202

Operation Forger, 195-196
Pearl Harbor attack,
  179-180
USS *Franklin* sinking,
  200-201
Wright brothers
  built first catapult, 149
  first airplane flight, 145-146

X-Y-Z

XFJ-1 Fury, 213-214
XO (executive officer), 17

Yamaguchi, Rear Admiral
  Tamon, sinking of USS
  Yorktown, 191
Yamamoto, Admiral I., 187
Yarnell, Captain Harry E., USS
  Saratoga, 165
Yorktown, 180

Zuiho (Japanese carrier), Battle
  of Midway, 188
Zuikaku (Japanese carrier), 180

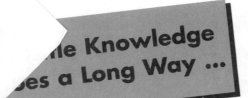

Check Out These
Best-Selling
COMPLETE IDIOT'S GUIDES®

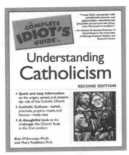

Understanding Catholicism
SECOND EDITION

1-59257-085-2
$18.95

Learning Spanish
THIRD EDITION

0-02-864451-4
$18.95

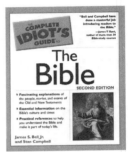

The Bible
SECOND EDITION

0-02-864382-8
$18.95

Feng Shui
SECOND EDITION

0-02-864339-9
$18.95

Playing the Guitar
SECOND EDITION

0-02-864244-9
$21.95 w/CD-ROM

Personal Finance in Your 20s & 30s
SECOND EDITION

0-02-864374-7
$19.95

Creating a Web Page
FIFTH EDITION

0-02-864316-X
$24.95 w/CD-ROM

Digital Photography
THIRD EDITION

0-02-864453-0
$19.95

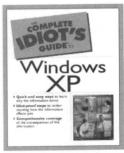

Windows XP

0-02-864232-5
$19.95

More than *400 titles* in *26 different categories*
Available at booksellers everywhere

ALPHA